Wisdom With
Understanding
is Better
Than Rubies

Lurine Karon Greenberg
Fine Arts Collection

THE FAULT LINE

THE FAULT LINE

Traveling the Other Europe, From Finland to Ukraine

PAOLO RUMIZ

Translated from the Italian by Gregory Conti

Published in the United States of America in 2015
by Rizzoli Ex Libris, an imprint of
Rizzoli International Publications, Inc.
300 Park Avenue South
New York, NY 10010
www.rizzoliusa.com

Originally published in Italy as *Trans Europa Express*
Copyright © 2012 by Paolo Rumiz
Published by arrangement with Marco Vigevani & Associati
Agenzia Letteraria
Translation Copyright © 2015 Gregory Conti
Book design by Tina Henderson

2015 2016 2017 2018 / 10 9 8 7 6 5 4 3 2 1

Distributed in the U.S. trade by Random House, New York
Printed in U.S.A.

ISBN-13: 978-0-8478-4542-2
Library of Congress Catalog Control Number: 2014944522

Contents

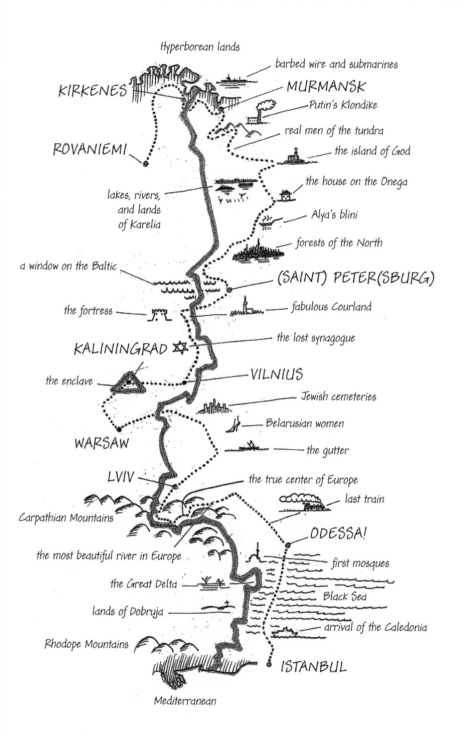

Hyperborean lands

barbed wire and submarines

KIRKENES

MURMANSK

Putin's Klondike

real men of the tundra

ROVANIEMI

the island of God

the house on the Onega

lakes, rivers,
and lands
of Karelia

Alya's blini

forests of the North

a window on the Baltic

(SAINT) PETER(SBURG)

the fortress

fabulous Courland

the lost synagogue

KALININGRAD ✡

VILNIUS

the enclave

Jewish cemeteries

Belarusian women

WARSAW

the gutter

LVIV

the true center of Europe

last train

Carpathian Mountains

ODESSA!

the most beautiful river in Europe

first mosques

the Great Delta

Black Sea

lands of Dobruja

Rhodope Mountains

arrival of the Caledonia

ISTANBUL

Mediterranean

THE FAULT LINE

Preface

You always go back to the scene of the crime. I suppose that's why on a rainy day in January 2014, I set out again for the land of rivers, lakes, and forests that I had traveled through six years earlier on my unforgettable "vertical" journey along the eastern border of the European Union. To "blame" for my return was the First World War. One hundred years had passed since it began, and I had realized in amazement that the line of its endless Eastern Front coincided in many places—the Baltic countries, Masuria, Ukraine—with my 2008 itinerary. The conclusion was almost automatic: the frontier of the European Union was not only located in the heart of Europe; it was also on a ruinous fault line.

Now, because earthquakes—including those of the geopolitical variety—tend to strike repeatedly in the same places, that long-term historical perspective inevitably consolidated the intuition expressed at the time I wrote this book, that a new Iron Curtain was forming, a few hundred kilometers east of the old one, which had collapsed in 1989. It now seemed even more plausible that countries like Ukraine, still Austro-Hungarian in the west and Russian in the east, were destined to be split in two, with grave consequences for the peace of the continent and the internal equilibrium of the Union.

This was confirmed by the events of 2014 in Kiev and its surroundings. By pure coincidence, the Ukrainian revolt exploded right before my eyes during my return to the Carpathians, changing all my perceptions. From then on, it was no longer possible to limit myself to the past, because the force of events obliged me to look at the present. Everything started to fit together like a puzzle. What I saw, for example, in the freezing-cold train station in Lviv, beyond the Carpathians, matched what I had been told in 2008, almost as a prophecy, by the student Maxim at the station in Khmelnytsky. A new conflict was in the offing, the country was on the verge of implosion.

Unlike my original vertical journey, my return to those places took the more banal form of a horizontal trip along the east-west axis of the great European roads, the rail lines, and the historic routes of armies. My aim was to verify, by navigating along the parallels, the findings I had made during that earlier extraordinary north-south core sampling. But the means of penetration remained the same: public transportation, particularly trains. They were not only a means for reliving the troop movements toward the front in 1914; they were also a good seismograph of the present. To understand which way the world is heading, you have to go to train stations, not to airports. But because diplomats prefer airports, their governments are no longer capable of foreseeing events.

I started out from Hungary, my staging area. There I sniffed the scent of a landlocked nation, proudly shut in on itself and haunted by claustrophobic nightmares. Budapest, nebulous in the endless Pannonian night, was the oversize head of a country whose body was reduced to its minimum dimensions a hundred years ago by the cynicism of Western politics. I remembered the solidity of the houses—still Hapsburgian—and its grandiose architecture, more monumental than Vienna's. Everywhere I looked, what came afterward was nothing more than a miserable crust. Everything indicated that 1914 had marked the beginning of a great unhappiness, which still endured today. Anti-Semitism was fatally reemerging, and people's minds were focused on the past. Politicians couldn't stop haranguing against the injustice of Versailles, the peace treaty that had deprived the country of two thirds of its territory.

The only way back to Ukraine was the night train for Moscow, a noble, snail-paced convoy of sleeping cars, which at the border with the former Soviet empire still had to stop, as it did in Brezhnev's time, to adapt the cars to the different gauge of the Eastern tracks. The instant I boarded, I felt as though I had entered a magnificent time machine. We headed into the pitch-dark plain, and from then on, everything became diluted and unfathomable. I saw armies marching blindly, searching for the enemy in the immense void of the steppe. The exact opposite of the Western Front, immobile in the trenches, concentrated in a narrow strip only a few miles wide. The Eastern Front was still the land of the Scythians and the Budini, the ancestors of the Slavs, whom the Persian emperors Cyrus and Darius had vainly attempted to rout on the boundless plains around the Black Sea.

I noticed that the Russian train personnel were gruff with foreigners and especially with the conductor of the only Ukrainian sleeping car. The reason was immediately clear to me: Kiev had seen the first incidents of street fighting that would shortly brew into a revolt, with people dead and wounded. The news was already racing from mouth to mouth; it had arrived on the wire of those cars and those tracks. Down at the end of the corridor, the conductor of our sleeping car was busy making tea in the samovar on the coal-fired stove, and I was reading the notes made by the soldiers on their way to the front: "It's all mud, mud, mud. Mud in the water, in the air, on the roads, in the pastures, in the fields, everywhere. Even the people look as though they're made of mud."

At midnight it was time to stamp passports, check visas, and inspect baggage. Then we heard the sound of hammer blows, screeching wheels, rattling chains, jacks. The cars were raised up one by one, and dozens of railroad workers appeared out of the rain to toil under the belly of the train. When the train started back down the track toward the Carpathians, trying to find its way in a thunderstorm, I heard the sound of the road to perdition, the same sound heard by the "boys of 1914" and, thirty years later, by the armies of the great totalitarian regimes, and then by millions of civilians—Jews, Germans, Gypsies, Poles, Ukrainians—torn from their homes and condemned to exile or extermination.

We were moving slowly, uphill, through ramshackle villages whose walls looked like papier-mâché, past lighted cemeteries and the ruins of collective farms, toward a dawn that was like a long howl. As the train panted its way up the mountainsides, the radio transmitted the latest news of the revolt, and that revolt, superimposed over my reading, evoked the same enemy: the legendary Golden Horde, the freezing cold of shelterless winters, the terror of the Cossacks' gallop, the vast armies of the czar. Forests, slow-moving rivers, sleet, reverberating bridges between Christian villages and the shtetls of the extinct Ashkenazim. I saw the locomotive winding through the brush, leaning to the right, and the line of cars following it with their magic-lantern windows. I was traveling in a different time, inside an archipelago of woods and downtrodden villages, with churches and ruins of synagogues, whose roofs were capsized boats.

Then, out of the cold and mud came Lviv, all of a sudden, with the meringue-like domes of a bonbon city and the iron roof of its old station. Those Hapsburgian domes, those Jugendstil wonders, which went into hibernation during the Communist winter, confirmed what I had understood in 2008. I was not at all in the East, but in the heart of the continent, in that Mitteleuropa that a great multinational empire, torn to pieces by the peace treaty of 1919, had governed with wisdom, avoiding ethnic conflicts and assuring the various peoples of Europe a providential buffer between East and West. Lviv could have been Prague, or even Trieste. I could see their common ancestry in the dormer windows, the trollies, the hot chocolate, the cafés of old Austria, the snow-sprinkled onion domes, the portraits of Kaiser Franz Joseph hanging once again on the tavern walls. No doubt about it, the Europe that I loved was still holding firm in the provinces, not in the great urban centers like Rome or Frankfurt. It was in places like this, on the margins of the Union and perhaps even outside its borders. I could feel it in Lviv just as I could in Odessa, Riga, or Lublin. It revealed itself in the old-style faces of the people, in the terrible secrets of the 1940s, in the uprooting of its peoples and its lost Judaism, but also in the people's nostalgia for honest politics and in their desire for a West, which as usual showed itself incapable of understanding. Never so much as in Lviv had I realized that the land of the single currency was losing its soul, sleepwalking in the theater of the new instability—the same somnambulism that in 1914 had sent Europe plunging into a war that nobody wanted.

Then the snow arrived from the steppe, windblown and fine, covering the vastness of Ukraine in a blanket, and it was soon impossible to distinguish among the dead. The whole country was one enormous cemetery under the blizzard. There were the soldiers of the Great War, the victims of the Holomodor (the Great Famine inflicted on Ukraine by Stalin), the Jews of the Shoah, the peasants exterminated by the Nazis, the deported prisoners of the Gulags, and they were now being joined, in the squares of Lviv, by the dead of 2014. The candles I had brought for the fallen of 1914 now passed effortlessly to the victims of the revolution of a century later.

The Ukrainians were putting thousands of them under the pictures of the victims, walking past them in an orderly procession, murmuring litanies. It was a peaceful protest. Their rancor was political, directed at the crooks, not at the Russians, and the word *Europa* was pronounced with the sweetness of a filial attachment that Brussels did not deserve. But on a giant screen, amid the crowd in Lviv, I could see, live from Kiev, the signs of a worrisome meta-morphosis: on one side, assassins, invisible in the sleet, positioned on the rooftops of turn-of-the-century buildings, and on the other side, hymns, agitated speeches, priests with flowers, patriots with crosses, the word *Ukraine* repeated ad nauseam. In the crowd, a mild-mannered old woman spoke terrifying words to me: "The revolution can't be accomplished without bloodshed."

I detested Putin's arrogance and his oil-baron blackmail. I saw the pro-Russian mercenaries terrorizing the people, but it was clear that in Ukraine, too, primitive nationalism was in ferment, fed by mass media in the service of the old and new power bandits. I could see them there; I knew their faces by heart: the perfect human prototypes of post-Communism. There was the imminent risk of a re-edition of the Balkan tragedy. The same old story: the palaces of power attempt to avoid paying the price of their failure by diverting the enraged masses toward ethno-national targets. A murderous trap into which had fallen not only naive and ingenuous ordinary people, but also the plenipotentiaries of the West.

Looking on, I thought to myself: the people here want to join Europe, but does Europe really need this archaic and intol-erant way of identifying with the nation? Or worse, isn't the EU already weaker and less united after the entry into the club of post-Communist countries like Poland, too susceptible to the appeal of crude, Wild West capitalism and enthralled by the divine notion of the nation? Aren't Catalonian separatism, the anti-Europe pop-ulism of the English, the explosion of xenophobia in France, and the bankruptcy of Greece already signs of Balkanization? How can a Europe that is so divided extend its borders to welcome still other turbulent countries?

I was running on steaming hot cups of tea toward the Dniester River and the boundless East, through a wild, unsettled landscape of pitched battles and the last great armies on horseback. In that whirling whiteness that had swallowed up millions of men, in the face of time zone upon time zone of steppes, cavalry raids, and caravans, I could feel my fear for the destiny of united Europe growing stronger. Peace was not written in our DNA; that's why this Union was indispensable for us. My journey to the sites of the Great War had reinforced my faith in alliance as the only possible antidote to decline and fragmentation. But it was a faith riddled with bleak doubts.

What legitimacy could we express as Europeans in the face of the great crisis of the Maghreb, the disaster in Syria, the authoritarian drift of Turkey? How could Brussels oppose the division of Ukraine after having consented to the separation of Kosovo from Serbia? How could the United States of Europe prevent the minorities—be they Russian or Ukrainian—from being ghettoized in the east or west of the country if in the Baltic republics, and thus inside the European Union, so many Russians had already been reduced to the status of "aliens"?

On my way back to Italy, I passed through Przemyśl, in Poland, on the edge of the border with Ukraine. Every hilltop around the city was a fortress. From the time of the Tartars all the way to the Second World War, the city had been the site of furious battles. Its bastions, made of white stone and red brick, devastated by neglect and ignored by the Poles, looked like huge toads nestled among the thornbushes. It was there, from those walls now become archaeology, that my Polish friend Tomasz Idzikowski pointed out to me, just a few yards away, hidden in the underbrush, the blue and white stakes and barbed wire marking the Ukrainian border.

Nothing, it seemed to me, better expressed the fragility of fortress Europe. It was all so clear! The external threats to the Union were in large part the consequence of its own internal fragility and contradictions. That barbed wire was useless as well as pathetic. So from atop those formidable ruins, I thought how good it would be for the Union in order for it to react positively, to have a healthy sense of its own precariousness. We'd just have to remind the Eurocrats that even the lords of the old empire must have believed their fortresses were eternal, as the new ones believe their bunker in Brussels is today. We'd just have to remind them of the madness of the Great War.

INTRODUCTION: JOURNEY'S END

THE TRAIN TO ODESSA is careening along at ninety miles an hour in the green light of dusk, hurdling copper-colored rivers, plunging south toward the Black Sea across the long, tilted plain of Ukraine. The compartment is quaking as though possessed by the devil, sending everything on the little table topsy-turvy, and the three-hundred-pound guy in the overhead bunk is snoring and tossing around so loudly that I'm afraid he's going to come crashing down on me. I've already been hit by his backpack, a shower of loose coins, and a bottle of mineral water. As we were pulling out of the station, he asked me, "Where are you from?" I answered, "Italian," and laughing in disbelief, he asked, "Why in the world did you come to this country?" I replied with a sigh, "Your country is a marvelous land," but he just turned his huge bearlike body on its side and plummeted into an instantaneous lethargy, anesthetized into a deep night of the senses.

The first stars, already sporting the fiery yellow of Provence or Turkey, are so luminous they make halos on the windowpane, like the celestial torches of a hallucinating Van Gogh. The Ukrainian giant is snoring but there's no way I can get to sleep in this mad race verging on derailment. The map shows the names of cities I've never heard of, Zhmerinka, Kolyma, Kotovsk. But no, Zhmerinka

I've heard before; Primo Levi passed through there after he was freed from Auschwitz, on the long train ride that took him to Belarus and then back home through the Balkans. The locomotive accelerates again. For more than two hours now it has been clinging to the same straight line—that's how it is in the East, from the Carpathians to the Urals, no curves and no tunnels. It's as though this train is trying to make up for the crazy zigzag route of the longest uninterrupted journey of my life, thirty-three days now, from the frozen Arctic Ocean to the Mediterranean, a giant slalom, crisscrossing the eastern frontier of the European Union.

Odessa! After thirty-six hundred miles of hinterland, the city calls out to me with the imperious name of an opera singer. It's the perfect embarcadero, the head of the line of the ferry that will take me to Constantinople, which in turn is the departure point of the train that will take me across the Balkans to Trieste, following the route of the Orient Express in reverse.

I'm not the only one in the compartment who's awake. In the other upper bunk there's a businessman from Kiev who never stops talking on the telephone, but his conversations are all drowned out by the clamor of the rampaging train: jolts, lurches, thumps, on the brink of a crash. In the darkness, the engineer searches for the sea as though hypnotized by the compass needle stuck on southeast, venting all the claustrophobia of this vast featureless landscape that is the Other Europe. The summer night is teeming with long-distance trains, glowing caterpillars heading south, to the tune of seventy or eighty hours of travel time, standing-room-only trains from Murmansk, Omsk, Yekaterinburg, and Baku.

What an adventure. And what encounters! A giant-crab fisherman and buxom vendors of blueberries and sour cream, a special-forces Rambo in Chechnya now turned priest, and a tenant couple living in a former synagogue turned into a barn by the Nazis. I've met a reindeer herder engaged in a desperate war against Putin's Gazprom, and a writer named Wolf in a solitary house amid the lakes in the wilderness of Karelia, north of Saint Petersburg. I've crossed paths with smugglers and submariners, young coast guard officers freshly promoted to be commanders of rust buckets in the frozen seas of the North. I've seen a bunch of women on a train sticking packs of DVDs to their thighs using Scotch tape as garters, and walking by a river, I met an old woman named Lyuba with three goats on a leash who told me her version of Genesis. In Ukraine, I looked on as a pack of thugs beat up a taxi driver who refused to pay for protection, and in a restaurant in Belarus, I watched the unbridled dancing of twenty young hairdressers, beautiful and happy to be there without men.

The heat is oppressive. The Podolsky Express is a Soviet rattletrap, hermetically sealed to prevent drafts and imbued with the stratified odors of generations of travelers. As a consequence, the doors to all the compartments are kept wide open to capture all the available air from the tiny windows along the corridor, the only ones that open. I exit the compartment into a billowing swirl of coffee-colored curtains; the train has been invaded by spirits sucked in from the surrounding countryside—Galician rabbis, Moldavian farriers, Polish cavalry squadrons, Gypsy violinists, Muscovite police commissars, and boatmen from the Dnieper. I try to walk straight but the jolts are too powerful. Direct lateral hits, as if a mallet were battering the side of the train. My face grazes the pairs of feet sticking out of the bunks, women's feet, children's feet, the feet of grown men and old codgers, Russian feet and Ukrainian feet, bare or with socks, all pointing out into the air, then I manage to grab onto the air vent and fill my lungs with fresh air. The night is hot and smells of grass; Ukraine is a warm mother.

Under the bunk is my luggage space with my backpack and shoes. That's all I have. Fifteen pounds of luggage, and it could have been less. I've traveled on trains, buses, ferries, and barges; I've traveled on foot and hitched rides. On some occasions I've regretted this decision—Rumiz, who was it that convinced you not to travel by car?—but I've always managed somehow, and I've always met someone who has been happy to lend me a hand. My state of need has made it easier for me to understand the human temperature of the places I've visited; the hardships have become stories, and the journey has worked itself out without my needing to plan anything at all. I started out lame from a recent fracture of my right foot, walked in pain for miles and then, after meeting a monk in the Solovetsky Islands, threw my cane into the White Sea, betting that I would make it. That has become a story, too.

The Slavic people of the East have big souls. To be treated as a friend, all I've had to do is be seen, with my Western appearance, as I get off the train with my white beard, backpack, and uncertain step. "Where are you going?" they ask me. "Where do you come from? Why aren't you traveling like a tourist? Aren't you afraid of riding on Russian trains?" All I've had to do is tell them I'm Italian, I'm going to Istanbul, and I'm not the least bit afraid of Russian trains, and the welcoming machine is set in motion. It begins with an invitation to tea, then the tea turns into dinner, and the dinner becomes an offer of a bed for the night.

Exhausted, Monika is asleep in the other lower bunk. In her backpack, shut inside her luggage space, are a hundred or so rolls of film. She always sleeps like a rock, but tonight her sleep is especially deep. She's been doing the work of three people. Photographer, Russian interpreter, interviewer—tasks she's able to perform simultaneously. Without her, I wouldn't have seen half of what I've seen. I wouldn't have met old Lyuba and her goats, wouldn't have received the confidences of a young Russian lad from the North just released from a forced-labor camp, would never have realized that a private home in easternmost Latvia was actually a former place of Jewish worship, with its basement still full of holy books, forgotten amid cigarette butts and shards of shattered glass.

I am heading into the Mediterranean night, the black night of the Black Sea, crossing the black lands of Ukraine, and in the forest of exchanges, I recite like a litany all the different shades of negritude. Karadeniz, Chorne More, *chernozyom, ochi chorniye*.[1] The darkness—what a marvel, the darkness after the overdose of light in the North; and what a blessing to imagine the sun going down into the sea while the tavern keepers of Odessa, Smyrna, and Istanbul, all aligned on the same longitudinal meridian, spread out white tablecloths on outdoor tables to the sound of pots and pans coming out through the windows of their old buildings. Lights, smells, prairies, and torrents have marked the segments of this journey on the edge of night, but more than anything else, it's trees that have punctuated our progress southward. First the birches, then the lindens, then the oaks, then the vineyards, then the plane trees, and then the fig trees. I'll never be able to forget the emotion of my encounters with my first linden tree and my first horse chestnut tree in Estonia. I said their names out loud like the name of a long lost friend.

I could have gone from south to north in order to avoid extreme temperatures and let the progress of spring and summer attenuate the rigors of the North. I chose to do the opposite, to use the calendar to extend the latitude. In this way, instead of thirty parallels, it's as though I've crossed fifty, and instead of one month, I've lived three, the ones that come between the end of winter and the beginning of summer. It snowed in Murmansk, just a month ago, and in order to cope I had to put on all my clothes in layers. Now I'm dripping with sweat as if I were on the outskirts of Calcutta. I realize that in this past month, I've seen unfold right before my eyes an unimaginable range of scenic backdrops. Frozen lakes and fields of grain, cold forest dawns and sultry Southern nights. A "vertical" journey that has dragged me toward the lower realms of the globe almost by force of gravity.

There are no maps that contain all of Europe from the Arctic Ocean to the Gulf of Sirte. From a longitudinal perspective, they are all partial maps, which seldom go farther north than Saint

Petersburg. This made it difficult for me not only to plan, but even to imagine my journey. Before my departure, a sense of the distances escaped me. The immense boreal lands were too shrunken, those closer to the Mediterranean too enlarged. So I had to make my own map, on a scale of one to one million, transferring pieces of various atlases onto a single strip of paper, long and narrow, folded like an accordion. I marked out my possible itinerary in red, thousands of versts[2] long, and next to it in blue the European Community frontier, and between the two lines there was a kind of courtship, with each endlessly pursuing the other. At the margins of the strip, as in a *dazibao*,[3] a slew of annotations drawn from books, Russian maps, notes gathered catch-as-catch-can from other travelers.

Since my departure, I haven't added anything more. I've had to concentrate too much on the going to spend time chiseling my road map. Nomads know this all too well: maps aren't useful for directing you during your journey, but rather for dreaming about your journey during the months leading up to your departure. It would have been blasphemous to add notes about things actually seen to my notes about the things I had dreamed about or imagined. So my map of the European frontier became untouchable, the representation of a different, imaginary journey. I dive back into it to re-evoke those magnificent moments of excitement and anxiety that mark every departure's eve. I lose myself in a forest of annotations. The synagogue in Grodno, the wizard of Lublin, the monuments of Pinsk, the decaying grandeur of Daugavpils. On the Russian-Finnish border I read, "Mannerheim Line, immense fortifications in the middle of the woods." Or: "Seto minority—Estonian language, Orthodox faith, pagan mentality."

Finally I doze off, and an hour later there it is, the first ray of sunlight darting in and out among the rows of poplars, gilding the blue mattress of dew covering the fields. It's already an Asiatic sunlight, wispy and warm, apricot colored, like the Anatolian high plateau. Meanwhile, the corridor of the car is filling with people who silently return their pillowcases and sheets to the conductor, a big, snarling Ukrainian woman in the proto-Soviet mold. The women conductors I encountered in Russia were better. Dressed like flight attendants, they were efficient, affectionate, almost maternal. The trains in Russia were better, too. Immaculate toilets, lace curtains on the windows, impeccable ventilation, and samovars restored like new. The decline of empires always begins on the periphery.

Five thirty a.m. We're slowing down amid dilapidated houses, acacia trees, hanging laundry. We barely have time to realize that we're coming into Odessa and we already have to get off the train. Platform number eight is full of people: vendors of strawberries, blueberries, and raspberries, ladies in pantsuits offering seaside apartments for rent—"Dacha na morya"—and school groups just arrived from mythological cities: Samara, Luhansk, Saratov, Kaliningrad. The whole of the Other Europe is gathering here in the early morning hours, under the dome of the station at the foot of the age-old plane trees of Odessa—the first of my journey—in a magnificent radiant sunlight, with no shouting, no arguments, in a liquid, patient flow.

Hungry as a wolf and breakfast at six, with fried cabbage, rice and meat rolls, unmistakably Turkish, and fish stuffed in the Jewish way with radish, the dish for which, in the words of Isaac Babel, "it's worth converting to Judaism." Detraining has gone wonderfully; I've already dropped off my backpack at the hotel and fended off the taxi drivers of Odessa, the most brazen in the empire when it comes to jacking up fares. I've walked across Pushkin and Uspenskaya boulevards and taken the measure of the nineteenth-century city with its rectilinear neighborhoods and their immense courtyards. I've encountered the latest night owls and the earliest street sweepers, sniffed the smell of coffee, salted sardines, and warm bread. On every block, somebody is washing the sidewalk. The whole of Odessa is engaged in its morning toilette. Odessa is Istanbul and Lisbon, Saint Petersburg and Trieste, all rolled into one.

On the streets, faces that are Slavic, Caucasian, Turkish, Central Asian; freckled blond beauties and Mediterranean women with defiant black eyes. A film passes before me with the extras who have peopled this adventure I've been on from the hyperborean lands of the North to the frightful ones of the Minotaur. Jews have been an essential part of the cast; from Saint Petersburg south, I've seen impressive signs of their presence-absence, and in fact, here they are, passing before me here, too, groups of three and four on their way to the synagogue on Osipova Street. I follow them, they let me go in with no checks, they give me a yarmulke, and then they get on with reciting their prayers in an adorable Levantine confusion.

But what am I saying, the East? Where I am now is the center. The belly, the soul of the continent. Moreover, this soul is completely outside of that bureaucratic scaffolding that calls itself the European Union. Even geographically, this is the center. On the Tibiscus, in Ukraine, I found an Austro-Hungarian obelisk that marked the midpoint of the continent from the Atlantic to the Urals, and from the Mediterranean to the Barents Sea. Even back then, they knew that Mitteleuropa was not to be found in Viennese cafés but much farther east, even beyond Budapest and Warsaw. The heart beats here, hundreds of miles beyond the ex–Iron Curtain, among the birches and the great wandering rivers, in a terra incognita made of forgotten peripheries.

On my do-it-yourself map, there are no nation-states, only historic border regions that have been swallowed up by geopolitics. Here are their names: Bothnia, where the frozen bottom of the Baltic melds into the tundra; Karelia, a labyrinth of rivers between Russia and Finland; Livonia, covered with lakes and fir trees; and listen to the soothing sound of Courland, with its lagoons and sand dunes battered by the wind. Look in an atlas for East Prussia, Latgale, and Masuria, I get chills down my spine just from pronouncing their names. And what do you say about Polesye, the flattest watershed in the world, the land from whose marshes it was once possible to travel by boat to both the Baltic and the Black Sea? Or the endless rolling hills of Volhynia?

And that's not all. How about Ruthenia, Podolia, or Bukovina? Try mentioning these names to a travel agent. They'll think you're off your rocker. But don't give up; show them the map. Tell them that these are real places that have rivers, cities, monasteries, synagogues, plains, and mountains. Tell them that you also want to see Budzhak, the last projection of Ukraine before the Danube Delta, a wild island of minarets in the middle of a sea of orthodoxy, an uncharted land of shepherds and Gypsies. Demand to visit Bessarabia, Dobruja, and Thrace. Reeducate the tourism industry; explain that with sky-high oil prices, travel has to become once again adventure and discovery—stay away from the famous places, choose the unknown peripheries, go back to traveling light. For thirty-six hundred miles, I haven't come across one tourist village nor even one Chinese restaurant. Italians fewer than few. All of this must mean something.

From Norway south, I haven't found any nations, only a slow transcoloration that is oblivious to borders and their ridiculous barriers. Poles in Ukraine, Jews in Belarus, Finns in Russia, and Russians in Latvia. The peoples of the frontier always surprised me; they never conformed to cliché, and they were always distant from the political and administrative centers of their countries. They did not echo Italians in saying "Moscow's a thief," but they weren't far from it. Everywhere I went, I found relics of the moving frontiers of past empires—Russian, German, Ottoman, and Austro-Hungarian—abandoned like erratic blocks in the middle of the Alpine foothills. In Ukraine, I saw a golden Madonna shining atop an ex-minaret. In the Carpathians, I came across tombs of soldiers from Trieste—my hometown—who from 1914 to 1917 had fought in the war for Austria against the czar; in Poland, castles built by Teutonic Knights; and in Belarus, titanic monuments to Stalin.

Do I want to go back home? Not in the least. And I know perfectly well why not. Every time I've reentered the EU during this zigzag down the zipper of Europe, I've felt disoriented and I've asked
myself, *What am I doing here?* Crossing the border into Estonia or
Poland, I had a burning sensation: to the west, my adventure would
be over, the scribblings in my notebook were bound to wither away,
and the air was tainted by that unmistakable blend of saccharine
Catholic respectability and obsessive Protestant "busyness" that
poisons my world. I felt an immediate distaste for its moralism, its
pharmaceutical cleanliness, its annoying flowers on the window-
sills, and its unjustified presumption of innocence. And its conviction that it is the brain and nerve center of a political space capable
of self-control, and not its stomach, susceptible to bellyaches of the
most banal origin.

In the East, things were better. More brotherhood, communication, curiosity. Primordial landscapes, more sacred places. On
its western border, my frontier displayed the heavy impact of this
closeness. It had a Slavic soul, the spirit of a great people that has
suffered and loved. Throughout my entire itinerary, the lingua
franca was Russian, and saying *spasibo* ("thank you") always worked.
Just one Ukrainian ticket seller, at the train station in Uzhgorod,
not far from the Hungarian border, barked at me that she was not
required to speak the fucking language of her ex-masters, so I answered her unperturbed in English, soliciting an even more ferocious response. Russians, Ukrainians, Belarusians, the difference
among them as far as I was concerned was like the difference between Serbs and Croats, sworn enemies whom Miroslav Krleža has
ironically defined as "Shit from the same cow pie, cut in two by the
wagon wheels of history."

"Look at this land, isn't it wonderful?" a Ukrainian peasant
woman asked me one evening in front of an ocean of grain, sway-
ing in the wind. "It could feed the whole of Europe," I commented.
To which she, as though talking to herself, said, "Then why are we

so poor? Why do millions of us emigrate? Why is there so much uncultivated land? Why do so many of our women go to Italy to take care of your old people?" Then, after a long silence, "I'll tell you why: we're governed by bandits. And you, over there in Italy, do you have bandits in power, too?" I avoided the question.

This journey to the East has been a bath of humanity. More than any other, this has been a journey made not by me but by the people I've met. Put another way, the journey has made itself, without any regard for my expectations. Maybe it worked because I didn't know very much before I left, and perhaps the most successful journeys are the ones you don't have enough time to plan. The ones you set out on without the ballast of a ton of books. Lightly. Carrying nothing except the experience of your previous wanderings.

Initially, I thought I would go as far as Cyprus, skimming past Turkey along the Greek islands that dot its shoreline, and maybe even go on to Alexandria, inhabited up to just the other day by Greeks, Jews, Italians, and the French. Now I realize I've already seen too much. I've skinned the Russian bear, filled seven eighty-page notebooks, and what I've seen is more than enough. I'm saturated. Seven notebooks and a series of accompanying drawings, to better fix details and landscapes in my memory, all gathered in a blue cardboard folder. I've patiently reproduced the labels of Eastern beers, bilingual signs, multicolored train tickets, trapezoidal antique maps. I can't go any farther. Odessa is a perfect terminus. I know almost nothing about this place, but I can feel that it contains within itself my entire journey. The road home starts here, on the shore of the Black Sea.

Mediterranean sunlight. We're anxious to plunge into the water to wash away ten countries' worth of dirt, and getting to the beach in Odessa is really easy. Just follow the stream of pedestrians carrying beach bags. I walk down through a grove of acacia trees, pass by stands of dried fish, baskets of ruby-red shrimp, and dusky-brown sole hanging on a line, and end up on the cleanest and most civil free swimming area I've ever seen. A populace of two million Russians and Ukrainians comes to the sea here, without invading one another's personal space, without strutting about to show off new swimsuits or sunglasses, without littering, without bickering, without screaming spoiled brats, and without playing deafeningly loud music. "It's like this because the rich, arrogant Russians are at the seaside in Italy," laughs to my amazement a still attractive seventyish woman with a glitzy red rose in her hair.

I dive in against the wind. The water is only slightly salty and vaguely oily. The sun is scorching hot, and in just two hours, I'm on the verge of a severe sunburn. Out at sea, way out at sea, a dozen or so containerships look as though they're already lined up for the Bosporus. Around eleven o'clock, the wind whips up from the south and, backlit by the sun, the water turns the color of pewter. Off in the distance, I can see some agitated movement down on the pier: a platoon of diving cormorants has signaled the presence of a school of sardines. There they are, wrinkling the surface like a light sunset breeze. Everyone has seen them, the fishing lines are already whizzing this way, without breaking the perfect silence. I'm surrounded by people it seems I've known forever. I sit down in the shade to write, at an outdoor table of a bar. I'm joined by a pearly-headed Cyrillic beer, and the story begins.

1. BOREAS

JUNE 2008, SIX A.M. The last bus in Europe is heading north through Finland toward Lake Inari, chugging its way through an immense landscape of water, stone, snow, and forests. Its ultimate destination is Kirkenes, the last piece of Norway before the Russian border, where my long descent south will begin. It's cold, in defiance of the season, and there is an air of funereal melancholy on board. Finns don't talk much, and they smile even less. The people of the woodlands live in terror that someone will smile at them, because in that ill-fated case, their code of good manners obliges them to come out of their cocoon and respond to the signal.

A ceiling of heavy clouds. No longer the cauliflower and bulging dragons of my latitudes, but banks of bloated herring, gashes in their flesh, ulcerating wounds, ash-colored tumefactions still warm and pulsing with flashes of orange light. No mountains: the landscape looks as though it has been planed by some planetary carpenter. The sunlight in Helsinki? It's already a dream, as is the Mediterranean. The Baltic? The tropics by comparison.

Why have I come here? I ask myself that every time I go away, as though it had been the supreme order of some czar and not my own free will that pushed me to leave home. Half asleep, I think back to the winter night when it all began, six months ago, next to a brook, in a solitary valley illuminated only by the moonlight.

It was December 20, 2007, my sixtieth birthday. The date coincided with the elimination of the Schengen Area border around Trieste,[4] and this geopolitical occasion set the tone for the party. We celebrated the fall of the border at a woodland inn fifty feet away from a pedestrian border crossing, with a couple dozen friends and a Balkan quintet. After the revelry, we turned our attention to the historic iron bar painted white, red, and blue, and with the help of a bunch of Slovenes, who at the stroke of midnight had popped out of the forest with searchlights strapped on their heads, we cut it into slices. Somebody poured champagne on the overheated saw blade, kisses were exchanged at random without regard for our countries of origin, and it was there, amid the smell of wine and slivovitz, as the iron bar was cut into souvenirs to the sound of an accordion, that my Jewish friend Salamone Ovadia cried out to the moon his strident prophecy: "And now, you old barn owl, you're going to miss this fucking border."

Moni laughed derisively when the last piece of bar fell to the ground accompanied by cheers. *What the devil?* I thought. There was no reason at all to regret the opening of the border. When it first went up, all it brought was misfortune, then with détente it had become a joke. Nobody took it seriously anymore, especially after the suicide of the ex-Yugoslavia, so it was only right that it should disappear. It was the poison fruit of a war brought on by the Fascists, and for decades it had separated Trieste from its natural hinterland, the hinterland that had made it rich when it was part of the Austrian Empire at the turn of the nineteenth and twentieth centuries. Why would I ever miss that damn iron bar? Now I could cross the border wherever I wanted. Separate microcosms were now reunited and I was free, free as the wind, to set out on foot, by car or bicycle, to recompose the severed topography of my world. Yet . . . I really started to feel as though I were missing something.

Something . . . but what? What was it that my friend meant to tell me with that derisive howl of some nocturnal predator?

It wasn't long before I understood. What I missed was the dream, the shadow line to cross over, the sense of the prohibited. Wasn't it the very presence of that border that first pushed me to travel? Didn't my wanderlust come from the claustrophobic sense of confinement in which Trieste had been closed on the exact date of my birthday, December 20, 1947? "What's on the other side?" I wondered as a kid, listening on an old static-filled radio to the voice of the Communist world carried on the airwaves from Budapest, Prague, and Belgrade. From then on, I had begun to navigate in that direction, toward the land of the storks between the Vistula and the Danube. First with my imagination, then—as an adult—on old trains, bicycles, buses, even river barges.

My home is a land of seashore, rocks, and wind. A place I inhabit more as a base camp than a city. Trieste is a place of refuge clinging to the north coast of the Mediterranean, a place that every now and again God enjoys turning upside down with his ladle, in a tempest of air and water called the bora. Trieste, with its furious continental wind, is my hiding place. Between one journey and the next, I'm on the lookout for nooks and crannies where I can't be seen. Taverns, penumbrae, ghosts, old bookstores, blind alleys, no stylish nightspots, and not even piazzas. I would like to sweep away all the obstacles that separate me from the sea. Go, go, a sailboat and I'm gone. A city to be used only as a boarding area, a place to leave from. A lookout, a balustrade from which to gaze at new horizons.

The Finnish bus snores up and down the slightly sloping road, past elongated shields of moss-covered rock, and right here, in these vast spaces, I realize that my little homeland is not a territory but a line, a frontier in itself. Since birth I've been poised precariously on that fault of mine like a tightrope walker on his rope. I'm a man of the frontier, situated between languages and cultures, between the sea and the mountains. In Trieste, there is nothing between the Alps and the Mediterranean, and even the local news and gossip reflect this extraordinary contiguity. On a street two minutes' walk from the center of town, an old lady adopted a sweet little puppy looking in the garbage for food, and not until several months later did she realize it was a wolf. A young goat, having come too far down off the mountain, had no other escape route than to throw himself into the sea, right there in the heart of the city, and several times the papers have run stories about Slovenian bears that have come to the edge of town to snack in local chicken coops. In Trieste, the industrial area backs up to a wilderness canyon called Rosandra, with sixth-degree cliffs, and that gorge takes you to the border in a half hour's walk. That's where the no-man's-land is marked by my inn with the iron bar; a place typical of the Cold War, still intact, where thirty years ago soldiers from the now defunct Yugoslavia used to stop in for some rounds of unauthorized drinking with the Italian tax police.

Once, during the Jewish feast of Purim, in which getting drunk is a licit activity, a Jerusalemite rabbi whose family was originally from my area gave me the best definition of my *Heimat* (home). "When a Triestian sits at the head of a dock and looks out at the sunset with a good bottle of wine in hand, well, that is prayer, great and blessed prayer." And if you pay close attention in those moments, he added, "the sea bristles with pleasure, the grass on the Karst turns to velvet, and women look at you with bursting desire. And the master of the universe, caressing his beard, says to you with satisfaction, and just a pinch of envy, 'My lads, you've got the better of me yet again.'" In other words, the magnificence of the place resides in its unique contiguity with antithetical situations. Seeing is believing. The distance between a mooring berth and the opera house is fifty yards, between your boat and a tavern less than thirty.

I am proudly attached to this shoreline of mine, where I have dreamed up all of my departures. There are nights, especially autumn nights, when the breeze kicks up, the air turns to glass, and the ferries to Istanbul weigh their anchors to pass in front of the freshly snowcapped Alps, when I really do have the sensation that God envies us mixed-blood bastards perched between worlds on this fabulous precipice. Standing at the head of a pier, without moving an inch, we can see Europe and Turkey; imagine the islands of Ulysses and the beer halls of Prague, where Bohumil Hrabal looked for his passengers; make out, among the ribbing of the surrounding hills, the front of the Great War, which intertwines with the Iron Curtain; sniff the warehouses of Serene Venice, packed full of goods from the East, and at the same time the wild smells of the steppes beyond the Danube. In the mid-1980s, when a Bavarian chancellor landed with his helicopter on one of these piers, he said, *"Unglaublich"* (incredible), because such was the synthesis of the different worlds.

So when the borders began to open and the rhetoric of globalization started dismantling the sense of the Elsewhere, slowly, in the spirit of contradiction, there began to grow inside of me, without my knowing it, a sense of nostalgia for a true border. I longed for one of those borders from days of old, with barbed-wire fences, glowering looks, searched luggage, and tense silence in front of a man in uniform scrutinizing your passport. Yes, what I needed was a long journey along a *limes*, a boundary path. That was my unexpressed desire that my friend Moni—transborder poet—had simply rendered explicit and no longer postponable.

So I had to leave, then. But for where? The Iron Curtain was gone; the fences had been replaced by landscaped parklets, museums, and cycling paths. In order to find some still untamed places, you had to go beyond that, to the eastern frontier of the European Union. Maybe that was where "another world" began. And so there was nothing more to do than imagine a borderline itinerary from the glacial Arctic Ocean to the Mediterranean, all the way to Turkey, or maybe even Cyprus. There would be no lack of surprises. Between Russia and Finland, the barrier separating the two worlds still ran alongside the fences of the big chill; the bunkers from 1940 had not been dismantled. Two steps from the North Pole was Murmansk, with the most mysterious submarine base in the world, the one from which the submarine *Kursk* set sail on its final tragic mission. There was Belarus, the last Communist dictatorship in Europe, and then Kaliningrad, a city of spies come in from the cold, surrounded on all sides by the European Union. Followed by Ukraine, with its elbow of the Carpathians crisscrossed by smugglers and the powerful remnants of its lost Jewish presence. And then, the Black Sea, with its frightful, unending silence. That was where I had to go.

Now I'm on a vertical climb, toward Boreas, the land of the last light. After Napapijri—the Arctic Circle—the Finnish railroad stops, and the only way to get to land's end is this soporific motor coach. The driver is a sort of harpooner, with a walrus mustache. He's been driving without a bump since six in the morning. The map says I'm heading north between two historic regions, Karelia and Bothnia. Two different worlds, it would seem, but I see the same lakes and snowfields left and right. The colors are all muted, except for a fuzzy down of tiny yellow flowers on the tundra.

Gray, on the other hand, is giving it all it's got, displaying an amazing array of shades and hues: the coal gray of the sunless lakes, the asbestos gray of the rocks, the rifle-barrel gray of the compact bank of clouds above the snowfields, the granulated gray—shiny as mica—of the still-frozen higher lakes, the coppered or reddish silver gray of the birches, and the nickel or opal gray of the sea when it bristles in the fjords, depending on whether or not the sun comes out. The streaks of windblown snow are the only thing capable of marking the humps in the terrain in a world without shadows. I can understand why the Finns and the Scandinavians love the flag: more than anything else, it is a salute to color, and therefore to life, in this mineral misery. Even the houses display the national colors of the North—red, blue, yellow, and white—like matchboxes scattered on the detritus of a mine.

For a while now, a fine snow has been falling. The shiny Scandinavian shield is all covered in flour. In the seat pocket I find a brochure with some maps of the area. There is also a more general map of the Northern Hemisphere as seen from the Pole. I've never seen anything like it. Eurasia, with its Siberian spine, is like an enormous cow with its hind legs kicking. India and Indochina are its hooves, and Kamchatka the tail. North America is upside down except for a bend down low, on the left, around the Gulf of Mexico. On the margins of the map, the equatorial lands are dilated as though they were under a magnifying glass, while the empires of the North—Russia and America—lose their arrogant magnitude. It's the vertical dimension of the world that is now beginning.

Before this I had seen only horizontal maps, and their highest level of grandeur had been revealed to me on another snowy day similar to this one, on Hungary's border with Ukraine, not long after the fall of the Wall. It was in the control room of the immense railway station in Záhony, where, with deafening creaks and squeals, the eastbound trains were lifted off the track to have their wheel trucks replaced to ride on the imperial-gauge Russian tracks. It was a cylindrical projection map of the ex–Soviet Union, which covered an entire wall, sixteen feet by ten, above the electric control panel for track switches. On the far right, beyond the Bering Strait, the western edge of America. On the far left, I managed to make out TRST, for Trieste.

I felt like an ant in the immensity of steppes and marshes where the rivers snaked along in leisurely meanderings before reaching the sea. My Europe was a miserable periphery. And the North, without the convergence of the meridians, was monstrously enlarged. Halfway down from top to bottom, on the fabled Trans-Siberian line, were the names of every single station, and there were so many of them that in order to fit them all in, they'd had to use a minuscule font. For lack of space and because the empire extended horizontally, the names of the places along the railroad lines were written vertically, forming a kind of long millipede. Never again have I seen such a representation of immensity.

I turn my general map of the journey in my hands and make a few discoveries. First, the European Union is six hundred miles wider than it is long. Second, as you move closer to the Pole, the spaces between the meridians get narrower, like the tips of orange wedges, and they narrow so rapidly that at the top all you have to do to change your longitude is take a step left or right. I am much farther east than it seems; my meridian cuts Turkey in two and goes on down to Alexandria. Third, the local maps here, rather than square, are isosceles trapezoids. On a notice board in Utsjoki, on the Finnish border with Norway, I see a map like this for the first time in my life. Fourth, in this contiguity of longitudes, time is deceptive. If it's eight o'clock in Norway, it's nine o'clock in Finland and ten o'clock in Russia, but because in the far north a piece of Norway inserts itself like an ingrown toenail between Russia and Finland, someone traveling east on a six-mile journey has to turn his clock back one hour and then ahead two hours, despite never changing direction.

The sea finally makes its appearance at Varangerbotn. The coach lets off almost all of its passengers as a snowstorm begins. A young man is standing motionless at the bus stop. He stares into the void, looking frozen; then he gives a sign of life, stretching out his hand as though to lean against the wall, only the wall isn't there and he falls to the ground in slow motion. So inert that he does almost nothing to break his fall, he hits his head and lies there on the ground quaking with what seem like epileptic contractions. I pick him up and sit him down on a bench. He's stiff and up to his hair in alcohol. I sense that I've arrived in a tasteless, colorless world of desperation. One of the other passengers explains to me that an ambulance will certainly arrive soon. Here everything is delegated to the state, even compassion. I have to get back on the coach. I've got a painful foot from a recent fracture, and sitting for such a long time has made it swell up like a ten-pound salami. As we pull away, I see the drunk leaning like a dead herring against a billboard with an enormous frost-covered crab, just pulled out of the water. Under it are the words GIANT CRAB SAFARI, and in the middle of all that wind and snow, the African word seems offensive, to be banned in these latitudes, a monument to the damnation of mass tourism.

We start climbing again toward the mountains and the Neiden River, sacred to the Sami reindeer herders, who, here at the place where they used to come to catch fish with their hands, built an Orthodox church dedicated to Saint George. The place that the Sami chose for their cemetery has been a sacred place for ages. It's perfectly situated on the border between sea and mountain, where the reindeer herders go down to the sea to meet the salmon fishers, who, vice versa, move upriver toward the mountain spring in pursuit of their prey. The place is contested by Russians, Norwegians, and Finns, without regard for the only real owners, the nomads of the tundra who do not recognize nations and frontiers. Result: the newly restored church has been closed, and it seems that nobody can go inside, not even the king of Norway. Its only rightful attendees are the ghosts of a people swallowed up by the snow, whose language, around these parts, nobody speaks anymore.

There are three of us left on board. The coach goes down a long road, and at the base of a fjord that looks to be a lake lies Kirkenes, three thousand inhabitants, colored wooden houses, my end of the line and my frontier. I get off into a stiff wind impregnated with the melancholy of a Welsh coal mine, holding on to my cane, wearing all of my few clothes layered like an onion. My God, where have I come to? There's not a living soul here. On the streets no one but fat, menacing seagulls, almost as big as eagles. The hotel is closed. I ring the bell; no answer. Rather than a hotel, it seems more like a precarious frontier barracks, a wooden building with no foundation, attached to the granite with pilings as to a muddy lake bottom. Am I in the right place? A portly taxi driver in his Russian mafia–style tinted-glass black Mercedes comes to my aid. He spits out mono-syllables without vowels, opens his door, jumps out, strides up the steps of the ghost hotel, and without a moment's hesitation, pulls out the keys from a box next to the front door. He opens it, shows me in, and grumbling, drives off.

I am totally alone, inside and outside the hotel. At eight o'clock in the evening, the social life of the town is over. Public offices and stores are open until three; all that's left is an exasperating wait for a night that never comes. In the lobby, the reception desk is bolted shut, as though the owners had emigrated years ago. The only sign of welcome is a slip of paper with my name and room number written on it. I realize that I've been left, on trust, to look after myself, and I go to install myself in a monastic cell at the end of the hallway. The door is open and the curtainless window looks out on the birch trees. At my latitude, the light would be that of five in the afternoon, but here it's dinnertime. To the north, at the far end of the fjord, a cold sun moves horizontally behind a veil of humidity.

I'm hungry; I go to look for something to eat. I limp my way to the only tavern still open, and there too I'm perfectly alone. It's a place right out of the English suburbs, but with something even more desperate about it, and when the young man behind the counter greets me with a brusque "What do you want?" as if to say, *Why the fuck have you come all the way here, to the end of the world?* I'm overcome with a desire to douse my empty stomach with a shot of vodka. Sitting there at my solitary table, I gulp down meat, potatoes, and beer, then I walk out to look at the water and discover with a throb in my heart that the last light of day is sucking me into a far-off void through a slit of pale yellow between the clouds and the tundra. The North. At two o'clock, I don't fall asleep—sleep is not the right word. I slide my wool cap over my nose and collapse into a tempest of dreams that tosses me about until morning.

The next day, the sensation that I've come unstuck in time gets stronger instead of weaker. What time is it? Ten o'clock? Six? Three in the morning? My watch says it's eight o'clock, but in the hotel there's nary a sound to be heard. Maybe I'm the only guest. I don't hear any noises of plates and silverware coming from the breakfast room right next to mine. But when I walk out into the hall, I see a dozen Norwegians sipping coffee in a cloisterlike silence, as though they were in the refectory of some monastery just before vespers. It takes all of my attention for my ears to intuit the hushed exchanges worthy of a confessional. So at that moment, just to break that soul-chilling ice and throw them into dismay, I call out a lusty *buongiorno* to everybody, and I enjoy the sight of those startled eyes lifting themselves with difficulty from their plates of fish, eggs, and onion, to respond to the new arrival with a nod. Only then do I find the strength to confront my black bread, herring, and coffee.

I have a whole day in front of me, and I pass in review the contents of my bag. I'm about to go into the belly of the Soviet bear with the lightest bag of my entire life. Fifteen pounds. There's an ultralight sleeping bag, four pounds of clothing, a dozen or so notebooks, stationery, medicine, a bedside book (Isaac Babel's *Odessa Tales*), ten maps, a pillowcase, some nuts, and an emergency canteen. The reduced baggage brings with it nightly laundry, synthetic fabrics that dry in two hours, layers of light clothing in cold weather, even miniaturized handwriting—something fairly close to stenography—in order to save paper, and a categorical refusal of souvenirs or purchases of less than vital necessity. Passport, visa, money, telephone—all are tucked away in a multipocket vest whose only defect is that it makes me look like a journalist. I learned long ago that traveling light instills calm, frees you from the superfluous, and allows for short-notice departures.

Back in November 2001, on the Khyber Pass, near the border between Pakistan and Afghanistan, if I hadn't given up my suitcase for a small bag purchased at the bazaar in Peshawar, I wouldn't have been able to jump onto the truck full of mujahideen heading for Jalalabad on the road to Kabul. There were about thirty of those trucks, and I had seen them coming a long way off, in a dust-raising convoy down the switchback turns, with their cargo beds full of men armed with whatever weapons they could find. In their thick beards and colored turbans, they were as euphoric as kids on a school trip at the idea of beating up on the Taliban. I had to decide on the spot, and when the line of trucks slowed down a few hundred yards from the border, I asked the Pashtun militiamen to let me get aboard. They laughed and said yes, so I jumped up into the back of the truck without giving any weight to a thousand utterly reasonable forebodings of an ambush. In five minutes, I was over the border with no checking of my documents.

The year 2001 was also the beginning of a great experience: the first of the journeys, which, ever since then, I've had the good fortune to make every summer on behalf of the newspaper *La Repubblica*. In that memorable summer, just two months before the eleventh of September that would change so many things, I went from Italy to Turkey through the Balkans by bicycle. In those lands, only recently escaped from the storm of ethnic conflict, I began my progressive renunciation of the superfluous. The first step came in the green campgrounds of Vojvodina, north of Belgrade. My two traveling companions, more expert cyclists than I, having noticed that I was wearing briefs under my elastic deerskin cycling shorts, made fun of me until I couldn't take it anymore—so much so that in a cornfield between the Danube and the Tibiscus, I took off my briefs and threw them into the Serbian sky as if they were a white dove carrying good news. The picture of that liberating gesture was to remain for me a symbol of my entrance into a new way of living: more nomadic, more free-spirited, lighter.

And now here I am, beyond the Arctic Circle, checking yet again to make sure that there's nothing necessary missing from my bag and nothing unnecessary in it. At the foot of my bed is my only pair of shoes, the survivor of a severe selection process. A week before my departure, I had selected six pairs, all thoroughly checked, and I had tried each pair for an entire day so as to avoid surprises. With a broken foot on the mend, I couldn't allow myself the luxury of a mistake, and in the end I opted for a low-cut shoe, light as a slipper, in which I inserted a pair of interchangeable made-to-measure orthotic insoles. *"Geld, Karten, und Papiere,"* an old Triestian named Fritz once told me, to remind me that three things are indispensable for a good departure: money, maps, and documents. I can now add *Schuhe*, shoes. A man with a good pair of shoes can respond to any kind of emergency. He acquires a better stride, becomes less clumsy, inspires more confidence. His erect position helps him think better, gives him a more rounded calligraphy, a more pleasing metric cadence. A good pair of shoes counts more than a pile of good books. And I must confess, I write with my feet.

There is something of the sublime in these technical trials on the brink of the big leap. You throw out a useless T-shirt, you buy a pocket knife, and maybe two new pencils (the only luxury I refuse to give up is stationery); you spit-shine some old shoes, and you chuck an unsustainable arsenal of certainties without struggling too hard to imagine what the future will bring. It's useless to try to prepare for everything; even if you do, the journey will do its best to upset all your plans. It all seems like a metaphor for life, a rehearsal for the final journey. Sometimes I think that people who have crossed a lot of frontiers are also better prepared to die. They don't fear the unknown as much as homebodies do.

In the Kirkenes Library, I find the northernmost Internet point in Europe; it's nice and warm, and I ensconce myself inside to catch up on correspondence. Among my other contacts, I try to find a Russian geographer by the priceless name of Kolossov, who, it seems, can give me some information about my "borderline," one of the most militarized places in the world. The keyboard of my workstation has no accents or apostrophes, Mediterranean embellishments that, I gather, are useless in a language in which everything is as clear cut as a hatchet blow. That far I can adapt, but the ø's and å's are too much, and on top of that, the instructions are not available in any foreign language other than Russian.

I look around for some help, and it comes in the form of an octogenarian, skinny as a herring, who has just arrived. He deposits his enormous backpack and springs into action on the keyboard as though that were all he'd been waiting for. That monitor seems to be his only contact with the outside world. He explains that he lives far away out on the tundra, all by himself, and comes down into town once a week to do the shopping. His name is Mette. Meanwhile, the workstations are occupied by an incredible sampling of humanity. A little Lapp girl with dazzling black eyes pops in from the reading room, followed by a refrigerator-size Russian and then by a Chinese man—a member of the only people more close-lipped than the Norwegians—who hammers away at the keyboard, letting out a series of little grunts; it's not clear whether of disappointment or satisfaction.

But the best is a mother who parks her baby carriage and baby outside (the thermometer is fixed on forty degrees), comes in, and after placing her baby monitor on the tabletop, starts typing. She doesn't bring the baby inside so as not to disturb the others. Can you believe it? This is Norway, the land of silence.

Down at the shoreline, the sun has come out, and Kirkenes is suddenly beautiful with its brightly colored houses and birch trees. In front of every house is a snowmobile, which is probably the only sure means of transport. Winter up here in this extreme region must be an extraordinary season. You can even walk or drive across the lakes, the rivers freeze over, and all you need is the stars to show you the way.

I hear the horn blast of the Hurtigruten cruise ship that is arriving at the end of the line after weeks of sailing along the serrated Norwegian coast. It sounds like all the pipes of a cathedral organ playing at the same time, and that thunderous boom, resounding through the mountains and echoing down the valleys, reveals the acoustic dimension of the fjord. The fjords are cathedral naves, fabulous sound boxes that send even the most minimal acoustic signal down every coastal ravine and gorge. I go to see the docking operation of the cruise ship. An army of timid trolls, bundled up and happy, comes streaming down a gangway, welcomed by a rubicund woman dressed in the national colors and waving the gold-crossed flag to announce that their voyage has ended. The ship's second officer is a magnificent young woman with short-cropped hair, smiling and full of life. Among the regional fauna of depressed males, the Northern woman takes command.

All around us are the sea, the mountains, the wind, and the little wooden houses—white, red, blue, or mustard yellow, in the style of Ice Station Zebra, and the inhabitants don't try to impose themselves by wealth or arrogance. On a street in the center of town, I knock on the door of the secretariat of the Euroarctic region of Barents, a border zone that includes parts of Norway, Russia, and Finland, and Mr. Rune Rafaelsen tells me about the demilitarization of what used to be one of the most heavily armed borders in the world. To me it appears to be just the opposite. On the ex-Soviet side, Putin is still flexing his muscles, and actually the area under surveillance is now several miles wider. Even a Russian who wants to enter it has to request authorization on his passport. For Westerners, the procedure for obtaining a visa is now longer and more costly than it was in Brezhnev's time. Back then, all you needed was a photocopy of your passport. Today you have to send in your passport itself, weeks in advance. Who knows why? Maybe back then everything was so programmed that the place itself, Russia, left no room for the do-it-yourself traveler. Now that moving around has become easier, the police are always on your back, and here at the border, it's even worse. For a thirty-mile-wide swath, from the border to a place called Staraya Titovka, everything is prohibited: taking pictures, asking for information, getting out of your car.

Now it's snowing hard. I'm all bundled up, walking against the wind on a frontier that if it were any more of a frontier, you'd die.

Kirkenes doesn't have one border; it has three: not only with Russia and Finland, but also with the ice pack of the Arctic Ocean, which in the winter comes all the way down to the entrance to the fjord. Old German bunkers cling to the cliff sides like motionless green lizards. Some of them have since been blown up and imploded, caving in on themselves after a quaking spasm. This is where Hitler launched his attack on Murmansk, the only northern Russian port that didn't freeze over, allowing the Allies to supply military aid to Stalin. That's why Kirkenes was bombed three hundred times and reduced to ruins like Dresden. And later, also like Dresden, it suffered the worst of the Cold War. Today the city is a shadow of its former self. In this cemetery-like silence, nobody would believe that, up until 1940, thanks to the nearby iron mines, this was a Klondike full of adventurers, restaurants with caviar, banking windows, beautiful women, and Eastern palaces with onion domes.

In the realm of silence, it happens that cemeteries speak, and the cemetery in Kirkenes is a special place. The gravestones ask, *Who are you who have come here to visit us?* Berglioth Hansine Kristensen, 1916–1938, mutters it; the query is repeated by Harry Jensen Fodt, 1918–1941, and along with him, Berte Marie Eliseussen, 1866–1939. I catch myself thinking out loud. I wonder if Amanda Thorbjornsen, 1892–1978, was as passionate as her name seems to whisper to me? What changed in the life of Gunnar Oistein Fjeld, 1918–1979, after 1945? Why does Ole Ulvang, 1878–1947, confide to me that he had a happy love story? And was Helga Eleonora Konstase Eriksen, 1887–1968, worthy of the matriarchal epitaph that remembers her? And who knows why, right in front of the grave of Andreas Lind Hanssen, 1876–1931, a hot-tempered seagull takes aim at me from his perch, spreads his wings, screams, and then attacks, grazing the top of my head? The dead are laid to rest just under the surface because the permafrost makes digging graves impossible, and the great beyond seems closer here than it does elsewhere. I walk around by myself in the dim light, and it feels as though, around every turn, behind every hump in the terrain, I might run into a ghost.

From the solitary lighthouse of Bokfjord, mythical *finis terrae* just a few miles from Russia, I'm looking north-northeast onto an ivory-colored window of open sea. A surface so flat I can make out a walrus fin three miles away. I wonder where she is at this time of year—the White Lady, the fata morgana, the ice pack. How is it formed, how close does it come to the shore in the winter months?

About nine hundred miles out from the lighthouse, beyond the far end of the Novaya Zemlya archipelago, lies another archipelago known as Franz Josef Land. The men who discovered those remote islands came from my home, from the east coast of the "Sea of Venice" (the Adriatic). Their names were Marola, Zaninovich, Scarpa, Lusina, or Catarinch—frontier names, "bastard names" like mine—and they amazed the world by all coming back alive from the white inferno that had swallowed them up for nine hundred days. A crew of fourteen sailors from Dalmatia, Fiume (Rijeka), and Trieste, who—after abandoning ship—returned home by a horrible journey on foot across the glaciers over a span of two winters at sixty degrees below zero. It was 1874, and those sailors and officers pushed themselves north to the highest latitude ever reached—82° 51' in the lonely archipelago that they baptized Franz Josef Land in honor of their emperor. Upon their return, in Norway, then Germany, and finally in Vienna, they were given a heroes' welcome, but still today the name of their commander, Carlo Weyprecht, from Trieste, is unknown in Italy.

In the Kirkenes Library, I found a number of books with references to his story. Even the Norwegians admit it: the first great scientific expedition to the North Pole was not made by their hero Nansen or by the American Perry, but by an indomitable German-born Triestian and his Adriatic crew. The English and the Austrians recognize his record; his name appears on the NASA website as one of the fathers of international scientific research. Vienna has commemorated him with posthumous awards, and the Austrian Academy of Sciences has published his letters. But Italy ignores him, and even Trieste, his adopted city, has not so much as a street named after him.

Bear with me for telling you all this. It helps me to explain to you where I come from. Those were the years when geographic fever was sweeping across the world and globes featured vast, still-unexplored white spaces. The North Pole was the biggest one of all, and Weyprecht, a lieutenant in his early thirties, full of scientific fervor, infected sponsors and institutions with his enthusiasm, raising all the money he needed. He had a steamship built capable of sailing in icy waters, sheathed it with iron, selected a twenty-three-man crew, and on June 13, 1872, set sail for the Pole with the added objective of finding the northwest passage to the Pacific. He happened upon an extraordinarily cold summer and was immediately trapped in the ice pack without any help from the Gulf Stream, which in normal conditions would have been able to open up a route for him through the icebergs for at least six hundred miles or so.

As a kid, I read a book about him, illustrated with old black-and-white drawings—dawn breaking on the ice pack and interminable nights illuminated by oil lamps. I remember a date, October 28. That was the day the sun disappeared to remain for months below the horizon line, and the pressure of the ice on the keel became so powerful that the ship was lifted out of the water to the sound of terrifying creaking and thumping. The darkness was so thick that, to overcome the men's depression, the commander invented all kinds of menial tasks for them to carry out and held classes for the crew as though they were on a training ship. At midnight on New Year's Eve, they all went out on deck with torches and sucked on pieces of frozen champagne, while a few polar bears tried to climb aboard.

The next summer they sighted new land, but the ice pack closed in on them again and the night of the second winter arrived. They had to wait another six months before they could explore the

Ultima Thule, where they baptized a promontory with the name Cape Trieste, after the commander's adopted *Heimat*. In Trieste, Weyprecht had become familiar with the Venetian dialect used by the sailors, had strengthened his scientific training, and had learned to appreciate the sons of those windswept cliffs overlooking the sea. They say that when he informed his fellow Germans that he wanted to take on the Arctic with a Mediterranean crew, they smiled at him with contempt. But he didn't let that discourage him and reminded himself that during Napoléon's retreat from Russia, the units that suffered the lowest losses were those from the Illyrian provinces: Trieste, Istria, Dalmatia, and Montenegro. On the ships of the Austrian Navy, the sailors least subject to illness were again the sons of the Dalmatian coast, tempered by torrid summers and hard winters, descended from the men who had defended Vienna and Venice from the Ottoman Turks.

In Bremerhaven, the German port on the North Sea, it's still possible to see today an obelisk in honor of the sailors from Trieste, Istria, and Dalmatia who defeated the Italian Navy off the coast of Lissa in 1866, under the command of the Austrian admiral Wilhelm von Tegetthoff, for whom, after his death in 1871, Weyprecht's polar steamship would be named. In Pola, now in Croatia but formerly part of Italy, I've seen a plaque, which, with not totally unfounded vainglory, exalts the "men of iron on ships of wood" who defeated the "men of wood on ships of iron." The iron men were the Austro-Hungarian enemies of Italy, but when sailing their ships, they spoke Venetian, and every time their cannons hit the target, they yelled, "Viva San Marco," in honor of Venice. *"Demoghe drento!"* (Full speed ahead!) is what Tegetthoff is said to have shouted to his helmsman just before ramming the Italian flagship, crammed with sailors from Liguria, Tuscany, and Naples—the Adriatic against the Tyrrhenian.

At the Battle of Lissa, Weyprecht also sank an Italian ship, and it is understandable why he ended up in the vast archipelago of our national amnesia. Italians don't know or prefer not to remember that the port of Trieste experienced its greatest flowering under Hapsburg rule. They don't know that my city invented the propeller and the first battleship with rotating cannons or that the enterprise of building the Suez Canal did not begin in Paris but with a pool of bankers and insurers in Trieste. It's unimaginable that they might remember reading somewhere that the first combat planes in history were designed in Gorizia, near Venice, and that the first torpedoes and the first experimental hovercraft were perfected in Pola. Under the dynasty of Savoy and the Fascist regime, Italy was Tyrrhenocentric, and because Austria was the heir of Venice, even the legend of the Serene Republic has been relegated to the lower echelons of our national consciousness—and with it, the story of the captains courageous of the North Pole.

Sleet. The weather is getting worse. The pilot of the motorboat that has brought me to Bokfjord gestures that we had better head back into port at Kirkenes. I ask him how the winters are in these parts. He replies that sometimes it snows nonstop for a month, and that's when they start having problems with the polar bears, which don't go into hibernation. But the worst time is the transitional season, when the weather changes constantly and crossing the frozen lake is no longer safe. The boat heads toward Kirkenes while a splinter of sunlight reveals a little church on the coast. The chapel of King Oscar II, it is in the village of Grense Jakobselv, the easternmost point of Western Europe, the Europe that you don't need a visa to visit. Set apart from the village, just a few yards from the shoreline, the church stands almost exactly on the thirty-first meridian. Around it, tundra and birch trees of all colors: brown, copper, tea, reddish brown, straw yellow, dirty silver, pure white. There's no monotony in their presence. Their leaves still haven't sprouted; the season is late this year, but little flowers all around indicate that nature is just waiting for the smallest signal to explode.

On an afternoon of alternating sun and sleet, I go to the airport to meet Monika, my companion. She'll be my escort all the way to the end of the journey. She's a photographer and a writer. Born in Warsaw, she speaks Russian, and on the frontiers of the East, the terrain of my journey, she knows her way around perfectly. She has an innate talent for making herself be accepted. She's been accepted by the Berbers of the High Atlas Mountains in Morocco, by Belarusians, Bulgarians, Sudanese, Iranians, Afghans, and Bengalese. For years she has gone in search of the lost peoples between the Baltic and the Black seas—Lemkos, Hutzuls, Boykos, Gypsies of every origin, the Gagauzi of Moldavia, the Tartars of Belarus, Caucasian Albanians and Udins—and peoples of borderline religious faiths like the Dönmeh in Turkey, practitioners of a hybrid of Judaism and Islam; or the Rifa'i Sufi; or again the Old Believers, a collection of Russian Orthodox splinter groups who have refused any modernization of the original liturgy. Her dense and varied biography bespeaks a woman who has lived for eighty years rather than her forty-two. When I see her coming down the stairs from the plane, I realize her backpack has even less space for clothes than mine, because of the bulky telescopic lens and dozens of rolls of film she has to carry.

The color of the sky is changing constantly. We leave right away to go looking for images, and the town, which up until yesterday was deserted, suddenly seems crowded. But with Russians. Herring fishermen, traffickers, miners, ex–political refugees. We can see they are Russians from a mile away because of their more aggressive walk, their Slavic gestures, the musicality of their language. To go from Norwegian to Russian is to enter a whole new world. With the Russians, the vowels take their revenge against the guttural consonants of the North; the i's triumph, frequent and variegated as the birch trees. Around town, the signs are often bilingual; I read in Cyrillic: Gostinitza (Hotel) and Klub Moryakov (Mariners' Club). On the hill, next to an antiaircraft shelter from the Second World War, there's a monument to the unknown Soviet soldier, which nobody dreams of taking down, even if only to avoid irritating Putin.

In the harbor, a dozen deep-sea fishing boats from Murmansk are napping at the dock, waiting to be careened. Mythological tramp steamers, flags flapping in the wind, arranged in rows of three. An extinct species where I come from. The Russian sailors greet us and, unlike the Norwegians, they're anxious to talk. So we're invited to go aboard the *Kolmykova*, a huge beast with a crew of thirty, specialists in autumn giant-crab fishing. To get to it, we have to cross over two more iron-laden tramps and three gang-planks. The captain—a mild-mannered man from Murmansk by the name of Nikolai—welcomes us in his slippers. He takes me up to the bridge and tells me that those monster crabs with claws up to six feet long are native to the peninsula of Kamchatka and were brought here about thirty years ago by Russian scientists. They thrived so well that they multiplied well beyond their normal rate and ate up everything, even the algae on the sea bottom. A disaster. Today hunting them down is a public service, even more so because they are exquisite, and restaurants pay through the teeth for them. "A nice problem," I say to the captain.

"I'd call it a succulent problem," Nikolai Alexandreyevich laughs, licking his mustache. Our conversation has gotten off to a good start.

He takes me into the cabin of the radio telegrapher and shows me on the computer some apocalyptic images of the fishing boat covered with ice in a storm-tossed sea. On the cabin walls, an icon of Saint Nicholas cohabits happily with the tits of a blond worthy of a truckers' calendar. The computer prints out a collection of frightening images of the armored monster of the depths.

The bearded telegrapher asks me where I'm from.

I say, "Trieste."

He responds, "I see, I see. We're on the southern coast of the northern sea and you're on the northern coast of the southern sea."

A geographic treatise in one sentence. These people are solid, modest, and happy-hearted. I say this to the captain.

"You know what we call the Norwegians, we Russians? *Zamorozhenniye*, the frozen ones."

I ask him how long their fishing trips last.

"Five to six months, nonstop."

"And the sea," I ask again, "how rough can it get?"

"Force nine."

"Ah, I thought the maximum was force seven."

Nikolai asks me to go up to the *fabrika*, the assembly line, which, out on the high seas, swallows up giant crabs from Kamchatka, cooks them, and freezes them for the restaurants of Norway. I follow him through a labyrinth of stairways and gangways and end up in the slaughterhouse, the first stage of the production line, bristling with sharp corners and hidden dangers, where the crabs are stripped of their claws and submerged in boiling water.

"Imagine working in here during a storm at sea. We wear gloves to pull the claws off; it's a job that can be done only by hand. Then we stick them in the cages and boil them. It's not easy, some of them weigh as much as forty-five pounds."

"How much do you earn?"

"A percentage, about fifty cents a pound to divide among thirty men."

"And how much do the restaurants pay?"

"Fifteen dollars a pound."

"That's a tough job, captain."

"Yeah, but you got to eat somehow."

During the summer, only six of the crew remain aboard. They are painting what in the summer becomes their second home, and I have to be careful not to get my pants smudged with orange paint. We go down to the stern, to the point where they launch the nets with their immense tackle. Some decapitated fish are hanging from one of the bulkheads, where they've been put out to dry.

Alexandreyevich pulls one off the line—the biggest, more than five pounds—wraps it in some paper, and gives it to me to wish me a good trip. In the North, a fish is an important gift, a traditional gesture of Christian charity, which in the Russian world cannot be refused. And because it will take me days to finish it, I decide to hang it from my backpack and carry it across the border with me; why not?—just to see the faces of the customs officers. I'm delighted; I'll ride my silvery codfish all the way to Red Square in Moscow, just like Mathias Rust and his airplane. My pockets are jingling with cute little Norwegian coins with a hole in the middle. We're off to the East. Between us and the United States, there is nothing but Russia.

2. BARENTS

THEY'VE SEEN EVERYTHING, these Russian soldiers on the lonely border with Norway: smugglers of furs or enriched uranium, businessmen in tinted-glass luxurymobiles, salmon fishermen, maverick geologists and metal merchants (northern Scandinavia is an open-pit mine), sailors from the high seas, and emissaries from Gazprom carrying top-secret dossiers. The Kirkenes border is not a place for tourists. It's crossed by a handful of people every day, all for a very special reason. But a Westerner with a fish hanging from his backpack is something the guards here have never seen. I'm talking about the dried cod I was given by Nikolai Alexandreyevich, the Kamchatka giant-crab fisherman, which I have stubbornly decided to bring with me.

The scene: a concrete pillbox in the middle of the snowfields, on the shoreline road of a still thinly frozen lake, a funereal gray layer of freshly spread asphalt, sparkling with crystals of mica. A deserted landscape, with no lines of trucks, no waiting cars, enclosed by a fence, sealed off by bars, surveilled by spotlights and guard towers. A traveler with an EU passport and a business visa arrives in this place with a shiny, pewter-colored fish, silver with copper highlights, covered in plastic wrap, hanging from his backpack, smelly as ten sea bass left out in the sun. He emerges from the tundra, presents himself at one of the most militarized borders in the world, and offers his papers to a guard as pressed and polished as a Coast Guard Academy graduate on his first day on the job.

At the time of Rust's memorable exploit, an infinite number of things were prohibited in Red Square. There was not one Moscow guidebook that didn't contain a list of that ocean of prohibitions. No running, no smoking, no singing, no disrespectful dress. But nowhere was it written "no landing." So the German landed his plane and provoked an uproar without violating a single rule. At this border crossing, also infested with restrictions, there is no sign prohibiting the display of a fish on entering. So I try it.

I know perfectly well that the soldiers might feel I'm making fun of them. With a simple nod of the head, they could make me destroy my food reserve, and they would be totally in the right. Western border guards make the poor travelers from the East throw all the food that arrives from that direction, considered impure or contaminating, right into the garbage. In doing so, they commit an act of sacrilege against creation that will certainly have evil consequences for this opulent Europe, an act that deserves any kind of retaliation imaginable. But this time the Russians are dumbfounded, almost respectful. Standing before them is a sixty-year-old man with a business visa and a dried cod. Nothing in their rules and regulations contemplates anything like this.

There were six of us who got off the bus. Five have already gone through the passport check and had their baggage opened. I'm the last. I walk through a tunnel with an endless number of incomprehensible prohibitions posted on the walls and mirrors above and below. At the end of it, a young soldier scrutinizes my passport for ten, fifteen, twenty minutes, without asking me a thing. There's no use in my asking questions; in Russia the fewer questions you ask, the better. For twenty minutes, all I can see is the top of his big Soviet-style fur cap. Then comes the stamp. I move on and put my backpack on the luggage bench at Customs, but the man in uniform gives me a cheerful wave of the hand and says, *"khorosho,"* OK.

I've made it through. Incredibly, I've made it through with my fish as my pilot. I've made it through all the controls, just like Rust's Piper Cub flying over the Kremlin. Who knows, maybe the Russians have somehow intuited the symbolic power of that beast on a line. For the first Christians, it was an icon, the savior fish that, according to an Eastern belief, piloted the ark in the Deluge. For the Jews, it is a sign of fertility, the jiggling gelatin of the Sabbath, the refuge food of the poor in this world of rivers that extends as far as the Bering Strait. Fish, multiplied by Christ like the loaves, an essential food for monks and ascetics. My real passport was that fish.

I change a €500 note, which is scrutinized by three different anticounterfeit machines, then we're back on our way. On the bus, two Norwegians with enormous Yukon-style fishing backpacks, a mountain of brand-new equipment with the labels still attached. They're going salmon fishing, and they're meeting a friend in Murmansk who's going to take them to the top of the world in his SUV. Their names are Rolf and Knut, and they look with dismay at my minimal bag. There's also a taciturn Russian girl awash in a sea of melancholy, and a young man, also mute, wearing a tie and jacket and carrying a briefcase. The bus has tinted windows, like a hearse, and a driver who never says a word, only hand gestures. That's fine with me; we Italians are expert hand readers, but the Norwegians don't understand and are frozen in their seats.

It should be over but it isn't. There are still more checks. Here Putin has no buffer states between him and fortress Europe, and the border is still the border of 1945, packed with soldiers, notwithstanding the rosy predictions of the secretariat of the Euro-Arctic region of Barents. I can confirm that in the last few years crossing the border has gotten even more complicated. Thanks to the cellular phone networks, my movements now are more accurately monitored than during the Soviet era. After the pillbox at the border, a second gate opens with the inscription ROSSIYSKAYA FEDERATSIYA, and the bus drives along the shoreline of the Pasvik River that flows down from Lake Inari in Finland. Between us and the water, a barbed-wire stockade. Finally, here it is: the old-fashioned frontier I was hoping for.

Beyond the militarized zone, another checkpoint. We get through this time, too. My fish has become our mascot, and it pilots us along a muddy road amid the anemic birch trees of the North. The only annoyance is when I try to write: the road is so full of potholes that my trembling notebooks will hold no more than six or seven slanted lines per page. Meanwhile, off in the distance, a trinity of smokestacks has appeared. It's Nikel, unmistakable, the city consecrated by Stalin to that single divine mineral. When Mussolini founded cities named for minerals, he at least added an inflection: carbon became Carbonia. Here in the Arctic, it's as though Mendeleev's periodic table of the elements had assumed totalitarian powers over the human population. Nikel is an ecological disaster. It is introduced by mountains of detritus and limbless, maimed trees, the tundra seemingly laid waste by enormous flamethrowers; apartment buildings ring the factories, and then horrifying cemeteries engulfed by dead trees, the gravestones enclosed by fences with little blue gates, surreal, one for each grave. The only human presence outside of the inferno is there in the cemetery, a crowd of little men bent over their loved ones sacrificed to the god of chemistry. Faces of Uzbeks, Mongols, Caucasians. A creeping deportation that continues even after the years of the Kolyma Gulags.

To the east, strange flat-topped hills like a cordillera or a tidal wave: heaps of detritus that occlude the horizon. At their feet, another socialist industrial city, Zapolyarny. Then, once again, nothing. We aren't allowed to stop, no pictures, no questions. We just keep bouncing along like crazy. Even sitting down you have to grab onto the handles to keep from falling out of your seat. On the sides of the road, which runs atop an embankment, carcasses of old cars devoured by rust. "Vodka," the driver says, pointing at them. What else, other than alcohol, can make you drive off the road in this desert of desperation? Here nobody bothers to remove old broken-down stuff. The tundra is crisscrossed with rows of crooked or ruinously fallen light poles.

This piling up of old stuff is not typical just of Barents. Even in Point Barrow, the northernmost town in Alaska and the United States, I have seen an immense open-air junkyard. Everything imaginable was on the roadside: whale skeletons, tail fins piled up next to old tires, oil barrels and wooden sleds bent out of shape by the cold; leviathan beaks, heavy as lead, next to jeeps with four flat tires; gigantic jawbones and rib cages, as big as two adult men, abandoned out in the open among rusted mufflers and snowmobile remains. Enormous bones of tail fins or rear paws lay covered with dust in courtyards among muskrats and frenetic lemmings—the latter being a sort of short-tailed, red-coated squirrel, scurrying over your feet like lightning.

Antler-headed caribou, hung out in the wind and rain to age, stared at me with their lifeless eyes surrounded by the ribs of junked boats; and then piles of wolf pelts, meat hanging on hooks to season on rooftops next to parabolic antennae; next to the front door, a pile of freshly skinned shinbones from who knows what animal. Not to mention fantastic tree roots, ripped out of the ground by a storm and carried there by the currents of the Pacific. Those tree limbs, contorted like Mediterranean olive trees, were the only things made of wood in that barren land—roots that might have come from Honolulu, Patagonia, California, or China. In the middle of all that wind and abandonment, not a living soul. Except for yours truly, who obstinately walked those deserted roads despite the bulletins announcing the presence of polar bears in the vicinity of the village.

We've been on the road now for seven hours, but Murmansk is still far away. Between one passing car and another, as many as ten minutes go by. A heavy, low sky and a diffuse sense of fear presses down on everything. We can feel eyes looking at us, and in fact, in the middle of nowhere, the signals on our cell phones remain perfectly active. Nature appears again after another fifteen miles or so. You barely have time to see a vegetable garden or two, cultivated by the people of Zapolyarny, and there's another military base, hangars for hundreds of tanks, platoons with backpacks fully loaded, on the march. After Pechenga—more factories and the most Nordic railroad station in Europe—more barracks and tanks in plain sight. There's even a monument to the tank. A MiG descends slowly, covers us with the prehistoric shadow of a pterodactyl, and vanishes among the birch trees to the southwest. A bathroom stop in a motel made of trailers poised on the terrain atop antisnow latticework grids. Superclean toilets with two women at the cash register who eat and chat as they keep watch over their realm. As they tear my admission ticket, they screw up their noses at the stench of Nikolai's dried cod. Evidently, they no longer smell the odor of the sulfur that permeates the air for miles around the factories. We get back on the road, riding along a river that flows down from dark brown hills. On a long bridge, there's a third checkpoint, then a sign indicating Staraya Titovka and the end of the off-limits zone, the one controlled by the FSP (ex-KGB). Only now can we get out of the bus, take pictures, go wherever we want. At least in theory.

Now the road is a toboggan run with curves and roller-coaster ups and downs, which back in Italy are called Russian mountains but here are called, unaccountably, American mountains. The bus threads itself into narrow ravines with monuments in memory of the conflict with the Germans from 1941 to 1944. A terrible battle for Murmansk. I ask Knut how people manage to sleep in the summer with these days that never end. "Simple, you don't sleep, it's a law of nature." That's what the Norwegians do. In the winter they go into a sort of hibernation, and in the summer they manage to stay awake for five or six days in a row. He explains that in the North, in the summertime, animals grow faster than they do in the southern part of the country. Meanwhile, the road turns even worse; the signs of the human presence in the landscape are only ulcers, wounds, landslides. Nature is offended more here, precisely where it is most vulnerable, than it is in any other place on the planet.

The northernmost city in the world suddenly pops into view, white with huge apartment buildings, in the middle of barren hills and sleet. We've found a room in a hotel for the provincial nomenklatura, named Polyarniye Zori, Aurora Borealis. My fish is looked at askance at the reception desk, but this doubles the pleasure of the shower and the cabbage and paprika soup, and the glass of vodka that ends the day. I'm rather tired, in part because of the constant light that hammers away at my retinas and keeps me from sleeping, in part because, at my age, traveling with a backpack and public transportation is a crazy thing to do. But it doesn't matter. It's in the transitions that you encounter the world.

It happens at one o'clock in the morning. In perfect silence. An incandescent sword slips through the window curtains, sets fire to the glass of water on the bedside table, then paints a white vertical stripe on the psychedelic blue wall. The sun. I turn over under the down blanket, and it takes me a while to realize where I am and what's happening to me. The sun. This isn't jet lag. It's not a waking up from an overly long afternoon nap, or even a hangover. It's the sun. The sun of the North. I'm in Russia, in Murmansk, on the fifth floor of the Polyarniye Zori, room 519, and the low light leaves me no escape, penetrates into the deepest part of my den, makes me furious as a bear rousted from hibernation. The only dark place is the bathroom, and I would shut myself inside there if I weren't too tired to reorganize my sleep.

I've also lost my sense of direction. The compass on the bedside table says something impossible: the sunlight isn't coming from the East but from the North. It's in the north that the sun reaches its lowest point, and it's in the north that it manages to transfix you the best. In the boreal lands the hour that blinds you is around midnight. I'm under the power of the luminous force that enchanted Weyprecht, hypnotized Fridtjof Nansen, Willem Barents, and Otto Nordenskjöld; the curse that killed Bering and other explorers of the frozen north. The North is a totalitarian dimension, and here in Murmansk, in these Soviet concrete bunkers made to crush man and give him no quarter, you feel it a lot stronger than in Norway.

And then there's this fjord, oriented toward the Pole in such a perfect way that in the dead of night the thirty-first meridian seems to come down out of the sky in person to transform the last sliver of the Arctic Ocean into a fiery mirror. Here it is; now the sword of light pierces a hole in the room with a laser beam. It has cut its way inside in perfect silence, like a knife through a frozen cake; it is a power capable of slicing through darkness with the relentless force of an icebreaker. By the time three o'clock arrives, I'm hungry; at four thirty, I give up on trying to sleep and start jotting down notes. The hotel is already awake anyway. The hallway is abuzz with chatter, shouting, excited knocking on doors, cellular ring tones. There are no sleeping pills equal to the power of the Northern sun.

But at five o'clock, when I'm fully awake, the damn crack in the curtains switches off, and the room plunges back into semidarkness. I go over to the window to figure out what's going on and I see that it's snowing. The sky is leaden; flour is blowing down in oblique gusts among the apartment buildings of Murmansk. In the North, a dazzling night of sunlight can be followed by a day of tenebrous gray clouds; and insomnia, by narcosis. The illusion of a real night makes me collapse into somnolence, and I throw myself back under the down blanket and dream of gigantic Russian women with pagoda-style hair, a parade of enormous die-hard Communist *matryoshka* dolls in army boots.

The dreams of travelers are the easiest to decipher, and I owe them all to the waitresses at the hotel, monumental and aggressive as gladiators, who waited on our table the night before. The pianist had such big breasts that I don't know how she could see the keyboard as she played *Prince Igor*. The waiters, on the other hand, were pale ephebic adolescents who responded to our orders in feeble voices, almost excusing themselves for existing. The dining room was full of spic-and-span Russian and American naval officers, visiting the Arctic naval base at Severomorsk. But in that case, too, the triumph belonged to their wives, oversize women in evening gowns garish in proportion to their husbands' rank.

We get up late, when the breakfast room has already closed, and, all wrapped up, we go down toward the seaside through a labyrinth of stairs chipped and broken by the ice. The snow is coming down mixed with rain, and Murmansk begins in a tangle of ugly train tracks, hovels, containers, mud, apartment buildings, and strange garages, concentrated in crumbling ravines. The asphalt is terrible, riddled with holes like the road from Norway to here. But the people move with elegance. The men look like professors; the young women glide over the cobblestones in their spike heels without spraining an ankle, and it's a mystery known only to the Slavs how they do it. I can feel myself being infused with slower times. Trains pass over the fish market: loaded-to-overflowing coal cars and military green passenger cars with curtains behind every window and a fuming smokestack at the head of every car, a sign that inside the heat is on. They rattle slowly down the track, and between one train and the next, the inhabitants of Murmansk have all the time they need to walk across the track, which skirts the city on an embankment parallel to the fjord.

Yes, the seaside. Vladimir, captain and teacher at the nautical college in Murmansk, explains to me that it is a strategic resource and not a place to promenade as it is in Saint Petersburg. He has sailed all over the world, but he has never been allowed to enter the base at Severomorsk. It's off-limits for him, too. He shows me a map of the

city and says, "You see, you can't go here, because it's the commercial port; here neither, because it's the fishing port; here don't even
think about it, because it's the harbor for the motorboats that patrol
the fjord." That's the way it is here in Murmansky Zaliv (Murmansk
Bay). Here there is no seaside, and so the people dream impossible
dreams of overseas. In this respect, the city incarnates perfectly the
oneiric dimension of the frontier.

Thanks to the last lapping tongues of the Gulf Stream, the
fjord of Murmansk is the only one on the Russian Arctic Ocean
that doesn't freeze in winter. Hitler bombarded it ferociously to
cut off Stalin's supplies. The photographer Yevgeny Khaldei took
memorable photographs of those days. One especially, a reindeer
under the bombs. That reindeer had become the city's mascot. They
had trained her to carry bombs to the front lines with a sled, but
then they abandoned her, in a precipitous retreat. She followed the
retreating trucks but then she gave up, and Khaldei immortalized
that very moment of surrender, in which the betrayed animal gives
up hope in mankind.

I read the signs along the street: LABIRINT food mart, RITUAL
souvenirs, FARAON beverages. The triumph of psychedelic and
New Age. In a bookstore, shelves of esotericism and astrology with
gilded covers, too full of color, glittering. Here, too, the market
encourages dreaming to keep people distracted from politics. The
future has disappeared from book titles; the past is in vogue. Ras-
putin, the extraordinary epic of the czarist empire, the Romanovs
killed by the godless evildoers. In the background, mystical melodies, elevator music. In the aisles, lots of security people, almost
no salespeople.

It's snowing again. On the ground, a batter made of compact
white dust and beer-bottle caps with unusual labels and colors. As
a kid, I would have collected them all, washed and shined them.
The frozen mud is a cemetery of empty bottles, and all over town
there are people collecting them, scientifically outfitted with

wheelbarrows, to sell them and buy more bottles for themselves, full ones, in a self-fueled alcoholic chain. In the puddles, the reflections of all kinds of women. Superelegant as mannequins, wrapped up like peasants, wearing fur caps or with towers of carrot-red hair piled on top of their heads, women with almond eyes above Tartar cheekbones. We come across three of them walking spritely in the wind with the stride of a grenadier and blue balloons in hand; Monika follows them and arrives at a wedding, a Russian wedding with snow, a blond bride, and men in gangster sunglasses.

We go to the train station to buy our tickets for the South and we suddenly become cognizant of the distances. A huge notice board displays the travel times. Vologda, 36 hours and 51 minutes; Adler, 76:16; Astrakhan, 65:39; Minsk, 45:24; Saint Petersburg, 27:32; Novorossiysk, 75:21. I begin to understand why nobody ever makes this vertical journey. I look at the map and realize that if I turned Scandinavia on its head toward the Mediterranean, using Denmark as a hinge, I would arrive as far as Tunis. I'm incredibly far away; I can't imagine how much time it's going to take. This north-south direction is disconcerting. Europe is really a vertical formation.

Here in the North, the frontier is a real mirage. There is no road that skirts it. You can get to it only on endless dirt roads that split off like the teeth of a comb from the shaft of the main north-south artery, parallel to the train tracks. The phrase POGRANICHNAYA ZONA is written everywhere: Border Zone. And the instructions for getting there are posted everywhere, even in elevators, illustrated with pictures of guard towers, wolf-dogs, fences, and soldiers in white winter uniforms, with skis and snowmobiles.

The station is a comfit-green neoclassical building, a color fit for an aquarium. Inside, no chaos, just a relaxed coming and going of travelers and two big stray dogs, respected by everyone, sleeping on the floor between the information booth and the ticket window. In the waiting room with a glass wall, a calm crowd and a quiet buzzing. The people eat, argue, chat. I start up a conversation with a literature professor and a strawberry vendor. Both of them exhort me with sweeping gestures to visit the oceanographic museum with the story of the mythical icebreaker *Yermak*. Here waiting and meeting are completely coincident. In Cuba, I recall, I once gave a ride to a mother with two children who had been waiting for six hours, under a bridge, sheltered from the sun. When I expressed my amazement at her patience, she replied, "Without that wait, I would have never met you."

It's June and it's as cold as March. Hard times for the poor. Outside a supermarket, Monika comes across a bearded street person of undetermined age. In Russia, the street people are more striking than those in the West. This man has a lazy eye and above it a horrible slash on his forehead, a wound that he has sutured himself, using wool thread. He looks around curiously with his one good eye from his pile of gray rags. He doesn't ask for anything, but Monika gives him a hundred rubles, worth about five dollars. He's overwhelmed with surprise, almost keels over from fear, then he gets himself together and responds with delight in his eyes. We also give him what's left of our smoked fish, along with a freshly purchased loaf of rye bread as dark as licorice, and a bar of butter. We do some shopping for ourselves: dried pears, cookies, and special dark honey made from buckwheat flowers, one of the flavors of the Other Europe, like pumpkin seed oil.

We're standing in a windswept square, waiting for a park ranger who has come down into the city from the nature preserve on the Kola Peninsula, our next stop. He's a Muscovite, transplanted to the tundra, enamored of the extreme territories. Before leaving home, I phoned him from Italy to ask, among various other things, if there were already a lot of mosquitoes up there. He replied, in a plaintive, timid voice, "Here it's snowing," and that phrase, coming to my ear from so far away, disturbed by interference, suddenly put me in tune with the other world.

While we're waiting, I take a look around that frigid square, shivering in my layers of lightweight clothing. At the bus stop, I've just seen a motor coach bound for Nikel, the end of the world. It was full of people steeped in dignified desperation. There is no shelter from the gusting wind. A decommissioned Soviet hotel towers over our heads. The name is written on the thirtieth floor: ARCTIC, in 3-D Cyrillic. It comes to mind that, in anticipation of warm summer days in the lake country, I had put some mosquito netting in my pack. Nothing could be more useless. Some summer this is. It's snowing to beat the band, the trees are stripped bare, the season is at least a month behind. Then I realize that I'm thinking of the Baltic Sea as if it were the Mediterranean.

We go to dinner with Ivan Vdovin—that's the name of the park ranger—and talk about reindeer and mines. Finally, a little warmth. An accordion player plays a heartrending piece by Vladimir Vysotsky, and our waitress brings us a soup called *solyanka*, plus a herring with beets. Ivan tells us about the plight of the Arctic reindeer herders, pushed off the land by the nuclear submarine bases on the Barents Sea, driven southwest by the nickel mines, cut off from Lake Imandra by the railroad, deprived of the tundra by the industrial pollution in Monchegorsk, robbed of their rivers by American salmon fishers, who have been given a twenty-five-year license to fish on half of the peninsula. And then there's the Yokanga, the most beautiful river on the peninsula, with the new shoreline villas of the Russian nouveaux riches, as well as the Swedish companies that have leased entire mountains for gold mining. Not to mention the poaching of moss, a vital food for the reindeer, of which hundreds and hundreds of tons have been exported to the West to decorate the tombs of the rich. "Europe decorates its cadavers with the reindeer's font of life," is the comment of Mariusz Wilk, a Polish writer transplanted to Karelia, north of Saint Petersburg.

Ivan studied mineralogy in Moscow. Then they sent him to work in the North, where he developed a passion for the Sami people. After a few years, he was given the job of managing the nature preserve near Seitajärvi, and then the entire Kola Peninsula. A huge task, almost hopeless, to be carried out with virtually no means at his disposal, but he keeps at it, explores his world as best he can, in the winter with a snowmobile, in the summer with a motorized deltaplane, an ultralight sport glider. The obstinate persistence of the Sami people to keep living in those latitudes, to the chagrin of all their enemies, is a sacred mystery, as is the survival of the antlered moss eaters. It doesn't take us long to size each other up; in these desolate latitudes, an encounter is a rare opportunity that must be seized at the moment it's offered. It's eleven o'clock; outside, the sky is ablaze.

SMOKESTACKS ON THE TUNDRA; mountains, rivers, and snow-fields under the black sky; a lake that collects water and pollutants as if it were a gutter. Then a small candy-coated city of boulevards and avenues, made of pastel houses in strawberry, pistachio, pine-apple yellow, and licorice blue, all with round decorations like the ones on whipped-cream cakes. Seen from its panoramic overlook, that's what Monchegorsk looks like, the center of ex-Soviet metal-lurgy, under a blue sky in the middle of nowhere, beyond a carpet of vodka bottles, lichens, broken glass, dwarf birches, rust, and barbed-wire fences.

We've arrived here on a bus full of women, after traversing a muddy, mining-country landscape scraped flat by glaciers and disemboweled by man. On the long, slightly sloping descents, the driver saved gas by shifting into neutral. The bus station we started out from, in Olenegorsk, was a wooden shack with homeless men gathered around the woodstove, two vigilant dogs, and a ticket seller with thick makeup, spike heels, and a halo of peroxide blond hair. On our arrival in Monchegorsk, a cabbie brought us up here to the mountains, to the overlook under a television tower, where you can see all the way to the Finnish border. Dmitri his name is, and he doesn't understand why we think there's so much worth seeing. I had reserved a half day of his services, but he laughs that two hours are more than enough for this place.

"What in the world is there to see in Monchegorsk?"

But there is a lot to see. At my feet is something new and unprecedented: nature that is sweet and meek, defenseless and violated without mercy, punctuated with mines like pus-filled pimples on an adolescent's face. "Cobalt, nickel, copper," the cabbie explains, patting his hands together against the chilling sleet, listing the minerals as though he were talking about the petals of a flower. The industrial giant: eleven thousand workers and twenty huge smokestacks, sealed off by barbed wire and guard towers like a Gulag. Here, mining cobalt, nickel, or copper is called *tsvetnaya metallurgiya*. I'm not sure if that means "light," "colored," or "flowery" metallurgy. In any event, the adjective is misleading. If there is a place that has nothing that's light, colored, or flowery, this is it right here. Enormous black pipes dripping over the lichens, chimneys spitting sulfur onto immaculate snow, mountains of industrial waste as high as the Andes, heaped onto the flower-carpeted pastures of the Scandinavian reindeer. Such is the Kola Peninsula: inferno and paradise. There are few places where Earth's suffering is more legible.

It's snowing and the sun is shining. A short walk from the smokestacks, the meringue city is almost beautiful, the last aesthetic effort of the regime before the monstrous apartment complexes of the Khrushchev era. It's made of three-story houses, decorated with neo-Baroque, almost Austrian, stuccos. Because of the latitude, almost all of them have parabolic antennae pointing downward, as though they were looking for the center of the Earth. The rest is boulevards, lakes, gardens, and silvery birch trees, still leafless. In the main square, with a bronze monument to the elk, a crowd of mothers, happy children, young men with beers in hand, and young women in wedding gowns who have just come out in their high heels from their wedding ceremonies in the town hall.

In the church, an elderly woman, sweating from the emotion, is ending her season of atheism by undergoing baptism. She's alone on her knees, in front of a brand-new iconostasis and a twenty-something priest who looks Mongol.

Toward evening we take the bus for the lake, which is the base camp for the last reindeer herders scattered about the Kola Peninsula. Lov is the name of the lake, and the road to it, a roller-coaster ride riddled with potholes, floats atop a water meadow formed on the permafrost at the end of the thaw. Here, too, the bus's engine screams uphill and goes alarmingly silent in descent, with the transmission in neutral and the brakes smelling of sulfur. I suddenly realize why we Italians call roller coasters Russian mountains. Anemic birch trees, army bases, barracks with parking lots full of armored vehicles, and strange monuments shaped like missiles pointing to the zenith. On the bus, a lot of muscular men with gym bags. They get off with a bouncing step in the middle of the birches, nowhere near a town. Soldiers, evidently. They all seem a little punchy from the never-setting sun, like one, long, endless Ramadan. We're hungry. Now we wouldn't mind having the fish we got from Alexandreyevich and gave to the homeless man in Murmansk.

After every downhill glide, outlined in the distance is a big white mountain, round-topped and treeless. It looks like the hump of a sperm whale and is the orographic center of Kola. I've read that it contains loparite, from which titanium is extracted, and that the town of Revda, at the foot of the mountain, is a dormitory town for miners. The high-altitude winds raise swirling banners of snow and light over the valley of mines, which are now in the process of being phased out. It is said that that mysterious basin is considered by the Arctic peoples to be the very soul of the peninsula, which constitutes the northeast closure of Scandinavia. The boreal lands are full of such spirits: the birch trees, small as shrubs, begin to thin out above two thousand feet, contorted by the wind like ghosts on the frontier of nothingness.

Kola is a land of extreme visions, white nights and black legends. Legend has it that in 1799 vampires invaded the land of the midnight sun and cut the population in half by sucking the precious blood of the reindeer herders. The invasion is still talked about today during nights of camping out on the wintry tundra. Around these parts there is a disease, caused by the latitude, called Arctic hysteria. It produces collective hallucinations and is tied to the shamanism of the Sami, the only inhabitants of the extreme lands, the ones where the doors open to the great beyond. A place beyond which only real men are able to look without turning back.

Waiting for us at the end of the line is Ivan, the park ranger from Russian Lapland whom we met in Murmansk. On the jeep that takes us to the lake, the radio is transmitting the voice of the Russian bard Oleg Mityaev. The closer we get to the lake, the more we swerve back and forth between ruts of watery muck. The lakes of the North are not like the Alpine lakes. Here there is no dry and linear beach, but a maze of woods, water, mud, and marshes, nontraversable either on foot or by car. The best time to explore them is in winter, when the ice and snow cement the surface. With skis you can go anywhere, and it doesn't matter that the nights are so long; you can navigate by the stars. The glowing snow beneath the leafless birches provides perfect visibility.

Vdovin explains that the mountains of Kola are terra incognita. For strategic reasons—the presence of metals for military use—their names are not even written in atlases. Every schoolkid from here knew the names of every mountain in the Urals and the Caucasus, but about their own area, nothing. In Russia, as everyone knows, it was better not to ask questions. So up until yesterday, those toponyms of the North were either unknown or, if known, unmentionable. Which only added to the air of mystery.

We're almost at the lake, but our jeep is in mud up to its doors. Now we can't even get free using four-wheel drive. Ivan ties a steel cable around a tree trunk, pulls out a sort of sliding jack, attaches it to the cable, and tells me to push while he activates a lever. I already know Russian mud. Years ago, in a steel mill under construction in the area of the river Don, a manager's car got stuck in the mud. He peremptorily called for a truck to pull him out, but in the effort the truck got trapped in the mire, too. Yelling and screaming, he called for a bulldozer, which was promptly swallowed up by the thaw-soaked earth. It took a bridge crane mounted on rails to liberate the three vehicles, to the cheers of a thousand or so workers, overjoyed at the defeat of their arrogant boss.

We're back on solid ground and finally arrive at the shore of the lake, still encrusted with ice. Ducks. Tracks of a white hare in the snow. We turn off the engine. Silence. And the reindeer? And the herders? "The Sami are a long way off," says Vdovin, looking toward the east. In Slavic, Sami, that is, Laplanders, means "loners," the "solitary ones." Ivan speaks to me in simple English. A few key words: "Far away, men very far away," and he points to an invisible line beyond the white mountains. "They know the stories, but they don't write them down. They only tell them, around a fire." He says, "They know the stories," but what he means is, "They know the secrets of life." Actually, the word reindeer means "life," because it contains within itself the secret of survival in the void.

The town of Lovozero is not made of little wooden houses, as would seem logical for a people used to living in tents, but of concrete apartment buildings. This is another product of environmental violation. When they were built, in the 1960s, the nomadic Lapps were forced to live in them and to adopt a sedentary lifestyle, with a consequent wave of suicides and alcoholism. Outside a building shaped like an Indian tepee, there is an evangelical service, with guitars and American-style music. Religion completely emptied of magic, reduced to music, morals, responsibility, behavior—the disintegration of the last frontier of mystery. Also the last toehold of a lost people.

When the service ends, a congregation of bony-faced people with watery eyes comes out. An old man with a cane—he barely knows I'm a foreigner—launches into a diatribe against thieves, bad government, and those who have betrayed the dead of the World War. "Today, everything's going to hell, nobody fixes anything anymore, our houses are falling apart . . . and Murmansk is a long way off. . . ." He adds, "I'd shoot those people," and he picks up his cane and holds it like a rifle, takes aim, and squeezes its imaginary trigger. "*Pum, pum.*"

At the Tundra Co-op, which processes and freezes reindeer meat, they confirm that the nomads are far away from the town. "Our herders are out beyond the lake, where the roads don't go." And then: "*Dalyeko*, far away," and they make the same quivering gesture that I'd seen Ivan make, to indicate a fascinating and fearsome place off to the east. Who knows, maybe that's where the real frontier is. Not the political frontier with Finland, which never existed before 1945, but the age-old frontier between the stationaries and the nomads. They go on to add: "That's where the secret of their culture is, their children are born there, in the huts and tents. They come here when they're seven years old, when they are already men, to go to school."

But here are Vitaly Startsev and his wife, Tatiana, pioneers of Arctic grazing. He is a fast-talking self-assertive guy full of pugnacious vitality. She is small, determined, and taciturn. They throw some birch logs on the fire and talk about the winter, about the herds that scatter in the Arctic night beyond the frozen lake for miles and miles, almost copying the geometry of the stars. When you approach one of those droves of down crowned by an entanglement of dead branches—antlers—a thousand glistening eyes take aim at you in the dark. All around, in the heart of darkness of Kola, the last frontier of European Russia, the pastors of the Great North are in hiding, the last caretakers of the reindeer, the symbol of our Christmas.

Tatiana has no doubts: "Those are real men. They're born in cabins on the tundra, together with the herd, and before going to school they learn to listen to the stories of their elders, to understand the thousand voices of silence, the mysterious signs of the long Northern night, the tracks of predators and the places where *yagel* grows, the dried silver-green moss on which the animals nourish themselves even in winter, digging under the snow. Only later will they go to the city, with no risk of being spoiled. The years spent on the tundra will already have changed them forever. Go! Go there yourself! There you drink at the font of wisdom, look nature in the face. What could be better than that? Isn't that civilization, too?" I hear a familiar creaking sound. A window opening to a new journey. A journey to be made as soon as possible.

The Arctic wind blows at ground level from the Urals, from the great plains of the rivers Ob and the Yenisei. It's excruciatingly cold, yet here there are things worse than winter. Bears, for example, which in April tear the calves to pieces and devour them. Wolves, which capture adult bulls, grabbling them by the tongue after exhausting them with the chase. Or the *rosomakha* (wolverine), a little devil with the teeth of a vampire capable of decapitating a reindeer in ten seconds. Then the mosquitoes and the horseflies, which suck the blood of men and animals through their mouths and nostrils. But the worst are the gnats, swarms of them attack a single victim, driving him mad. Here, the summer is horrible, that's why the transhumance is done in reverse: the herds go up in the winter and down in the summer because with the sea breeze there are fewer insects.

But the insects and predators, Vitaly assures me, are nothing compared to man. Since everything in Russia has been put up for sale—forests, rivers, fisheries—the reindeer have been under attack. Even they—symbol of the Nativity—are now the most recent victims of the massacre of our natural resources. Poachers, tourists, the nouveaux riches, motorists, agents of the multinationals—they all come here, and the slaughter ensues. "Today, everything that is nomadic gets in the way of the culture of exploitation. Our seasonality irritates those who want to do business year-round. So the reindeer die off, forgotten, while Moscow and Saint Petersburg, Oslo and Stockholm resonate with Christmas carols and the blasphemous mill of consumption grinds up the billions."

The cattle raiser tells us how, one day in January, east of Lovozero, a band of Muscovites showed up on snowmobiles, with thermal suits, navigators, satellite phones, and laser precision rifles. First they exterminated a herd just to take the antlers. Then they invaded a herder's cabin and drank themselves into a stupor, breaking up the furniture to feed the woodstove. "Starting a few years ago, we've had to pay people to guard the *izbas* [log cabins]. Our land is endangered. They want to turn it into a hunting reserve for the rich, enclosed by fences and protected by armed bouncers." Just as in Italy but even more brazen.

It starts to snow. Vitaly is tense, a man at war with the system. "They open up new roads, terrify the animals with helicopters. In the past, there were soldiers who would massacre a herd with machine guns just to carry off a tongue or a thigh, the premium pieces. There was a submarine base in Ostrovnoy (aka Gremikha) with a hundred thousand people. Today it's a base for poachers who come in on the ferry from Arkhangelsk. They shoot at anything that moves, leave behind broken bottles and cigarette butts, raise more havoc than pigs, and they are given carte blanche in exchange for money."

Tatiana throws some wood on the fire and opens a map of the territories served by her cooperative, an area as big as Connecticut. The long parallel spaces of the transhumance between the mountains and the sea are well marked by contrasting pale colors. She shows us a Gazprom pipeline that is supposed to supply Germany from the Arctic via the Baltic, going right through those passages. Not long ago, a huge deposit of platinum, titanium, gold, silver, and copper was discovered, and there too they're going to build a railroad for a Canadian multinational. Then on Mount Leshaya, in an old Gulag, they're about to reopen a molybdenum mine financed by Anglo-Irish capital.

Vitaly is not afraid to talk. He wants the whole story to be known, hopes that the rich West will help him, at least in the name of the sanctity of Christmas. "If Gazprom and the other two mines join forces against us, good-bye reindeer. Write about it. We have asked that they build infrastructure that is environmentally compatible, but I'm afraid they won't listen to us." He outlines the stages of an implacable siege. "They want to take away our concession over the forests; they have bought our slaughterhouse, and now they've even sold our fluvial fishing rights. Let's not talk about the fishing in the Barents Sea; it's all in the hands of the multinationals, while the local people have only the right to a minimum quota of fish."

When it comes to tourism, it's open warfare. It spreads like an herbicide, with the corrupt complicity of the usual *chinovnik*, the local government functionary, described perfectly by Chekhov. Here water and land, lakes, rivers, and hills are all mixed together in a labyrinth, and here for millennia, hunters have also been fishers. Well, now, while for the "natives" fishing is limited to the minimum for survival, the largest bodies of water are handed over for twenty years to be managed by an English company, which organizes luxury camping tours for salmon fishing. One and a half million acres of forest have been put up for sale, forests where the reindeer have been grazing for millennia. Rivers with legendary names such as Rynda, Olyonka, Kharlovka, Varzina, and Sidorovka have been given in concession to foreigners, and Santa Claus's reindeer constantly find their passages to the seaside blocked. "Russia no longer belongs to the Russians, believe me."

Tatiana lights a candle under the icon of Saint Nicholas. She explains that the reindeer give everything they have: fur, meat, milk in the dead of winter, building materials (bones and antlers) even where trees don't grow. They are uncontaminated animals, the quintessence of therapeutic purity. They spread out on the land so as not to use it up. They eat moss, mushrooms, dry grass, and when there's nothing else, even algae from the sea. They draw their strength from the womb of the earth. They don't need vaccines because the cold kills off the most tenacious germs and prevents the spread of infectious diseases. Kola is one of God's gardens. But the global has no respect for the sacred, and the herdsmen know no peace. For them there is no Santa Claus to save the day in his sky-blue sled. The very countries that celebrate him are killing off his symbolic animals.

In the languages of the Great North, the Arctic peoples are known by a name that means simply "man." They live in the great void, almost always alone with their animals, and they never think even in tribal categories, let alone nationalistic or imperialistic ones. Man has no need of adjectives to be recognized in the great white spaces. It's not important that he distinguish himself from the other men, only from the bears, the wolves, the hare, or the reindeer. When he leaves the great solitude to return to the world of supermarkets and mobile phones, it happens that he feels more like his animals than the civilized bipeds that he meets on the street. "When I go into the city," Vitaly smiles, "the people horrify me so much that it's not hard for me to feel a sense of brotherhood with a reindeer. Or even that I feel, quite simply, that I am a reindeer."

Tatiana cuts a slice of salted reindeer meat and a golden loaf of bread. She explains: "People here didn't know what bread was before the Russians came. And a lot of Russians came here during the Stalin years to avoid the Gulag. Those who were threatened with arrest moved of their own accord to the less desirable parts of the country, and Kola was one of them. Otherwise, there's no way to explain the large influx. There aren't just miners and soldiers." Vitaly's grandparents came to Lapland from Arkhangelsk and brought with them their knowledge of bread. Vitaly: "I remember them well, Ivan Mikhailovich and Anna Mikhailovna, always in love. They came to the Kola Peninsula in 1938. They made me fantastic pancakes."

On the street, it's dismally cold and wet. Packs of stray dogs, very well behaved, with blue eyes, are out looking for food, and women are hoeing their gardens, preparing the soil to plant potatoes. But the climate has changed, spring is late in coming, as are summer and winter, too. The reindeer are reluctant to move until May or even June, to avoid being swallowed up by thin ice. Fresh snow is scarcer and scarcer while ice continues to accumulate, and for the animals it's increasingly difficult to dig down to the dry lichens. Everything has changed for the herds and consequently for people as well. Slaughtering season has moved from November to January/February, months that overlap with the early stages of the reindeer's pregnancy.

In a food market, I run into a Sami hanging out by the draft-beer tap. He greets me like an old friend, and under the withering gaze of the woman behind the counter, he afflicts me with his fantasies about the billions of rubles that he is infallibly going to earn by selling the antlers of his herd to the Americans. To do what with? I ask him. "A new, amazingly potent, natural Viagra. Potency, potency!" he exults, making the umbrella-up-the-butt gesture with his arms. He rattles on about microchip collars and ultrasound against mosquitoes, new devilish tricks to save his animals from extermination, and he's completely unconcerned that I don't understand a word he's saying. The woman pours us another beer, and meanwhile outside another blizzard is howling.

"Naturally you are Finnish," says Tatiana Vasilyevna, concierge of the only hotel in Revda, a nowheresville on the bare mountains of Kola. And she looks at me calmly as she arranges her light blue dressing gown.

It's ten o'clock at night. Instead of the moon, there is a giant orange sun lighting up the woods with a stupendous copper glow, but all the same, finding a place to sleep at that hour is not easy, especially in Russia, especially in out-of-the-way places like here on the last frontier, especially with someone like Tatiana Vasilyevna.

"Actually, I'm Italian," I reply, imagining that it will make no difference. I'm standing in the snow, hungry as a wolf, holding my flaming-red EU passport, freshly renewed in order to avoid any problems with the Russian police, and inside it a costly business visa, which frees me from the obligation to register at local police stations and authorizes me to make a double entry into the lands of the federation. So everything is in order.

Behind us the streets of Revda are utterly deserted. The only sign of life is a terrorized mouse that scampers over my feet. Fifty yards up the street, the strawberry-red sign of a supermarket with no cars parked in front. In the empty parking lot, a loudspeaker is broadcasting something indistinct and grating that is supposed to be music. There's also a civic-minded election campaign poster of a man with the face of a gangster and the slogan WITH ME THE FUTURE OF KOLA. Just beyond it, the endless forest. Meanwhile, I've pasted on my face the most respectable expression I can muster.

There follows a moment of silence. The hotel is a prefabricated, two-story building, cube shaped, in gray brick, thirty feet away from the prosecutor's office. Exactly as in the Wild West, the saloon is two steps away from the sheriff. The atmosphere is right out of the Klondike in the gold-rush years. The same ramshackle houses, the same alcoholic haze, the same streets with people looking out at you from behind the curtains. There's also the jail, surrounded by hedges and barbed wire. In effect, there's not much difference at all. Here, too, there is an El Dorado of precious metals. Only the woman with the pagoda hairdo reminds me that I am in another world.

I tell her again: "Italiano, Italian, European Union." Under her old-fashioned hair bun, Tatiana's face suddenly comes to life with an expression I recognize: panic. Soviet panic.

She hisses: "Italiano? It makes a difference, and how! Russia has a bilateral agreement with Finland, which gives Finns the right to equal treatment. They can come here to fish for salmon. But Italians, my God, Italians, they've never been seen around these parts. You'll have to go somewhere else, leave, no, come in quickly before they see you."

The woman pulls us into the reception area, which is also her kitchen, where until a moment ago she was dozing in front of the television. Black and white, obviously. She looks at me desperately.

"Naturally, you are registered with the police."

"Naturally, no, I've just arrived here, and at police headquarters the police are sleeping," I say, sitting down placidly in an armchair. I explain to her that we have just arrived from Lovozero.

More terrorized silence. Vasilyevna looks at me as though I am a catastrophe, as though our unannounced arrival meant sure arrest for her, deportation, and Gulag.

"Disaster, disaster. It's not permitted. Only in Lovozero are there hotels for tourists . . . authorized hotels."

"Ma'am, the last bus for Lovozero left three hours ago, and now we're stuck here. But don't worry if it's a problem for you. We have sleeping bags, and we can sleep in the woods." I'm bluffing, naturally, our sleeping bags are very light. We would freeze to death. I'm hoping to make a breach in the wall by showing our determination.

"Well, then, let's do this: stay here if you like, but from this moment on, you can't go out again. If they see you, I risk a fine of 800,000 rubles. It would take me a lifetime to pay it." I notice that the woman is trembling. Outside it's snowing again. Fine crystalline flakes and wind accompanied by the usual orange sunlight.

"I'll just make a quick run to the supermarket. I'll buy myself a sandwich and a beer, after which I swear I won't go out again until tomorrow."

"Go ahead, but don't speak in your language. If they notice that you are a foreigner, they'll file a complaint against me, and nobody will ever be able to get me out of paying the fine."

I tell her I don't feel comfortable keeping her in anxiety, and in the meantime the poor thing throws herself into a vortex of telephone calls. She tries to find some high-ranking official who can free her from her anguish. Three, four, five calls in both directions. The voice on the other end of the line is always female and equally nervous. Our arrival is turning into a problem of diplomacy.

A few minutes go by, and when I'm already imagining the arrival of the police, the phone rings again, and a voice enunciates the longed for, liberating monosyllable: "*Da.*"

In the Soviet world, people's fate was suspended on one of two monosyllables: *da* and *nyet*. It was not a choice between doing and not doing but between paradise and damnation. Here in the Arctic, it seems that the old world still hasn't disappeared.

"*Khorosho!*" As the nightmare fades away, Tatiana is transformed; she jumps to her feet and pirouettes toward the kitchen and the hallway. OK! We can do it! Hell yes, we can do it! She's happy for me and for herself, and a sort of halo lights up around her head. Electrified, she shows us our room, the lace curtains and the view of the mountains, the common kitchen at our complete disposition, the toilet and the shower in the hallway, all for less than ten euros. Tatiana's happiness is threatened only by the menacing face, in black and white, of Vladimir Putin, who has in the meantime appeared on television.

"My God," I say to her, "that man never smiles. We have a head of government who laughs all the time." But Tatiana does not take the bait, and she defends her hero. "Under Putin everything is better. Salaries have gone up, the roads are safer, and you can go home late if you like." Now she can go back to her armchair to enjoy her programs while outside the red lighthouse of the sun lights up again. It's eleven o'clock, and it's free rein at the supermarket, where, wandering down aisles packed with things we've never seen before, we manage to put together a dinner composed of chives, sour cream, cucumbers, eggs, black bread, algae with herring, fermented beets, and Baltika beer. A lovely brunette at the cash register bids me a blushing farewell. "Come back again."

The only sound heard in the hotel that night is the scraping and tapping of our forks against the ceramic plates.

News of the arrival of foreigners with backpacks has made the rounds, and already the next day, I receive an invitation to dinner by no less than the pope of the local Orthodox parish. An odd type, they say, who saves young people from alcohol by giving them lessons in self-defense. It seems he's as big as a freezer and has played goalie for an ice hockey team. Ivan the park ranger adds a key detail to his saintly pedigree: "Father Leonid was a Rambo in the special forces." Everybody in Revda knows about his picaresque conversion. He had gone into business, and when his partners started killing one another, he realized it was time to respond to the call from above.

We set off on foot toward his house, walking on the edge of the forest. Ivan and his wife are with us, and in that immense silence, we notice that we are chatting with one another in whispers. The apartment buildings of the city of miners have their lights on, and I like to imagine them full of humanity and stories. I feel a hidden warmth in this Russian North. But on those empty streets, I feel like a man alone in the universe. I repeat the names of the cardinal points in Russian: *sever*, north, desolate asperity of the Gulag; *yug*, south, a funnel that sucks you down toward the bottom; *vostok*, east, like the launch of a catapult; and *zapad*, west, the sound of falling head over heels.

Batyushka Leonid opens the door on the second floor of a shabby condominium, and the surprises keep on coming. Inside there are three more giants like him, men from the Russian special forces but still in service. Strewn everywhere are sleeping bags, gigantic backpacks, automatic rifles, mess tins, ropes, spring clips. The three of them, together with two young boys, have established their base here for climbing the local mountains. Along with Ivan and his wife, we have brought our contribution of food for the dinner, and now we lend a hand to help set the table. On the table, apricot chicken, bulgur salad, smoked reindeer, Arbatski Dvori salami, vodka, the usual licorice-black bread, and the inevitable herring.

Outside it's snowing like Christmas and inside it's bitter cold. "It's always like this. When it's warm for three days in a row, they turn off our heat, and they don't give a damn if the winter temperatures come back." Leonid the bear recites the Paternoster and imparts his blessing, slicing the air with his enormous paw. "And now, *ne stesnyaite,* don't be bashful and dig in." Nothing honors and warms the Russians more than an elaborate toast, and since everyone is looking my way, I realize it's up to me to begin. I raise my glass of vodka and look around at my extraordinary group of table companions. In Italy, nothing like this would be possible or even imaginable. Priests and soldiers, a fascist combination. Here, no, the three soldiers seem like quiet Alpine guides.

"Dear friends, your language is not unfamiliar to me. At the gates of my city, the Slavic world begins, and on this table there are things that have names that I know: *khleb,* bread, *voda,* water, *maslo,* butter. But do you know what women are called where I come from?—*babè*" (pronounced bah-BAY). A wave of laughter; in Russian it means the same thing. "And when you want to say that a woman is a really beautiful woman, do you know what we say?—*babôn.*" Even louder laughter; the word sounds incredibly funny in Russian, full as the language is of terms of endearment and diminutive forms. I explain that I have the good fortune of having a fantastic profession that allows me to meet wonderful people, "people like you"—and I bolt down my glass of burning water in a single gulp.

Now it's Leonid's turn. "Brothers, it's cold here, but the cold is warmed by our friendship." Monika translates his words in my ear. She's happy, too. "Politics keeps running forward without caring for anything. But now we are here among simple people, united by our faith in Christ. So I raise my glass to our guests from far away, knowing that we will carry them in our hearts." And down goes another glass. Out of the corner of my eye I see Vdovin and his wife beaming with happiness that our meeting has gone so well.

Out come olives, French wine, and Italian Gorgonzola. We eat in noisy good cheer. The three soldiers drink no alcohol, but they drink down our words. I tell them the story of the Triestian who discovered the archipelago of Franz Josef, the last piece of Russian land before the Pole, and that the day of my sixtieth birthday saw the fall of the frontier around Trieste, so I decided then to come up here to the North to find another one.

The smallest of the Rambos is moved. "Sixty? You're halfway. I wish you a long life and the chance to tell many stories." As with the Jews, here a hundred twenty years is considered to be the right life span for a patriarch.

I'm feeling so merry that I explain to the pope my pagan theory of hibernation. The Alpine peoples and those of the North, who from time immemorial have experienced the reawakening of bears at the end of winter, are naturally prone to believe in the truth of resurrection. Even before Christianity. Didn't the shamans dress as bears?

Another of the Rambos takes a long look, in silence, at the map of the journey. He's stretched it out on the floor to get an overview of the whole itinerary. He calculates, mutters to himself, and then bursts out: "But you're crossing Europe vertically?"

"Fantastic!" I say to him. "You've given me the title of the story. Vertikalnaya Europa." And the discovery obliges Batyushka Leonid, already euphoric over the hibernation revelation, to unleash a new toast to the health of Europe and of its hidden soul on the red line of longitude.

4. WHITE SEA

THE MURMANSK–NOVOROSSIYSK TRAIN—twenty-four army-green cars—is rolling south, muffled and soporific, among ice-encrusted lakes and rivers swollen from the thaw. Violent yellow light to one side, the Finnish border to the other, gray sky overhead. Every now and again it snows. I doze off under the gray blanket of the Russian railroads. I can feel the train's musical score filling up with muted bass notes. Everything becomes syncopated, even my notes on the page. At Olenegorsk, where we boarded, an elegant blond in a forest-green duffle coat (almost the same color as the train) sat superbly erect in the gusts of snow, alone on the bench of platform number two, saying good-bye to a man and crying like Anna Karenina. On the other side of the steam-frosted glass, I watched her disappear on the horizon, still sitting alone on the bench, and her image seemed to embody Russia.

Now the sky has opened up again; a yellow light shines out of the woods and illuminates the whole car, which is thumping rhythmically through the birches with a crisper double beat. On board, it is lethally hot; the passengers doze, chat, and munch without letting so much as a crumb of bread fall to the floor. It's morning, but all of them, even those who boarded at Olenegorsk like me, have already picked up their fresh sheets from the conductor and made their beds. Russian trains are an endless eat 'n' sleep, a long rock-a-bye nap through the forest. The ride can last as long as three days. They travel thousands of miles like an express train but stop every twenty minutes like a narrow-gauge local. Imagine an interregional from Glasgow to Palermo or a local from Montreal to Miami. If you're already punch drunk from the sleepless sunlit nights, taking to your bunk is the only way to live through these distances and these Siberian tempos.

I jot down: blouses, froufrou dressing gowns, muscle Ts, leotards, slippers, baby bottles, well-mannered children who play quietly with toy cars and say *"dobry dyen"* (good day) when I pass by. The second-class compartments don't have doors, but there are no intrusive looks. They all mind their own business, and if a woman has to change her clothes, it is common practice to turn away. There is a solidarity among the passengers that is unthinkable in my country. Monika moves in this intimate space with an extraordinary delicacy. She doesn't steal even one snap. Before taking a picture she excuses herself with her eyes, engages in dialogue, smiles, explains who she is. She manages to strike up a relationship in just a few seconds. Then she captures the image of a mother nursing her baby next to the window, of a man stretched out on his bunk reading a book of poems by Osip Mandelshtam, and of a pallid girl combing her waist-length hair, looking sadly out the window. For my part, I've got to deal with a fat guy who, while he's climbing up to the overhead bunk, does a full split in his pajamas, right over my head.

Every car is governed by a uniformed conductor, more often than not a woman. What a waste of personnel, I thought at the beginning, but I soon changed my mind. Our traveling functionary has a million things to do. She gets off the train at every stop and stands on the edge of the platform, welcomes new passengers, notifies those whose stop is coming up, serves hot water from the samovar located at the end of the corridor, checks tickets, keeps the bathroom tidy, hands out mattresses, sheets, pillowcases, and pillows, and helps the handicapped, the elderly, and children. She's much more than a ticket checker. She's a shaman who takes you to the mysterious tundra, a dispenser of security, an affectionate and tireless guide. The forests pass, the teakettle grumbles, and she arrives with a fuming glass of tea in a pewter cup-carrier with a drawing of the Smolensk Thunder Tower on the side.

The Imandra station, between a lumberyard and an immense lake. The stopped train snores for two or three minutes. Four wooden houses and, in the distance, white-capped mountains. A dream. Ah, to get off here, alone with a backpack and an inflatable canoe, knock at the door of a house and ask for a bed. Then go off and paddle your way among sandy islands ringed by thin ice toward an infinite horizon of birch trees, go through the passage from the lake to the river and then to another lake, lose yourself in the maze of rivers and lakes, all on the same level. The rivers here have changed direction. They don't flow north any more but toward the White Sea. They're swollen and cobalt blue, turn to froth in little rapids, and in the meantime the low light has turned even yellower.

Imandra, what a magnificent name. No roads pass through it. Its only contacts with the world are the train and the ferry. I look for it in the fragment of the guidebook to Scandinavian Russia that I've brought with me. Nothing. Not a word about what I'm looking at outside my window. Guidebooks are pages of nothing. Only banalities. Accomplices in the forgottenness that has descended on these territories. They facilitate destruction with their silence. I tear out those few pompous and useless pages, roll them into a ball, and throw it into the waste can. Yes, it's better to travel asking information from the people you meet, and maybe the perfect journey would be made blind, without so much as a map. Making your departure just by getting on the first train that's going your way.

The Arctic Circle meridian is still far away but almost imperceptibly I begin to feel the South. The tundra is thinning out; patches of tender green crop up in the burned brown of the lichens on the granite. The rest is still lakes, forests of naked birches, aquatic labyrinths. My face is glued to the window. I can't pull my-self away from the landscape of the North until Andrei, forty-five, dressed impeccably as a member of an orchestra, wakes me from my spell and asks me about my journey. I tell him about being a war correspondent in the Balkans and Afghanistan, and since he too had gone to Afghanistan twenty-five years before as a soldier, in the region of Kandahar, the question is not long in coming:

"What do you do when you're walking through a village, you see a boy playing in the middle of the street, and then that boy shoots you in the back? Tell me, what do you do to that boy?"

I remain silent.

"We pulled out of Kabul, and now the British and the Ameri-cans are there making the same mistakes we did."

"We Italians are there, too," I tell him.

"You're something different. . . . You don't have a colonialist approach. Your Alpini left behind a good memory of themselves everywhere they went on the river Don." He asks how we're trav-eling in Russia.

I answer, "With a backpack, on buses and trains. Without res-ervations. Asking advice from the people."

"You're brave," a woman who has overheard our conversation chimes in. "We Russians are full of bandits."

Andrei: "But no, you'll be fine. The majority are good people, like everywhere else, really."

More lakes and woods, but the undulation of the terrain has become more nervous. We're entering Karelia, with its thousand lakes between Russia and Finland. A gray house with POLYARNY KRUG written on the side indicates the passage of the Arctic Circle. Our train is running on the right track, the normal left track is occu-pied by a convoy of woodsmen who are clearing a sixty-foot swath on either side of the line. Now the metamorphosis of the landscape has accelerated. The prairies are strewn with erratic boulders. The spaces expand, the meridians widen more decisively, the light is yellower, the taiga (forest) greener, the trees more robust.

The station names have more vowels. Knyazhaya Guba, Knäsö, Poyakonda. At Loukhi, three young anglers come onboard. They come from Kalevala, and that name, as soon as it's pronounced, resounds like a rifle shot through the compartment. Kalevala!—the land of the epic of Väinämöinen, the *Iliad* of the North, the legend of the boatbuilder bard. Now the train is navigating between swollen blue rivers, all flowing southeast. Anton, a young angler who has been to Italy, tells me that Kalevala is a good place to live. "There aren't any new Russians or busloads of Western tourists who have soaked up all the fishing licenses on the Kola Peninsula. The roads are terrible, and the rivers are the best way to get around. A wilderness paradise."

Where am I? In Europe or out of Europe? What are the boundaries of my world? The river Don? The Urals? The river Bug? Or this *pogranichnaya zona* (border zone) with barbed-wire fences and guard towers that runs alongside the train? And what if Europe were nothing but an unreachable mirage, as Witold Gombrowicz said, for those from the East who go looking for it? Or what if it were a slow becoming, a progressive thickening of ethnic groups toward the land of the sunset, beyond which lies nothing but the endless ocean? The Arctic peoples I have just encountered on the Kola Peninsula—are they or are they not European? And what about Karelia, where does it belong? To be sure, my world does not correspond to the conglomerate of banks that is the EU, nor to Catholic-Protestant civilization. People say that Christ is the symbol of the West. Why not Zeus then? And does Bethlehem, which is in the Middle East, belong to some anti-Christian world?

I'm actually not on a frontier at all, but in the middle territories, where millions of people have been torn away from their homes, and regimes have left heaps of ruins. But I'm also in the lands where, as Monika says, the gods talk to one another. Where Christianity is infused with the shamanic magic of the North, where the faithful prostrate themselves as though they were Muslims, and rabbis have cohabited for centuries with the onion-domed bell tower. I look around me at this train full of young people and children, and I think that maybe the real sign of where I come from is senility, the white beard with which I stubbornly insist on traveling like a kid. Here in the lands of the Sarmatians, the Slavs, the Finno-Ugrics, of the Parthians and Dacians, I feel that I belong to a world that is falling apart, drowning in perfect unconsciousness. Like the Roman Empire.

Some brutish policemen come aboard wearing camouflage uniforms. They stride through the car with the conductor, looking for something. In a compartment near ours, there is a young man dressed in black, tattoo, boxer's nose, short hair, big hands and red knuckles, his eyes hard and tender at the same time. He doesn't sit down; he's tense, restless. He torments a set of rosary beads in black wood and looks insistently at Monika and her cameras.

She gets over her embarrassment and takes him by the hand. She makes him sit down, asks him why he looks so serious.

He says, right out, "I just got out of jail. Two years."

"Are you going home now?"

"Yes, but I don't know what's waiting for me when I get there." It's clear he's afraid of something, or someone.

"Do you have a family?"

"My parents abandoned me when I was three." He holds his hand at knee level to show how tall he was. "I spent ten years in an orphanage."

In Russia, everyone knows that orphanages are the ideal place for criminal recruitment.

"Have you got a girlfriend?"

"Yeah, a girl from Belarus. She wrote to me in jail. But I've never met her." He shows me a letter, then a picture. "Pretty, eh?"

He sighs and looks out the window into the woods. "Now it's full of blueberries and strawberries. Soon it'll be mushroom season."

"You like the woods?"

His yes is a crisp nod of the head, like an act of submission. Then he takes his rosary and puts it in Monika's hand. "This is yours," he says. Then he looks at me, standing there in silence. I ask him if he made the rosary himself.

"Yeah, I made it, but not for punishment. The priest told a lot of people to make rosaries as penance. But I didn't trust that guy. He used to be in the KGB. I made my rosary because I wanted to."

I take it from Monika's hand. Black, solid, with fifty beads and six crosses. I tell him it's a splendid gift, that we'll keep it forever. I rummage through my jacket and offer him the only thing I have to give him. A Swiss Army knife.

"Here, my friend, this is our gift to you. But first you have to give me a kopek. Otherwise it will bring you bad luck."

He digs the copper coin out of his pocket and holds it out to me. I tell him about my kids, gone far away from home to find work, and his eyes tear up again. Every time I tell him something that goes straight to the heart, he turns his head so we won't see that's he's upset. I look at him closely. His eyes are far apart, of a rare deep green, with golden sparkles. His smile is embarrassingly sweet.

I notice his strong neck and ask him if he has ever boxed.

"Yeah, but I was a chump."

I tell him my father was excellent. Lean and agile, he could knock me down with only the slightest movement of his body. His eyes tear up again.

The train is pulling into the station at Kyem, jumping-off point for the Solovetsky Islands. We're getting off here. We say good-bye. "Do me a favor now and keep out of trouble." We give him our address and phone number. He writes down his for us. Alexander etc. I see that he lives in a village nestled among the great lakes. A land of enchantment, which, however, terrorizes him.

Now the train is stopped in the rain. From platform number two, I look back at a young man dressed in black, looking out from behind the window, pretending not to cry.

"Maybe we'll meet again," Monika calls out to him.

He smiles: "Well, the world *is* round, isn't it?"

We cross the tracks of platform one, our legs turned to mush from sadness, our black rosary in hand. Alexander. We'll carry in our hearts forever the gaze of this orphan with the tender heart, stranded on a troubled road.

Looking at it from the wharf, the ferryboat for the Solovetskys—the monastery islands turned Gulag—looks as though it's suspended like a hot air balloon. Climbing on board makes me dizzy. It's floating there in the void between the equally gray and horizonless sky and sea, and its tethering lines seem to be the only thing preventing it from taking off and flying away. "Sometimes the White Sea and the Northern sky blend into a single mass of light," I had been advised on the way here. It's true. It's drizzling, cold, the lack of shadows has flattened all the features of the seascape, and today, boarding ship for the other world really does seem like a metaphysical experience.

"Wait here and don't ask questions," the woman at the ticket window on the wharf freezes me in my tracks. I had simply asked her if she could give me some information about the schedule, but in Russia questions often bring out the *Homo sovieticus* who sleeps in every public employee who works behind a window. The timetable says six o'clock, but, damn it, it's now seven, and another passenger has heard that the boat will be departing at nine thirty, which inevitably will become ten. I calm down. No one on board is complaining. Time is suspended. The boards of the embarcadero are the same ones used by Stalin's prisoners, and the village of Rabocheostrovsk comes peeping out of the mist: fifteen birchwood houses blackened by time. On a promontory, the chapel where they have just filmed *Ostrow—The Island*—perhaps the most beautiful film on spirituality and madness.

Fifteen years ago, the Solovetskys became monastery islands again, and their fame attracts throngs of sinners in search of grace—beggars, theologians, prophets, disillusioned businessmen, the gravely ill, mystics, and bamboozlers. Standing on the dock is Viktor Ivanovich, Ukrainian, born in 1940, a gray overcoat and a forest of gray hair, a man who travels all the time, sleeping in train stations and hermitages. He looks me right in the eye like the prophet Elijah on the dock in Nantucket before the *Pequod* sets sail in search of the white whale. "You are not Russian!" Then he explains: "Russians have the look of a martyred people, and you don't have that look." Then he takes flight: "God is good for body and soul, and I feel great. God is on my side and God is strength. Alcohol is death."

Then, calm as can be, "There's going to be a war, very soon, it will break out during the Olympics in Beijing. We don't have much time." I don't take him very seriously, but he certainly seems sure of himself. He says everybody knows, in the monasteries, that something's about to happen. He asks for a contribution for his ongoing pilgrimage. I hand him a few rubles. Then he goes on: "My life is in God's hands, and God is not to be understood. God is to be felt, and I feel his presence. Since 1983 I've been living as a monk. Before I worked in Norilsk, where lumber arrived from half of Siberia to be exported." I ask him if he's ever been beaten up by some drunk young Fascist. He says no: "They've never thrown me out of a train station, where I spend my nights between one monastery and another. And I've stopped defending myself from violence. I don't defend myself from anything anymore. I've forgotten how to do it."

The wooden hotels next to the harbor, in one of which we spent the night, are tourist traps where the sacred is mercilessly profaned. Inside, techno music. Outside, brutish shaved heads in dark suits and expensive cars. They're the local gangster bosses. That's obvious from the rooms in the cottages: Western prices for broken door handles, trashed toilets, showers that leak brown water. To escape from this underworld degradation, we stayed up late last night, walking around the area in a fiery light that inflamed the railroad tracks, the same ones that had brought dissidents sentenced to the Gulag to their destination. The wind carried such a strong smell of freshly cut birch trees that the whole of Karelia seemed to be lying on a bed of sawdust. We felt as though we were walking around a gigantic lumberyard.

Finally, we're off. A long rumbling starts up, like a submarine. For two hours we are immersed in the luminous gray of a glass of anisette—a flat, oily sea. Then, after the third hour, the onion domes of the kremlin, enclosed behind huge walls, flown over by formations of ducks, come out from behind the curtain, toward the bow of the main island. We've brought along an emergency backpack in case we decide to stay the night. We have toothbrushes, a knife and dried reindeer meat, pumpkin seeds, and a book of Russian fables. But it's a tough choice. The Solovetskys are a place that steals your soul, where it's better to stay a month or not to stay at all. We are inside a maze of churches and hostels for pilgrims, teeming with men and women dressed in black, and the maze rests on glacial masses so formidable that Mycenae and Machu Picchu don't measure up. In addition to this, the Solovetskys also manage to be Elsinore together with Constantinople. Denmark, Byzantium, and Siberia all rolled into one.

Roman Catholics ought to come up here, to the sixty-fifth parallel, to see what faith means in the world of sunlit nights. I'm taking an exploratory walk around the perimeter of the walls. I did the same thing the first time I went to Jerusalem. It's a sort of courtship dance, a preamble. Monika has gone looking for monks inside the kremlin, which used to be a prison. I go wandering around with a pilgrim's walking stick outside of the fortress, among lakes and beavers, browsing monks and cows, *izbas*, and grazed fields. The sun is shining now, and the windows of the massive perimeter bastions seem like watchful eyes. One especially, square with a pyramidal roof, which looks like a hat. It seems miraculous to me that orthodoxy, born in Byzantium, somehow found the strength to come all this way.

Wedges of ducks fly over the wood while the monks take their cows out to graze. But among the houses in the old village, I come across some cottages with English names: Welcome and Green Village. After the heroic years of the reconstruction of the monastery, we're already in the package-tour era, and I'm afraid this place, still infused with spirituality, might decay even faster than Athos, the sacred mountain of the Greeks, disfigured now by internecine wars between the monks and by slush-fund scandals, not to mention the diabolical plague of cell phones, which has broken forever the prayerful silence. I stop at the edge of an inlet where the sea is as still as a lake. I slice a piece of dried reindeer and fraternize with an enormous cat who has sniffed the aroma of my snack.

I'm walking on an undulating terrain covered by a velvety green carpet and strewn with erratic boulders, struggling again, as I did among the Sami of the great North, with the sensation of passing through a world on the verge of extinction. In front of the weather station, I say hello to a passerby, and sure enough, she introduces herself: "Nadyezhda Leonova, voice teacher." In Russia, don't ever say hello to someone if you don't have a few free hours on your hands, because that someone will respond to your greeting and will invite you to fraternize. Now that I've said *zdravstvuitye* to Nadyezhda Leonova, that's enough for her to invite me into a shed where some monks are building a wooden boat. It's a historical replica of the *Prepodobny Zosima*, the *Saint Zosima*, the ship on which Peter the Great sailed here. She explains to me that the blessing ceremony will begin in just a few minutes.

So that's how Monika and I were able to be in attendance at an extraordinary event, just the two of us along with the inhabitants of the Solovetskys. A monk enters the workshop, as gaunt as an icon, an effeminate voice, someone the wind would easily carry away. When he puts on his vestments, bright yellow, he is transfigured and unveils a quiet magnetic force. He utters a monosyllable and the onlookers hush. "That's Herman," one of the shipwrights says to me, standing stiffly at attention, "the man who, fifteen years ago, re-populated the islands and began the restoration of the monastery."

"Alexander, Pavel, Andrei, Nikolai, Mikhail, Vassily."

Now Herman calls upon all the saints, makes mysterious signs in the air, immerges a gold cross in a basin, launches into the lit-any. Nadyezhda and her friend Larissa respond in chorus. The men, bearded and speckled with wood chips, genuflect, get back up, re-peat the theatrical Russian sign of the cross, and slowly it appears that the boat is moving away from the shore and that the czar in person is sailing with us toward a brightly lit sea. At the end, Her-man sprinkles us with a sort of brush dipped in holy water. But it's not a blessing; it's a shower, and I'm soaked down to my belt.

We finish celebrating around a table with steaming hot tea and pastries—pirogi—made with a berry called *groshinka*, saturated with the aroma of fir trees. The monks and shipwrights have the faces of whalers. They tell us that the monastery was founded four centuries ago by a monk whose name was also Herman. Then it was a Gulag, and after the Gulag an army base. Finally the new Herman came and began restoring the chapel in order to have the minimal necessary space to say Mass. Since then, there has been a proces-sion of monks and volunteers who year by year have restored the churches, the dormitories, the museum, the printing shop. A lot of the new tenants on the Solovetskys are people who come from far away and decide to spend a part of their lives here, as a vow.

"Throw away that cane," the *hegumen* (abbot) with the long ashen-gray hair exhorts me as he bids me farewell. "You can make it on your own." I promise him I'll do it at the earliest opportunity. "Come back," Nadyezhda urges us, "this is a sacred place," and she tells us of the sunlit nights, or better, a special thing that in Russian is called the "white silence," and of God who inhabits the Solovetskys. The prisoners who came here were not afraid, because they could feel this spiritual energy. "Here, the prisoners had more hope than in the other concentration camps of the North." By now the little ship of Peter the Great has brought us together, taken us to the symbolic heart of the Karelian epic: the boat that is run ashore and transported from lake to lake, the same one that in the times of the Vikings sailed up the rivers of the Balkans and down the other side of the peninsula all the way to the gilded domes of Kiev. We are all a people of voyagers.

At six in the evening a mustard yellow light descends over the islands to exalt every wrinkle in the terrain. The weather is magnificent, and even the launch *Tuman*, the rust bucket that's supposed to take us back to the mainland from a crooked wooden dock out of Mark Twain's *Old Times on the Mississippi*, is shining like a goldsmith's display case. Onboard, another extraordinary court of miracles has already gathered: a small woman with Tartar cheekbones and boots; a guy with wild eyes and a silvery scalp, carrying a riding crop; a blond with reindeer gloves and a blouse wide open in the sun; a bearlike man dressed in camouflage togs who looks as though he just got back from Chechnya; and an old Scottish woman, wizened as a dried cod.

At the stern, there's a kitchen with doors and windows that open out on the sea, and a fish soup on the fire. Amidships, two windowed sitting rooms with a bench on the inside perimeter, which obliges everyone to face one another and talk. But get a load of the crew: an entire family. The maxi-size mother rules over the kitchen and cleans the salted cod on the side of the ship, using water from the lake. The father smokes behind the helm. The older children go up and down, to and from the engine room. The youngest—Losha, thirteen—helps out everywhere he can. He's a tough and sweet boy who is already a sort of vice head of the family. Hang in there, old *Tuman*; when they replace you with a hovercraft, all of this magic will go with you.

The departure is a wheezing, gasping cough, a delightful

throat-clearing of rust and salt, with a trailing skein of seagulls and, towed behind us, a frothing bulk-loaded pontoon pulled by a steel cable. Water and sky have again changed color together. The water blue, like a large river, the sky blue, puffed out like a jib in the north wind. At the stern, the distant kremlin shines white on the island bristling with pine trees. On the port side, three large dolphins, white as the Holy Spirit, act as our escorts. They're called *byuna* ("pallid ones"), and an excited young girl shouts out their name, leaning forward into the wind like a figurehead.

But when the fish soup is done to a T and the aroma has stoked everybody's appetite, right then we hear another shout. I don't understand what it means; all I can see is the guy in the camouflage togs pointing his binoculars into the sun back toward the islands, already vanished below the horizon. Now all the passengers are looking in the same direction and shouting the same name.

"A sea lion!"

I see him too now, his presence marked by some overhead sea swallows; the birds form a turbine around the school of fish that he's preying on. He looks like a big white dolphin, a little mountain of snow that emerges and disappears.

"There are two of them!"

"No, three!"

I see them; there are also some babies. The white hump of the leviathan glistens in the blue.

Wind, excitement. I open my map of Vertikalnaya Europa, spread it out on the deck of the bow to determine our position. The map is eight feet long and a foot and a half wide, and a small crowd gathers to see it. They recognize their world, rediscover their places, and add new ones. So right there in the middle of the White Sea, we're deluged with the advice and suggestions of the pilgrims to the Solovetskys. "Go to Kizhi, on Lake Onega; it's a forest of wooden domes. Go when there's a full moon; go to hear the morning prayers." Another almost cries out, "The island of Valaam!"

and as he names it, he crosses himself three times, so great is his reverence for the place. He points to it on the map, in the middle of Lake Ladoga, with its monastery. But already another hand, a pale feminine hand, is searching farther down, and a finger points to Novgorod. The woman asks me for my pen and adds a note in Cyrillic on my map. Another revered place of Russian orthodoxy.

But it's not over yet. The gorilla in camouflage reveals that he's Ukrainian. He bends over the map, stretches his mug toward the Carpathians, and says, "Pochayiv, the holiest of churches, where the pilgrims arrive on foot and stay overnight in the church." Outposts of the faith that have somehow survived the Stalinist repression, territories on the frontier that Monika has been exploring for twenty years. I realize that the map could be much longer. Passing by Mount Athos, it could go all the way to the rock-hewn churches of Cappadocia, the crib of Christianity, where half a century ago Islam stifled the sound of the last church bell. In my mind's eye, I see again the labyrinths of rocks and torrents, hear the roosters again, calling each other from valley to valley, see a ray of moonlight thrust like a sword into a hermit's cave on the side of a mountain. And then, even farther down, next to Bethlehem, I can see the Greco-Palestinian monastery of Saint Saba, solitary and fortified, at the top of a gorge, sandwiched between Jews and Muslims. At the foot of its walls, an immovable custodian refused entrance to Monika because she was a woman.

Everything starts to come together. From this vertical journey, it emerges quite clearly that Catholicism and Protestantism are living in their safety zones behind the front lines. The faith on the front lines is Eastern Orthodoxy. The hand-to-hand conflict with totalitarianism and rival monotheistic religions is not the stuff of priests, popes, and cardinals, but of solitary patriarchs, archimandrites, and hegumens like Herman, forgotten by Europe in their turreted outposts of the faith. I can see again the patriarch of Istanbul, in his office under the portrait of Mustafa Kemal Atatürk, whispering words of coexistence while from the Bosporus to Hagia Sophia, the cry of the muezzin annihilated all other sounds for the vespers prayer. An acoustic competition with no hope of victory.

"Go to that frontier," I was told years ago by Enzo Bianchi, prior of the Bose community in Piedmont. He added with his ardent eyes: *Those lands are a volcano of wars, vitality, and faith.* I was leaving with Monika on a journey to the Holy Land, and there, too, looking at a map covered with notes, helpful hands rushed to indicate the fortresses of the faith, and their recommendations exhorted me to go beyond Jerusalem, toward Saint Catherine's monastery in the Sinai and onward along the Nile, to the Wadi el Natrun monasteries, where they grow grapes and olives. Monika made the rest of that journey on her own to the land of the Copts, to the desert monasteries, all the way to the high plateaus of Ethiopia, to Lake Tana and to the African Jerusalem called Lalibela. Now that journey of hers back then and this one to the borders of the European Union have been fatally joined.

I realize that the map of this vertical journey should be twelve feet long, go all the way down to the heart of Africa. I fold it back up, and meanwhile at the stern, a small mirage has come into view. The desert and the northern sea have a lot in common, and now the most distant islands, toward the east, rise up on the horizon as though it were an air cushion, and if it weren't for the serrated rim of the fir trees, they would be dunes in the Sahara in the incandescent hours. Beyond the white wake of the launch cutting a swath through the cobalt surface of the water, the last strip of water has taken on the color of the sky, giving the illusion of a horizon lower than the islands. I'm traveling in a world of visions, where God doesn't let himself be caged in by catechisms, but remains unsayable, incommensurable, undefinable behind the incense that envelops the holy icons and the regal doors of the altars.

Now the last light of day has lit up the tree trunks on the nearest islands, which are suddenly inflamed, taking on the same rum tint of a Spanish doubloon minted in Martinique. That's when I let go of all of my doubts, grab hold of my cherrywood cane, and throw it as far as I can, into the waves. It spins through the air, plunges into the water, sinks, and reemerges to be painted red—it, too—by the fiery sunset.

5. KARELIA

ONCE AGAIN A TRAIN for the South, direction Medvezhyegorsk. It's windy and rainy outside, and it's delightful to stay under the covers and look out at the Baltic–White Sea Canal that's running along next to us with negligible changes of level, from lake to lake, river to river, through water meadows, peat bogs, and springs. The double beat of the wheels on the rail joints is slow, heavy, soporific. The stations have high-sounding names: Byelomorsk, Sosnovets, Krasnaya Gora, Spalovaya. The immense canal was dug by prisoners of war and inmates of the Gulags. In the beginning, the barges were pulled through it by hand from the shore, a drudgery worthy of the era of the pyramids, but the totalitarian nature of this place was not enough to crush its human inhabitants.

In Medvezhyegorsk, I see, for the last time, timetables for the Murmansk line. All the trains go up there or come down from there. Twenty trains a day, some days even more. The woodstove in the waiting room is crackling. Outside, the rain is coming down in waves, and I can feel that I'm coming out of the vertical dimension to initiate a long, wearying zigzag. Then there's the assault on the bus for Velikaya Guba, our next destination, on Lake Onega, where Monika is hoping to meet a Polish writer who is said to interpret even better than the Russians the soul of these places.

A person who lives in an *izba* on the lakeshore. We would have been overwhelmed by the crowd if the bus driver, realizing that we were unschooled foreigners, hadn't intervened on his own initiative to get us a place.

As we're pulling out into the rain, I realize that we are not on a bus but in some sort of submarine. A heated cabin for fifty people, sealed shut by dark glass windows, beaded with water vapor, whose visibility has been made even worse by pleated green curtains, swinging back and forth in a vaguely hypnotic rhythm. And then villages whose names are all the same, labyrinths of birch trees, sleep-inducing ups and downs with women coming and going in the rain. The route is a slalom between forests and lakes, all pointing southeast, which if you look at them on the map, says Monika, look like "a newspaper where an ink pot was overturned."

It seems that we've arrived at land's end, but no, the serrated coast of the Onega deceives us by elongating even farther, stretching out into infinite archipelagos, lakes, fjords, and promontories, all desperately alike. We read the names of the various towns with care. The road signs point to Uzkiye Salmy, Myagrozero, Velikaya Niva, but of Velikaya Guba not even a hint. Plus, the signs give you no sense at all that you're nearing some kind of urban center. In this immense sylvan landscape, all they do is separate one forest from another. Struggling to keep our eyes open, we look attentively at every sign of humanity: a sawmill, a bridge, a police station. Then the migrant within me realizes that we are no longer heading southeast, that is, in the direction of the "ink spill," but we have turned east. So I ask a fellow passenger where the devil is this blessed Velikaya Guba.

"But that stop was four miles ago!" the woman shouts, as though the responsibility for the error were hers. Inside the bus rolling on through the woods, there is a flash of dismay, which immediately turns into a wave of fraternal alarm for the two lost foreigners. From the back of the bus, the Russian woman makes her way up to the bus driver—"Alexei, stop! Now!"—and he slams on the brakes in the middle of the woods, gets out, helps us find our backpacks, explains the way to go, and then takes off again on a slalom between mud-filled potholes. There's just one thing he didn't tell us: we'll have to go the whole way on foot because at that time of night—nine o'clock—there's not a living soul traveling through the forests of Karelia.

This was a fix we'd gotten ourselves into. What were we thinking of when we decided to take a bus to this godforsaken place, just to look for some writer by the name of Wilk, that is, Wolf, surely a misanthrope, somebody who's come all the way here just to escape from Poland? Monika, who has read two of his books, made me curious by telling me that he sleeps on his woodstove like the Russians of yesteryear, that he doesn't have a telephone. He lives on fish, the potatoes and onions from his garden, and boiled water from the lake. But now that we are here, alone in the subarctic night, exhausted in the middle of the forest, dragging our backpacks on wheels, I'm overcome with desperation.

If only this guy lived in Velikaya Guba, which is, after all, the last administrative center on the north coast of Europe's second biggest lake. No, the oddball has settled down on the farthest outskirts of town, at the end of a maze of little woodland roads. The people on the bus had tried to explain the road to us: "Go on foot until you come to a little wooden church dedicated to Saint Simon, the patron of vagabonds. Ask in town, everybody knows where it is. The Polish guy lives right near there, with his wife, Natasha. You can't miss it!" But I haven't got the least bit of confidence. If we got lost on the bus, we'll surely get lost on foot.

It is at this point that out from the absolute silence of the forest, under a rainy sky, comes the car of Judge Maximov. Walking along with my gimpy gait, I've already been swearing for a mile and a half, and it seems too good to be true that this late-traveling automobile, the only car in circulation in the entire district of Onega, is passing right by us as we're walking on the gravel, dragging our backpacks behind us. Oleg Maximov looks to be around forty, speaks decent English, and immediately bends over backward for us. He clears the backseat of piles of court documents and files and invites us to get in. He can't believe that a foreigner of my respectable age is hitchhiking in Russia. He says it's dangerous; there's no telling what might happen. I reply that in Italy it's worse. Nobody would ever have picked me up in the woods after dark in such a deserted place.

Oleg: "You're a wise man. I could see that as soon as you came into view, from the way you were walking." They say things like that in Russia. They put their heart in your hands right off the bat. One time in Italy, on a train, I met an elder caregiver from Smolensk who, after five minutes of conversation, asked me if I was happy. It wasn't just formal curiosity; she really wanted to know. Obviously, it had been years since anyone in Italy had asked me a question like that.

Velikaya Guba is a forgotten piece of old Russia on the shore of Lake Onega. Having grown up around the dock for the ferry to Petrozavodsk, today it is a small conglomeration of colored *izbas*, together with the remains of an old sovkhoz (expropriated Soviet farm), a country library with the samovar always on the stove, an alarming monument to the Soviet heroes from the secret services, and a small psychiatric hospital, which may have had some connection to the KGB.

Next to a small food store, the magistrate picks up a young boy who knows how to get to where we're going and takes us on a dirt-road roller-coaster ride all the way to our destination, a solitary heath on the lake, surveilled by skeins of *chaikas*, the seagulls with a supernatural squeal, immortalized by Chekhov and unbeatable in vertical diving. Nothing at all to do with our marauding omnivorous seagulls. The *chaika* is a genteel beast that flies light, like the Holy Spirit, and certainly symbolizes it much better than the dove, unworthily promoted by theologians to the rank of God's bird.

By now it's eleven o'clock, and it's frigid, but Mariusz and Natasha's house, next to the chapel of Saint Simon, is burning in the evening sunlight. The Northern sky is like that: when it catches fire, it repays you for all the gray it has afflicted you with for days, weeks, or months. The chimney is smoking, so there must be somebody home. We bid farewell to the judge, but before he goes, Oleg makes us a present of a bottle of the elixir of Onega as a down payment on an invitation to his house for dinner in the next few days.

Now we're on our own in the wind. The "burning" house creaks, wind gusts whistle through the cracks, and as it opens, the front door sounds a long lament like a boat in a raging sea. I make my way forward, tottering on the loose boards of the most dilapidated entryway I've ever seen, and knock on the door, to my left, of what I imagine is the kitchen. It feels like a ghost house, but no, the odd couple is there, just finishing their candlelight dinner. Blond Natasha Vladimirovna, sitting next to the *pechka*, the wood-fired stove with a crackling fire, invites us in with a big smile. To get to know a man of the North, you have to understand his house, but since the heart of the house is always the *pechka*, the fire is always where you start. Next to the fire is where you are born and where you die. Around the fire is where encounters are sealed.

Mariusz struggles to come out of his wolf-man silence, and then he loosens up and talks. The stove is big, six feet by nine, as tall as a man, and is always in the "women's corner." The pagan idol stood there, in the feminine heart of the house. That's where offerings were made. But when Christianity arrived—a late discovery for the Russians—it became the "impure" corner and, in contraposition, the corner opposite the fire came to be known as the "holy" space. The religious icons were placed there. The *izba* is a concentrate of symbols. The ceiling is a blend of soot and larchwood resin where once the stars were painted, while the tree trunk at the apex of the roof is the Milky Way. The *izba*, therefore, is a representation of the cosmos in a world where until yesterday a shepherd was before all else a medium, someone able to interrogate the great silences of nature.

It's midnight, and the horizontal sunlight, doubled by the reflection off the lake, fills the house, enters even into the mouth of the *pechka*, as though to light the fire. It's something inconceivable in the Mediterranean world, a sacred mystery that Sergei Yesenin described better than anyone and that Mario Rigoni Stern, author of *The Sergeant in the Snow*, discovered to his amazement in 1943, on the front of the river Don. But it is only the beginning of the journey into a blazing constellation of symbols, which only now, after millennia, are losing their meaning and are calling for a poet to ensure they will be remembered. As Wilk tells it, "At the moment of birth, the door of the *pechka* was opened to propitiate the passage of the newborn baby, and if some burning coals fell out, they were gathered up to prepare an infusion for the mother." When the baby was born, he or she was placed immediately on a mattress on the roof of the stove-mother, cozy nook and perfect reproduction of human warmth. It's made of clay, the same biblical paste from which humankind was fashioned.

The idea that all of this is being lost deeply concerns Mariusz and Natasha, and they feel they have been called to a mission to save it. She has opened a school of weaving and traditional cooking in Velikaya Guba. He focuses on this age-old heritage in his writing to save it from oblivion. The Pole has now definitively come out of his diffidence and is talking in torrents. "By now almost no one lives here on a permanent basis. The lake has become a vacation spot, and the people have all bought Canadian woodstoves. The Russians are losing their memory of what it meant to spend a winter on a Russian stove. You know, when it's forty below, you can sleep naked on top of the stove. Every now and again you go out, make a hole in the ice, pull out a bucket of water and take it home. That's the extent of your relationship with the outside world. You're hungry? Make a hole in the ice and fish. Have a fever? You treat it with a wet blanket and juniper branches covered with berries. There's talk of a certain Ivan who never left his bed on the *pechka* all winter long, not even if he was summoned by the czar."

Now the lake is bristling from the Arctic wind. The sunlight has turned metallic.

Mariusz: "The season is behind, but that's better for you two; there aren't any *parmaks*."

I ask if he's referring to neighbors.

"No, they're enormous flies with monstrous eyes. If they bite you, you're cooked. They only live for ten days, but those ten days are frantic. They take aim at you from miles away, come at you like a cloud, and throw themselves at every part of your body that you've left uncovered. If your horse gets bitten, he goes wild with pain and there's no way you can control him. Those flies are bloodthirsty. They call them the locusts of the North."

There's a leather shaman's mask on the wall, called a *skoromokh*. Wilk puts it on and imitates the sound of the wind. Karelia is drenched with paganism, and the Christian world has rather precariously superimposed itself on it with its own array of icons, incenses, and tenebrous chants, also drenched with magic. All around the lake, the shields of granitic rock, smoothed and scratched by countless glaciers, are full of prehistoric graffiti: salmon, swans, beavers, geese, ducks, bears, reindeer. "There's a hunter on skis, bow and arrows in hand, chasing after a reindeer. They could be the oldest skis ever represented by man," Wilk observes. "But the most moving image is the one of a Great Mother, traced around a fissure in the rock in the position of the vagina, the barycentric symbol of Earth's fertility. Christianity—just imagine!—interpreted it as a sign of the devil, and carved a cross over that sinful body. It's not hard to understand why the Karelians were fiercely hostile to the first evangelizers."

I'd be happy to stay here and confabulate until morning, but my eyelids are dropping like roll-down shutters, and I retire to the attic with Monika, on two ramshackle beds with springs, in a freezing-cold room, far away from the maternal warmth of the stove on the ground floor. It's a cold for long underwear, which I don't have. My lightweight sleeping bag offers a precarious refuge, twenty-eight ounces of salvation folded up in the bottom of my backpack that, when opened, creates an air space sufficient for survival. Sleeping without a wool cap is unthinkable, so I slide mine over my balding head down to the tip of my nose. There's a bucket of lake water in the hallway for washing face and hands and cleaning the pit toilet behind the little door of a draft-filled water closet. But in these temperatures, hygienic rites are performed in a hurry, and I know as soon as I get into it that I won't be leaving my den until eight tomorrow morning.

The wind whistles through the cracks; the *chaikas* sail over the roof, screeching. With even the slightest movement, the bed twangs like an out-of-tune piano. Maybe that's why one of the wolf-man's four cats, a sly little Russian devil, decides to sit on my feet and huff. I don't know how, but I sleep like a rock, dreaming in Cyrillic.

In old Russia, don't let yourself be fooled by the phrase "go to see the neighbors." It can involve walking for miles. Mariusz and Natasha's neighbors live in the locale of Sibovo, the most god-forsaken village on the lake, about four miles from Wilk's house, reachable only by a mud path where you have to go on foot or with an off-road vehicle. The *izba* is caulked like a boat, and the lady of the fire is Vala Fyodorovna, a robust woman, cheerful and vivacious. As soon as she sees us pop out of the woods, she runs inside to put out on the table everything she has: candies, smoked fish, marma-lade, brown bread, and butter. Then she goes to stoke the fire, but not without asking me my father's name. To us it might seem like a superfluous curiosity, but for Russians to get to know you, they must absolutely know this fragment of your genealogy. They are sure that behind every name, and especially behind a patronymic, there is a saint, a miracle, a story. A key to your personality.

"My father's name was Pyotr. And I am Pavel Petrovich."

Vala responds with a big Russian smile. Then she goes to check on the bread that's rising in the *pechka*. She dances around the fire with the skill of a midwife, handling the baker's shovel as though it were a pair of forceps, then comes to the table with a samovar that's huffing, puffing, and whistling like a locomotive. Her husband, Jura, has already gulped down two glasses of vodka and is talking happily about the growth of the beets in his garden. He goes into town only to buy salt, sugar, cigarettes, and vodka. Everything else he makes at home. For fish, there's the lake, and in Russia, with all that water, fish is not something you buy but something you catch. Especially at this time of year.

The house is bubbling over with that slightly manic gaiety that bursts out in the brief Northern summers, when all farming activity is condensed into three months.

Vala: "I'm fifty-eight years old and I feel young. And with a mad desire to go to Italy."

Her husband, laughing: "I'm sixty-two, and if you go to Italy by yourself, I'll hit you in the head with a hammer and send you to your grave."

She's holding an icon. "You see this, Pavel Petrovich? This is the only survivor of the many that we used to have around here. Thirty years ago, some tourists came from Moscow. They got drunk, robbed the icons from the church, and then set fire to it."

He changes the subject: "Our cat has disappeared. He was perfect for mice. Now I don't know how to find a new one. Kubais, his name was, after one of Yeltsin's corrupt ministers. You can't imagine how nasty he was. The minister, I mean, not the cat. He stole everything we had. The treasury bonds he made me buy I ended up selling for two bottles of vodka."

Vala has a brief conversation on her cell phone. Then she explains: "You know? I can only answer calls with this damn thing. I can't make a call with it; my fingers are too big. One time I pushed three buttons at the same time and it stopped working. The people at the store couldn't understand how I'd done it."

Jura: "Today I have to plant the potatoes and buy some firewood. I'd better get to work."

I ask him why he has to buy firewood when the place is surrounded by woods. The dialogue starts to flow fast and furious. Monika translates as fast as she can, between a piece of candy and a cup of tea with honey, while the fire crackles with seasoned birchwood.

"Good question. The woods used to be owned by the state, and then that effing privatization policy came along."

Vala reprimands her man: "Watch your language!" Then, turning to me, "You know? Last fall I saw some bear tracks right outside the house. There was fresh snow on the ground and the prints were clear. I knew it was a bear because the dog was barking in a strange way."

Jura: "I swear I wasn't drunk that night. When I went out and saw those footprints in the moonlight, I said to myself, *Who is this crazy guy walking barefoot in the snow?* Bear prints look exactly like human feet!" Everybody laughs, including old Katya, just arrived from town for a visit, with some pastries and a big lemon for the tea, which fills the room with the aroma of the Mediterranean.

Vala points at her husband. "You see that guy there? When he was courting me, he had to row fifteen miles across the lake. When I wanted to see him, I would steal a horse from the kolkhoz [collective farm] and ride ten miles at a full gallop. That was desire. Today, with their cell phones, they have no idea what desire means."

Jura: "I'll say! Just thinking about it makes me want to take another roll in the hay."

She laughs. "What can you do, Pavel Petrovich? That man and I have been together for thirty-eight years. And Jura is a real muzhik. There aren't any more muzhiks among the young people today. Jura Fyodorovich was born here, on this *pechka*. His father pulled him out of the birth canal, not some midwife."

Jura, who has had a little too much to drink: "What are we effing talking about? Bears? Horses? Children? I'm totally lost."

More laughter, then a toast just between us men.

We talk about the kolkhoz, which turns out not to have been so bad. Vala: "My brigade was good. Cows, potatoes, and good schools. Today there aren't any cows, nobody grows potatoes, and the schools don't teach anything worthwhile. The kolkhoz is finished, and the countryside is finished, too. Look how overgrown it all is. The cowsheds are all closed. It makes my heart ache to see how bad things are. But who wants all of this?"

Jura: "But come on over to have yourselves a sweat in our *banya*! You can't live without a *banya*. We're crazy about it; as soon as we can, we fire it up. It's not only a way to get washed. It's our culture."

I ask how you can tell if it's too hot.

Jura: "Easy, when your ears roll up. Then you have to throw yourself on the floor, where the temperature is cooler. And cover your head with a wool cap."

Vala: "But in Italy don't you have the *banya*?"

No, I tell her. At most, there are saunas.

"But how can you live without it? It tempers the body. If you use it right, you never get sick, I swear. Last year my husband didn't do it, and he got sick right away. The sauna isn't the same. There's no lake to jump into afterward." Turning to her grandson, who has just come in. "Just think, Vadim. In Italy they don't have the *banya*!"

Vadim: "Really? What pigs."

Jura brings to the table a loaf of bread fresh out of the oven. It has an incision on the top in the form of a cross. He asks me, "What do you do for work?"

I tell him I write.

"Well, then, be sure to write good things about us. Listen, would you like a fish? We've got a refrigerator full." He opens the fridge and pulls out a bucket of pickled fish. He takes one out and wraps it, still dripping, in newspaper and hands it to Mariusz.

I tell them about the present of the dried cod we were given in Kirkenes by the Russian Nikolai, the captain of the fishing boat, that guided our glorious crossing of the most difficult border in Europe. "Of course they had to let you through." Jura laughs. "Fish don't need visas." Right, just try to build a fence in water. Water is the last free space in this world, where everything is privatized and stolen.

We go out to the lake. A skein of geese is crossing the road to go drink. Another fantastic treasure of Slavic peasant culture.

Jura: "Mind you, don't ever call a lady a goose. It's an offense to the goose. Geese are hyperintelligent. If a platoon of five hundred geese perceives a threat, they divide up into small groups. They keep pastures like golf fairways because they don't tear out the grass but clip it with their sawtooth beaks. And if they get rankled, they know how to defend themselves. That beak is worse than three bee stings. To get the better of them, a predator has to attack at night, cut their throats, and leave them to bleed to death. The fox and the *rosomakha* know that perfectly well."

I tell them that the goose was introduced into the cuisine of our Po Valley by Jews who came there from Poland. While the Christians celebrated the end of the harvest in November by roasting a pig, the Jews, on the feast of Saint Martin, November 11, sacrificed a goose. Today goose has become a dish of fine restaurants, and it is said that those who don't eat it on Saint Martin's Day won't earn the "beak of a penny."[5]

Vala: "Look, Petrovich, look at the wonder of our Onega. Here there's no need for cinema or TV. You just enjoy the lake. Look at how the old wooden houses turn red at sunset. Architects from all over the world come here to study them."

Me: "Rather than architects, what the houses needed are some good carpenters to fix them up. There's an extraordinary cultural heritage here that is going to ruin for lack of maintenance."

Jura: "True, we can see them falling apart right before our eyes.

They've been officially designated as historical monuments, so the owners are not allowed to do any work on them. Look at the house owned by Yevgeny and Alida Pechugin, that one behind ours. One day the broken part pulled back and brought the sound part with it, and the whole thing collapsed. People here don't have the money to do the kind of restoration that the preservation authorities would like."

My God, I think, *the mechanisms of swindling are the same everywhere. Simple and predictable. Yet nobody does anything about it. Not in Italy, either.*

———————

Farewells, kisses, wishes for the future. Jura waves his arms high and wide from the door to the steaming *banya*, his towel around his neck. He has to work off a flask of vodka with a nice long sweat. The potatoes and the firewood will have to wait till tomorrow. We walk back to the Wilk house, fish in hand, and for the entire four-mile trek, each of us will be enveloped by a swarm of mosquitoes, instantly awakened by the smell of our warm bodies and the pickling. We wave our arms comically and uselessly to keep them away. "In another week, it'll be a lot worse," Mariusz consoles us.

On the edge of the woods, on the right, the remains of the sovkhoz "Progress" come into view, stripped bare by privatization as though by a plague of grasshoppers. Until the 1990s, it was thriving and prosperous and was known as the Millionaire. Now the roof is gone, and most of the bricks have been stolen. Its cowsheds used to house more than two thousand dairy cows. Today, says Wilk, they call it the City of the Dead. Only oblivion can save this town from the fury of the thieves. Churches, farms, *izbas*; they would carry everything off. The Church of Santa Barbara, five centuries old, has been saved only because nobody knows about it, and you can get to it only by boat, in a hidden corner of Lake Yandoma, about twelve miles from Velikaya Guba.

Monika has started up conversation with a peasant woman named Gala, bent over at the end of a little dock on the lake, about fifty feet away from her little wooden house. She's intent on activating the pump she uses to water her vegetable garden. She tells Monika that her mother died recently and she has been left alone with her garden. "Come in," she tells her, and she invites her in to see her treasures, all affectionately addressed by diminutive nicknames: taters, carotelles, strawbabies, peasies, and so on. "Explain to your readers that it's a sin not to cultivate the earth," she says to Monika, and her elementary truth startles me. Why don't our priests thunder from the pulpit against this first of all sins? Why don't they say that the earth will go to ruin from abandonment? Gala explains that the watering has to be done with care. This plant shouldn't be drowned; this one, on the other hand, can be watered abundantly. A complicated geography of dedication, concentrated in an Eden no larger than nine hundred square feet at most.

Slogging through the mud on the way home, we talk lightly about heavy subjects, such as the sense of returning, the special dreams of the traveler, and the polar vision of the world, which belies the pretended grandeur of empires. We go through them one after another like fresh cherries. With our salted fish as our trophy, we talk about the difference between a traveler and a vagabond, about Taoism as the definitive expression of shamanism, about the relationship between the sweetness of the countryside and the vocalic softness of the Russian language. Then, once again, about the concept of the frontier, of borders, of this Europe of ours seen longitudinally, and finally, the theme of the difficult separation from the book, the father of all imaginable journeys, which, when the time comes for you to go off to confront the world on your own, can become a sort of cumbersome ballast.

The conversation continues around a table covered with all manner of God's bounty: canapés with slices of hard-boiled egg, cheese, beer, cucumbers, beets, and Jura's salted fish, nicely laid out on a serving dish with chives. Just before midnight, when a fantastic yellow light invades the room, illuminates every crumb left on the tablecloth, and lights up the deep womb of the stove, Mariusz unloads on the table a mountain of books, a worthy dessert after such a marathon of ideas. The mountain is made of fifteen illustrated editions of a single work, the *Kalevala*, the *Iliad* of the North, a gargantuan serving of epic that would make any *Lord of the Rings* look pale by comparison. A fluvial composition, made for these woods and conceived in these woods. It was on the shore of this lake, Mariusz Wilk recounts, that the *pechka* builders and the taciturn people of woods came together to define themselves reciprocally and generate fascinating bastard fruits. Karelia—if you haven't seen it, you can't understand the essence of this frontier land of woods, lakes, and rivers, where the boat is the only sensible means of transport but which is the heart of an epic that left its mark on history, just like the epic *Gilgamesh* in Mesopotamia. In a town on the northern edge of our frontier, Voknavolok, there is an old woman by the name of Sandra Remshu, who is still able to sing the saga in the original language—the last of her kind, perhaps, in all of Karelia, Finland included.

I leaf through spellbinding pages of icons, gold leaf, lithographs in black and white, where Byzantium and the Great North, the Gothic and the Orient, are wed in a natural way: streamlined boats like dugout canoes gliding in the moonlight, fights to the death between warriors clad in animal skins, fires burning in the night, flaming sunsets, lakes, constellations, endless forests. I enter into a world where there is no division between land and water and maybe not even between life and death. In the Great North, the road you will take depends on the tracks you've left behind you in the snow. Everyone has his own path, the Sami say, and if you know how to find it, your passing into the other world will be imperceptible. The Arctic peoples, whom Wilk has known and described, believe that there is no difference between the world on this side and the one beyond, and that in both there are reindeer.

Here, too, in Karelia, where rivers, lakes, and gulfs form inextricable labyrinths with minimal changes of level, the separation between land and water, forest and open sea, is labile. On the Onega, the equation between moving from place to place and embarkation is so perfect that they don't speak of "sailing" with the boat but of "going" with the boat. Instead of "building" a boat they speak of "sewing" a boat, in evocation of a sophisticated operation that was once executed almost magically, without nails. The bard in the saga of *Kalevala*, old man Väinämöinen, was before all else a builder of boats. Song and sailing, war and hunting in the woods, are the same thing in his epic. Pier Paolo Pasolini knew by heart the death of the hero Lemminkäinen, killed by a boy motivated by jealousy. It even seems that Pasolini carefully constructed his own violent death inspired by that thousand-year-old poem.

On the shores of Lake Onega, I come to understand a lot of things about the history of Russia: the voyage of the Scandinavian ships from the Baltic all the way to the area of Kiev; the naval power of Peter the Great built on the iron mines of Petrozavodsk; the epic of the Danish, Finnish, and Saxon carpenters and shipwrights who not only built the first large sailing ships of the empire of the czars, but prepared the way for their transport via land all the way to the White Sea and the Gulf of Finland, a mysterious itinerary that nobody has since been able to reconstruct; the descent of the Viking boats to the Black Sea, beyond the imperceptible watershed that separates it from the Baltic, in the land of diverging rivers known as Polesye; the pharaonic and obstinate foundation of Saint Petersburg at a cost of blood, sweat, and tears; and the attempt to Europeanize Russia, a world created on a different, irremediably Asiatic scale.

We are so enthusiastic about Mariusz's library that he makes us a present of a precious "mini" edition of *Kalevala* with black-and-white wood engravings by Miod Miecew, a work of illustration that took eighteen years to complete. A little marvel, perfect for my backpack. But because on a journey lightness is everything, reciprocating a gift with a gift becomes a question of spatial economy and therefore of survival. Up to now, with every gift received, I've had to liberate myself of something. I received a smoked fish and I gave a knife. A handmade rosary replaced a salami; a little book on the Solovetsky Islands slipped into the space freed up by a map, by then no longer useful, of Norway. The whole meaning of life is contained in these renunciations of the non-indispensable. Here on the Onega, the epic of *Kalevala* demands an important eviction, and the choice is soon made. I give away my mosquito net, which will certainly be more useful to our two friends on the lake in the days of the *parmaks*, the vampire-insects of the North.

In Velikaya Guba, the explosive power of the brief Northern summer is concentrated in the beehives of Adel Dinislamovich Khasanov, a geologist who lives at No. 5, Street of the Geologists, a beekeeper born in the "land of beekeepers." That's the meaning of the name Bashkiria (in the modern Republic of Bashkortostan), a mysterious lost region in ex-Soviet Asia. For two months, from mid-June to mid-August, this man with a Turkish face and name doesn't sleep, so he can take care of his bees. "Please excuse my disastrous garden," he responds to our attempted approach, "but I don't have time." He has us rapidly don suits and protective hats with wide flaps and mosquito netting, then he asks us to follow him to a row of red and yellow beehives on the edge of the woods. Amid the neurotic buzzing of the worker bees, Adel almost has to shout to make himself heard. He uncovers the boxes one by one to make sure everything is in order.

"In Bashkiria the summer is long and it's easier to work, even the bees are more relaxed. Here the ice doesn't melt until the end of May, and the bees go at it like crazy to collect as much as they possibly can. By the time autumn comes, I believe they're exhausted, as I am." Adel searches inside one of the hives, practically dives in, and he can't find the queen. He gets upset, then he spies her in a corner, next to a pile of royal jelly. He shows her to us. She looks to me like a fat slave girl in the middle of a harem. "I like my work, but there's too much to do. I don't have time even to notice that it's summertime. In two months, if the season is good, I produce two thousand pounds of honey. I've got twenty-five hives and thirty thousand bees."

"Today, they're upset," he adds. "They get this way when the weather changes. They're meteoropathic animals," and in fact they swarm together to form a cloud around our face nets, making a noise that sounds like a prolonged short circuit. We go in the house to drink a bit of birch and raspberry tea with molasses. Adel puts a piece of wax and honey on the table, plus some bread with marmalade made from a forest fruit whose name we don't understand. I ask him about bears, if they come near the house in search of some sweet honey. He says they come, and how!—and every time, it's a problem. The bees fight back like mad; they defend themselves in every way possible. They are a strong race that holds out for a long time in winter. To be sure, it's better for a man to meet a bear in the woods than a cloud of irate bees.

In the Slavic world, bees and bears are so intimately tied that around these parts—and not only these—bears have taken their name from honey. The word in the eleven time zones of the Slavic world is *medvyed*, and it comes from *myod*, which is the word for honey. The bear is a totemic beast in Russia and the surrounding countries. In 2001, when I was pedaling toward Istanbul with two friends on a beautiful ride through the Balkans, I met a tough-ass Ukrainian who was cycling around the Black Sea on a bike with a bearskin seat. It was all I could do not to genuflect like a Cheyenne before a medicine man or a totem pole.

So it's *medvyed* from the Bering Strait to Slovenia. And because I hail from a city on the Slovenian border, which is the country with the highest density bear population in all of Europe, I've seen them a number of times on my cross-border jaunts in the countryside. One day, I tell the Bashkirian, I crossed the border on a bicycle heading toward the Isonzo River, and I stopped for a snack next to a truck that a Slovenian beekeeper had turned into a mobile bee-hive. When they retire, a lot of Slovenians outfit one of these hives-on-wheels and move their bees around according to the flowering periods of the various plants. I struck up a conversation with the man, who was taking the sun about thirty yards away from his self-propelled farm full of mountain honey, when we heard a loud noise and noticed that the truck was moving up and down. The door of the hive was open.

It was clear. A bear had gotten inside. "And now all we can do is wait for him to finish," the Slovenian said, resigned. After a while the brown beast stuck his nose out, surrounded by a cloud of irate bees but nonetheless in a state of ecstasy and totally indifferent to our human presence. He was drunk on honey. He came down the access ladder and staggered back into the woods, followed futilely by the cloud of bees. Adel laughs and mutters, "Yes, that's exactly how it is." Try as he might, he can't bring himself to hate the beast that halves his earnings. The bear, he says, is many animals in one. Like a lion, he downs mammals much bigger than he; like any ru-minant, he pillages crops; he steals grapes and fruit like a monkey; nibbles on berries like a blackbird; plunders anthills and beehives like a woodpecker; digs up tubers and larvae like a pig; and catches fish with the dexterity of an otter. And he eats honey like a man.

The frenetic beekeeper finally sits down and takes a break from his incessant activity, but only to talk about bears and honey. One day, I tell him, we saw one at the edge of a clearing shining bright with the first snowfall of the season. He was rocking back and forth and his front paws were making strange signs in the air. It was hard to tell if they were intended as threats or only as a sign of annoy-ance or anxiety. Then he got back down on all fours and started moving in our direction, still shaking his head. There were three of us, on skis. We had come there from a town on a trail several miles long. Obviously, we didn't hang around to understand the bear's intentions. We turned on our tracks and were gone, faster than the wind. We skied for a good twenty minutes without looking back, and the first two in the line never, and I mean never, had time to check if the breathing they heard behind them was a companion or the bear. The last in line, me, logically stayed glued to the end of the train for fear of remaining alone with the beast, and keeping that tight formation we skied faster than we ever had.

Adel laughs at this scene out of a Walt Disney cartoon. I tell him that at the time I laughed, too, once the fear had passed, but I remember that we were all left feeling a mixture of reverential dread, attraction, and a profound sense of mystery, as though we had inadvertently crossed a shadow line. Personally, I became certain of one thing: the bear was now my totemic animal, irritable and cuddly, gluttonous and unpredictable. Since then, my life has been marked by repeated and memorable encounters with bears. I feel them as they are coming back, in this Europe that is going back to the wild and filling back up with woodlands. I follow their movements in Italy, from Abruzzo to the Maritime Alps, to the province of Trent. I've seen them migrate to the northwest of Bosnia, escaping from the war and the mines. And here, with the Bashkirian of Karelia, I feel at home. The inhabitants here all have a little bear in them. And the Russian women, unlike their Western counterparts, love their bear-men rather than obedient apartment-dwelling puppy dogs.

I've learned in my travels not to ask too many questions. It's better to talk about yourself. Offer something of yourself and your own story so that the dialogue turns into a bartering of firsts. I tell the beekeeper that in the late 1960s I went to the mountains of Durmitor, in the wild heart of Montenegro, to climb a few mountains, but I came down with a fever and spent two days alone in my tent while my friends went off to climb on their own. In the delirium of 102°, I brought our reserves of food into the tent, without thinking that it would have been better to hang them from a tree limb. That night I woke up to a strange noise and saw the shadow of an animal projected by the moonlight onto the side of the tent. A bear, no doubt about it. It was clear that he was about to come in, so I did the only thing possible. I jumped to my feet yelling and waving my arms in such a way that the whole tent moved, like a specter in the shadows. It worked. The bear disappeared, I hung the food on a tree, and my fever vanished instantly from the fright.

Adel praises the delicacy with which his historical antagonist gathers blueberries, opening his paws like a comb, so as not to ruin the plant. Nobody would ever guess that this same animal, maybe even the day before, had eaten an entire calf, leaving only the skeleton. "Sometimes you can mistake them for men," he says, "they leave similar tracks in the snow." Then he jumps to his feet, turns toward the yellow-red line of the hives and asks us to lower our voices. "Hell, I hope it's not him. A bear comes if you invoke him. That's what our old folks used to say. A bear is a shaman in disguise." The Bashkirian walks slowly and stealthily over to the hives. But no, everything is quiet. He looks at his watch and says good-bye. It's late for the loads of things he has to do. And we leave the house of the bear-man to head back to the house of the wolf-man.

Out on the windswept lake, the hovercraft is going southwest in the middle of a wilderness archipelago with no roads, a place where only the onion domes of the wooden churches, reddened by the setting sun and surrounded by birch trees, tell you that you're not in Quebec but in Russia, near Finland. Karelia, land of free frontiersmen, land of peasants, poets, and shipwrights exempted for centuries from serfdom because they were effective defenders of Holy Russia.

The *Cometa* is an enormous sparkling mackerel skimming over the surface of the water, and everything on board—hostess, aerodynamic sheathing, disco music, and whiskey on the rocks— is designed to yank you painfully away from the warm *izbas* of

Velikaya Guba and push you to the West, toward the marmoreal Petrozavodsk—the factory of Peter the Great—which comes into view on the horizon, sleek with Scandinavian order, against the pink evening sky.

On the way, we stop briefly on Kizhi, the island with what is claimed to be the most beautiful wooden church in all of Russia. I would have time to see it, but on the only mooring dock there's a cruise ship called the *Karl Marx*. The sacred place has been invaded by American tourists, so we decide instead to enjoy that cathedral of the North from afar, with its architecture that belongs more to Istanbul, Samarqand, or Tabriz than to Warsaw, Hamburg, or Salisbury—places where the perspective direction of our nave doesn't make sense, because everything is vertical. In Russian churches, you're not supposed to look toward the "far end" but "up high," as you do in the Hagia Sophia in Istanbul, a thousand years older than Saint Peter's in Rome.

One day it happened that the gold, incense, and chants of Byzantium sailed up the Dnieper and the Volga toward the forests of the North. The Christianity of the Greeks, threatened by the advance of the Turks, penetrated inland toward what would become the Third Rome (Moscow), discovered the land of the long shadows, and encountered the great soul of the Russian people. The cross married the birch, and the Byzantine liturgy absorbed from its new world the legends of that salvific wood and the primordial forest. It was then that the icons born on the Bosporus came to know the shipwright and the wood carver's chisel, acquired relief, lost abstraction, and found rough-hewn corporality. The gleaming gilded tablet had already become sculpture, a ligneous talisman.

The passage to carving was not at all, as some have written, a concession to the illusionistic corporeality of the West. It was a Russian product, which married the hypnotic power of the Byzantine icon to the peasant soul of the land of Rus, made of anthropomorphic masks, dragons, the prows of the longships of the

North, or fantastic creatures from the rivers, the woods, or the crops, carved to keep away the cold, famine, and storms. What was born of this wedding were not idols, but holy images of an unimaginable miracle-working force. Today we can see the product of this dazzling contamination: portable churches for travelers; long-bearded saints who agonize sitting down, wrapped in a black mantle; others with swords drawn against dragons or beating the devil with a chain; painted iconostases pullulating with images; patron saints of mountain springs wearing the sweet countenances of matryoshka dolls; royal doors carved with a precision of a Persian bas-relief.

I think back to what I saw on the Solovetsky Islands. That's where I put away forever the stereotype that sees Orthodox iconography as something cold, algebraic, obsessively conservative, immutable, and fixed to its Greek archetype. Instead, on the monastery islands in the middle of the White Sea, I saw the explosion of a decorative art that was warm, almost floral, of an unexpected and overflowing physicality, even similar, at times, to the images of the rubicund cherubim that you see in certain Alpine manger scenes. In the land of the long winters, the medieval was grafted onto the Baroque without passing through the Renaissance, whose carnal verisimilitude was incompatible with the Orthodox soul, much less with the spare solemnity of its origins.

After opening the books of the Kalevala, I am crossing the Onega with the sensation of a new epiphany coming to fruition. I think again of the royal doors, those openings in the iconostasis, where the faithful can peek through and see, beyond the isthmus that divides (or joins) Heaven and Earth, the terrible instant of the sacrifice, with the knife of the pope cutting into the bread. The doors were the hinges of Eastern spirituality, far more mystical than ours, and the abbot Pavel Florensky—executed by Stalin in 1937—defined their symbolic meaning with Pythagorean precision. But it is not true that the royal doors were initially decorated only with pictorial representations. As early as the thirteenth century, in Hilandar, and later in Novgorod, Pskov, and even Ioannina, capital of Epirus, there were doors enriched with bone inlays or wooden reliefs of torches, garlands, fabulous leopards, or birds-of-paradise.

I look out at the endless forests and think that much of this production in wood is rooted in the Russian tradition of the cult of the tree, great symbol of the sacred. The tree, with its roots that reach down into the shadows of the nether regions and its leaves that open toward the light of the cosmos. The tree as the chaos of the primordial forest but also as the order of creation; as original sin (the forbidden tree of knowledge) but also as flaming pilaster planted in the middle of celestial Jerusalem, precursor of the victorious cross. This could already be seen in Bulgaria before the year 1000.

The body of Nicholas of Myra, Eastern Orthodoxy's saint of saints, is replaced in the Russian world by statues, which are the repositories of the same extraordinary miraculous expectations that surround his mummy preserved in the cathedral in Bari. In carved icons from the sixteenth century on, the "source image" from Bari is always present. In general, statues of saints were not only objects of veneration, but also of ire, in the case of unfilled expectations on the part of the faithful. In Sicily, it was customary to put a salted sardine in the mouth of a saint who had failed to interrupt a drought. In Russia, worse things happened: Ivan the Terrible had the statue of Nicholas of Mozhaisk beaten with a cane, guilty—so the czar said—of having supported his Lithuanian enemies.

Some years ago, at a magnificent exhibition of Russian wood sculpture in Vicenza, I saw the statue of Saint Nil Sorsky (Nilus of Sora), who died in 1554 on the river island where he had spent his life in prayer, in opposition to the vast accumulation of wealth in land and serfs owned by the Church and monasteries. It is said that, sensing his end was near, he dug his own grave and lay down inside it, but then, as the moment of passage was beginning, he reemerged with a terrible strength, pulling himself up on crutches in order to die sitting down. For penance, he had decided that he would never lie down while alive, and death caught him in a posture coherent with this choice. The statue I saw showed him on his knees, eyes closed, crutches coming out of his armpits, with a talismanic force rivaling any two-dimensional painting.

In 2005, in Greece, I saw Saint Parasceve (Agia Paraskevi), protectress of the waters and of fertility, virtually unknown in the Catholic world. I saw her in a convent dedicated to her name and populated with fantastic floral images, as well as peacocks and all kinds of birds, which, according to their pious caretakers, were meant to represent the Garden of Eden. On the mountains near the Bulgarian border, that dark icon with two sweet eyes looked out at me from the semidarkness, from the other side of a mountain of silver offerings for grace received and a wall of jewel cases jammed with relics mounted on silver studs. She struck me dumb with her helpless grace, reincarnated in the superb sweetness of a woman of the East.

The landing dock in Petrozavodsk is almost Finland. Faces that are rounder and more washed out, the monumental cleanliness of the historic center, and people conversing in a muffled, almost whispered, chirping. Full-bore West: rushing professionals armed with briefcases, androgynous women on cell phones, the Latin alphabet again on billboards, and a never seen density of ATMs, able to distribute—get this—dollars! In the Internet cafés, there's even something resembling a middle class. The only genuine hotel, a ship named *Debarkader*, outfitted for overnight stays and moored at the pier, is booked up, so we're forced to resort to the pretentious Kareliya, with its higher-than-market rates and the inevitable, irritating tomblike marble, an affront to the millennial culture of birchwood. I should feel right at home, but instead I can feel my heart tighten. It seems that our adventure is already over.

But luckily, on the lakeshore walk, there's Anatoly Fyodorovich, who squeezes melancholy from his accordion, sitting on the wall between miniskirted girls with strawberry lips. Monika translates the heartrending verses, such as "The train leaves and you're all alone in a cloud of snow." Instead of a hat for donations there's a margarine tub. I drop in fifty rubles (four dollars) and Anatoly goes crazy, singing the old favorite "Katyusha" in a klezmer arrangement. It's Saturday, the whole city is on the waterfront for the evening stroll, and a quartet of lovely ladies out on their own surround the accordion player and sweet-talk him: "Come on, play us 'The Gypsy Girl,'" and then they start dancing with their arms spread wide, tapping their high heels, in a circle, Greek style. And when our guy squeezes out from his bellows "Other Peoples' Weddings," a hammer blow of melancholy that would knock out a bull, they pretend to be upset: "It's so sad, damn you. But we'll pay you just the same." Naturally, they keep on dancing, tied together in a tango, and laughing heartily.

Old Russia, stand firm. Once, during stopovers in these ports, characters like Anatoly boarded cruise ships with painters and cantors, to bring a little of their culture to the passengers. Today, under Putin, the onboard entertainment is karaoke and the Miss Cruise Ship contest, and the "new Russians" are ashamed of their pioneer tradition. One time, during a cruise on the White Sea, an Italian friend of mine named Marina was invited to come up to the microphone and sing. When she started to sing the Italian Communist resistance anthem, "Bella ciao," she could see the chill come over the faces of her Muscovite dinner companions and the total indifference of the Americans who were eating with them. When she protested against the waste of food by the newly rich passengers, who at breakfast threw handfuls of whipped cream and chocolate at one another, overturning trays of food, she was pushed and shoved and threatened, while not one member of the staff or crew came to defend her.

Alya Andreyevna, seventy-four, a widow, sky-blue eyes and

dress, is cut from a whole different cloth. She appears like an angel at the front door of her house, at the end of Prospekt Kommunistov, an old-fashioned street with wooden houses and backyards, which we are walking down in search of the real Russia. This woman, whom we will always remember as "the queen of the blini"—the legendary Russian crepes—is chatting with one of her neighbors, Sofia Pavlovna, and can't resist the desire to invite the foreigners to her house for tea. All around her, cats and happy children chase each other among the woodsheds and the well-kept lawns of the condominium. In simple words, she tells us the genesis and the denouement of her world.

"Once there was nothing here. Then Peter the Great came and built the factories. Then there were the wooden houses. Now the time has come for houses made of cement, and I'll have to go there, too. Very soon they'll come here with a bulldozer, and they'll tear it all down. It's a real shame. I've been living here since 1947, and I know everybody. But come in, my friends."

We enter a small, comfortable, and orderly apartment. On the kitchen sideboard, there's a picture of a man. I ask her if that's her husband.

"No, that's my son. He died in February. He was forty. Now I live for my grandson. I cook only for him. His mother isn't up to it. But come, sit down. I'll make you some Russian blini. I was just stirring the batter. All I have to do is fry them."

She moves frenetically, lights the fire, and if she could, she'd roll out a red carpet. In an instant, the table is set with a white table-cloth next to an *abat-jour*. Monika takes Alya's picture as she raises her eyes heavenward, her left hand holding the frying pan and the right evoking days gone by.

I tell her she has marvelous eyes.

"If you knew how they were once! Big . . . and deep. Oh hell, the blini aren't the right shape. See? I've got guests and instead of doing things right, I start yapping."

She dances, bringing to the table a delicacy that is called *varenye*, a marmalade of forest berries and honey. It is used to sweeten the tea, which here is not sugared. Then brown bread and homemade butter. Russian hospitality is all right here in this food and this warmth.

"I always have something ready, you know, for whomever might come. But fewer and fewer people are coming, and then I have to give stuff away. But you eat, eat some more; men have to eat more than women."

She serves up seven blini on my plate and bids me eat *ot dushi*, "from the soul." Then she tells us about her microeconomy of barter in which nothing is thrown out.

"My neighbors bring me more fruit than I can eat, so I make jams and marmalade, which then become gifts."

We sing the praises of the flowers that she has planted in the common garden.

"Ah, once they were much more beautiful. These days the young people drink too much and break everything. The flower bed is all broken, and if I yell at them, they insult me. It's incredible. They live like wolves. They've got no sense of limits. And they don't know the difference between good and bad. My heart aches for them."

I say that maybe wolves are better; at least they have a sense of the pack, and they don't throw away food.

Meanwhile the neighbor, Sofia Pavlovna, comes in without knocking to join us, carrying some chocolates.

"See. Sofia and I understand each other. We know the value of every kopek. We give ourselves to others. But young people today know only how to take. Between us and them, there's a *basaya raznitsa*, an enormous difference. Maybe our grandchildren will be different, but I'm not too sure. Tell me: how did all of this happen?"

I tell her that it's a disaster in the West, too. But it doesn't matter to me. I'm happy to be here with her. We tell her that it's lovely to be there at her table.

"I'm happy, too. When a foreigner passes by, I can't resist. I ask him where he's going, where he's from, where he's staying."

The samovar is steaming, and it's getting dark out.

"In 1941, during the German attack, there was nothing left to eat. My mother and brother died of hunger and cold. I managed to escape. They put me together with some other orphans in Saint Petersburg, put us on a boat on the Onega and sent us up the Volga until the war was over. My father was at the front. He made it all the way to Berlin with General Zhukov. Then I came to live here, and for forty years, I worked in a nursery school. It was an extraordinary collective; we all gave our souls to it. They were hard times but beautiful times. Even today we are still united. Every so often, we get together, and the comrades say to me, 'Come on, Alya. Bring some cucumbers and your blini, and if you have time, bring a few pirogi, too.'

"I love children. And you know what? I have a recurring dream: children in trouble, and I can't do anything for them. So I wake up with a start, and in that exact moment, I realize that life is passing me by. Ah, time goes so quickly. Each day just like the others. I get up and take my time getting washed and dressed, do something, and it's already two o'clock. In the afternoon, I talk with my friends, and the day is done."

We've got to get on our way so we won't miss our train. Another painful good-bye. Ciao, Alya. You'll always be in our hearts. Your story explained Russia to us better than a stack of books. And a half hour later, as we're leaving Petrozavodsk, on a platform crowded with young people on their way to North Karelia with inflatable canoes, hockey sticks, paddles, bicycles, and complete sets of camping equipment, we already feel the void left by her absence. "Are you going to Peter?" the kids ask us. For them, Saint Petersburg has already become a person, an uncle or a brother. "I love Peter," says an architecture student who is doing an internship in a firm. "I'm crazy about Peter," echoes a young sunburned blond who's trying to put her mud-speckled bicycle on the train after pedaling through the wilderness lands on the way to Arkhangelsk.

We'll be in Peter in a night, but now we're still looking for the frontier, the train for Suoyarvi. We want to attempt the circumnavigation of the biggest lake in Europe, Lake Ladoga, nearly all the way to Finland, and then go down to Saint Petersburg from there. A killer itinerary with no reasonable connections—purposely to impede you from exploring the militarized border with Finland— with endless layovers in Suoyarvi, Sortavala, Khiytola, and Vyborg. A soft departure, with platforms full of people saying good-bye. Attractive young people, better than the metropolitan tourists who trash Alya's garden. The conductor is pretty, with sweet Baltic eyes, and she's more elegant than a flight attendant. The samovar next to her bunk is already lit.

Ah, Russian trains. We're entering a world of endless forests. Monika falls asleep instantly. She's got a capacity for sleep that I have envied since the start of this journey. A militant sleep, the deep sleep of those who work. I, on the other hand, need to perform long rituals. I fold down the sheet, straighten the blue blanket, set down on the table the little illustrated book of the epic of *Kalevala*, close the pleated curtain, stick my stuff into the chest whose cover is my bunk. Another hour goes by before I am in my dream together with the boat *Väinämöinen*, Alya's blini, and Anatoly Fyodorovich's accordion, as the train heads toward Finland under a green sky, searching for the impossible night of the North.

6. BALTIC

FAREWELL, WILD KARELIA, lacustrine archipelagos and labyrinthine rivers. When I see from the train window the immense walls of Vyborg, the Finnish port taken by the Russians in 1944, I'm struck with a strange anxiety. I'm changing orbit. With a malevolent magnetism, the great centers and flows of the EU periphery are tearing me away from the terra incognita, where I have been joyously hiding out for the last two weeks, and pulling me toward known places. After Khiytola, my map of the North—a highly detailed one-to-a-million scale that I bought in Norway—has become useless to me. Now I belong to the greater Europe, "my Europe." I've now entered the one-to-five-hundred thousand map that I usually consult, the one that still has, on the upper right, old Leningrad.

The circumnavigation of Lake Ladoga, fully half as big as the Adriatic, turned out to be an act of pure railway masochism. Forty-five hours and six minutes from Petrozavodsk to Saint Petersburg, of which thirty hours and eight minutes were consumed by layovers at four different places, sometimes just a mile or two from the Finnish border. Stations in the middle of nowhere, under military control; villages out of this world, inhabited by Asians deported by Stalin to occupy the houses abandoned by the defeated Finns. People, I've been told, who feel secure only in militarized confinement.

Now, heading south from this "oversize" space, I'm passing into a world whose scale, horizons, and dimensions I know perfectly.

I'm leaving vertical Europe to reenter horizontal Europe. Now all the train lines begin to run perpendicular with respect to my chosen north-south heading. The frozen pole star of Murmansk vanishes from the train schedules. Now it's a lot more common to see Berlin, Warsaw, Kiev, Leopolis (aka Lviv, Lvov, and Lemburg).

This train is running faster than the others. Even the noises it makes are changing. It no longer sounds a double beat of the wheels going over the joints in the track, but a single beat, loud, hammering in the rain. On the far shore of the Baltic Sea, the star-spangled flag of the European Union is already drawing us back toward Estonia.

But in Saint Petersburg the magic of the journey seems surprisingly renewed. The names of the stations—Baltiyskaya, Push-kinskaya, Dostoyevskaya, Ladoskaya—conjure up mythological distances, and the throngs of humanity that fill them, condense in just a few hundred yards the immensity of the empire. Time zones upon time zones of ethnicities: Mongols, Caucasians, Central Asians and Siberians, peoples of the Baltic and short-headed natives of Khorasan, agitated head-turning beauties from Lake Baikal, Greeks from Crimea, women with that fabulous Circassian pallor, Turks with Astrakhan hats. On the subway, midshipmen from the naval academy, Orthodox nuns, micro miniskirts, drunken hooligans, old men absorbed in their books, happy campers. Handsome faces of a mature people that has known suffering more than any other.

On the Baltiyskaya line, a young invalid from the war in Chechnya with a bony, ferocious face, pushed from car to car in his wheelchair by a less than reputable-looking young man, literally extorts a "toll" from the passengers after yelling out a threatening appeal for solidarity. Police are everywhere, and the officers are of two kinds: black American-style uniforms or else muscle-bound giants in gray. Instructions not to leave bags unattended are posted everywhere you look, a precaution against terrorist attacks. Taking pictures is prohibited, but with her little noiseless Leica with no flash, Monika performs miracles.

At Baltiyskaya Station, half empty, we discover that Estonia is now farther away, the frontier more of a hassle, and visas harder to come by, especially in the last year, since the Estonians tore down the monument to the war dead of the Red Army and Putin vowed never to forget it. But it is above all since the collapse of the USSR followed by the independence of the Baltics, that train connections have virtually disappeared, and today what used to be the pieces of the union of fraternal peoples are reachable only by bus. At the ticket window, they detour us to the square in front of the station, where there's a sign inscribed with the words BUS EUROLINES, YEVROPEISKY EKSPRESS, LINII. In just a few minutes, there is supposed to be a bus departing from there for Tallinn, capital of the land of the Estonians.

We run toward the bus with our backpacks. The engine is already running, and we ask the driver if it's possible to get off at Narva, the first town over the border. An awesome place, we've been told, with a Swedish fortress and a Russian one built by Ivan the Terrible, facing each other from opposite river banks, and a road that pierces the frontier, running through the crenelated castle walls. The most scenic entrance anywhere into the star-spangled federation. One of those foreboding *limites*, with memories of the comings and goings of Russian, Swedish, and German armies. On the castle on the left bank, there is a plaque that commemorates the breach made by Peter the Great, who conquered the city in 1704.

"Narva?" the ticket seller asks in surprise. "Nobody gets off at Narva. I wouldn't even know how much to make you pay."

Inside the bus, drowsy women and some children. The windows are striped with rivulets of raindrops.

"Let's say five hundred rubles."

And here we go under the overcast sky, already Protestant,

Berliner, Hanseatic, toward the hard languages of the Finno-Ugric world and the vocalic diaereses of Central Europe, along landscapes flattened by the wind and the blitzkriegs. We're traveling across a terrain that's perfect for generals and large-scale military maneuvers. In the rain, even the Orthodox churches lose their Byzantine force and take on the Gothic verticality of the fir trees.

At the last Russian town, we decide to get off and go the rest of the way on foot. If the two checkpoints are as close as they seem, crossing the border on foot is the best way to avoid lines. In fact, the bridge over the Narva has a lane for pedestrians, who, on the Estonian side, have an entrance just for them. We cross the river in the company of cyclists and old women with bags, young men in black blousons, globe-trotters, and some odd types with no baggage, lit cigarettes between their lips, and their hands in their pockets. Our return to "Europe" is superb, the Narva a deep green color frothing its way to the Baltic. On the left bank, on the towers of the Swedish fort, some seagulls are screaming.

"Passport, please."

The Estonian police are condescending and vaguely irritating, like the Slovenian police. The newly admitted members of the EU are the most zealous in applying the rules of the club. But surprisingly, beyond the checkpoint, the city is still Russia. I try to pronounce two shameful monosyllables in Estonian, but the people passing by laugh and say "Don't understand." I discover that in all of eastern Estonia, Russian is still the lingua franca, because of the many ex-Soviets who have remained on the Baltic. I hear the same Slavic music on both sides of the river, and under the bridge, anglers from the western and eastern shores wade waist deep into the water and risk getting their lines tangled if their casts are too long.

The sharp sunlight is coastal, reminiscent of Lübeck and Travemünde. The architecture of the fortified bridge calls to mind the Bosnia of Višegrad in the novel by Ivo Andrić, *The Bridge on the Drina*. By now we're in deep Central Europe. The ravens, big and black, are the same as the ones on the Polish plains and in the Balkans. The sight of the first stork, the first linden tree, the first oak, and the first horse chestnut tree makes our hearts skip a beat. While the signs of technological modernity of the West darken my mood, the encounter with the trees of the South warms my soul.

Something completely new appears on my horizon: a pretty little hotel with reasonable rates and a concierge who speaks English. In Russia, I had no choice: either forgotten provincial ruins or overpriced penitentiaries for the rich. The cleanliness is a step up, too.

The city looks like a drab pharmacy, and everything seems a little fake—a city of doorbells, a Legoland populated by timid gnomes with a tendency to solitary drunkenness. Under the hegemony of the Estonians, close relatives of the taciturn Finns, the Russian minority has two survival strategies: assimilate and don't call too much attention to yourself, like Antonia Timofeyevna, who is chatting with a friend on a bench; or ostentatiously display your identity, like the two seedy-looking gorillas who are parking their flaming red Mazda with the 900-RUS license plate in front of a restaurant where they act as though they own the place.

There's some far-off music in the air, a band playing the notes of a marching tune that's suddenly very German. The Gs and F-sharps bounce off the walls of the fortress and the Russian river bank before the musical parade appears at an intersection of the main street. Horns and drums play as they head down to the river to a yacht club to inaugurate an upcoming regatta. A girl with the Latin phrase NAVIGARE NECESSE ("to sail is necessary") printed on her chest explains to me that, before confronting the Baltic Sea, the boats sail down the Narva in procession. Other sailors display slogans in Cyrillic. I ask one of them, "Are you Estonians or Russians?" He responds, "Russians, Estonians, Bashkirians, Uzbeks, Germans, Jews, we're all in the same band. Does music perhaps speak a language?"

And then the sea. My first glimpse of the sea since the Arctic crossing to the Solovetsky Islands. The beach on the Baltic ten miles north of the city of Narva is wild and windy. Dunes, strong wind, and waves that sound like Niagara Falls, a continuous rumble rather than the oscillating rhythm of the surf. The mouth of the Narva, with a lighthouse, radar, and the last roof terrace on the frontier, is a perfect literary environment. Seagulls standing with their faces to the wind, dunes with a barrier of gnarled trees and a strip of yellow grasses combed by wind gusts like fields of barley. Just inside the estuary, a dam semidestroyed by hurricanes, rusted boats, and a small shipyard for fishing boats. No signs that say Warning or Prohibited. Nothing military baring its teeth toward the powerful neighbor.

Slightly upriver, there's a Russians-only yacht club, with turbo–folk music and sausages smoking on the grill. Russian songs, Russian menu, Russian alphabet, Russian beauties. Once, the Soviet nomenklatura came here to enjoy the Mediterranean of the North.

We sit down for a late afternoon beer at the river's edge, and a young Estonian from Tallinn, invited by friends to the Slavic party, smiles at our interest in this marginal place: "The real Estonia is not here; it's farther west. It's older, and also more modern." He doesn't understand that we are tired of the claustrophobic West, and he can't manage to understand the sense of this journey along a line of peripheral places. He'd be even less able to understand how I'm dying of nostalgia for the shores of Lake Onega and the steaming *banya* in Velikaya Guba.

Off to the northwest, toward the invisible Swedish coast, our journey's first windswept sunset explodes. Little gulls doing the flight of the Holy Spirit, and then a sea of violet heath rippling in the wind. I think back to my frontier and feel an emptiness in my soul. A void close to humiliation. How is it possible that the European Union has expanded by six hundred miles on the Baltic and by only twenty miles on the Adriatic? Why can a Berliner cross four ex-Communist countries without showing his passport and a Triestian can do the same only with the country of Lilliput, tiny

Slovenia with its two million inhabitants, a neighborhood in Beijing? Yet already in the 1970s, where I live, the Iron Curtain had become a joke compared to the situation in the North. In the middle of Germany there were guard dogs, the Vopos, Checkpoint Charlie, and chevaux-de-frise. Where we were, the Curtain was full of holes: sailing vacations in the Dalmatian islands, cross-border shopping without the thrill of possible customs controls. What did we care about expansion? We had already expanded abundantly.

What happened? "It's all the fault of the Balkan War," they tell us in Rome. The only explanation from the Italian foreign ministry is this knee-jerk response. If united Europe at our latitude finishes just beyond the Carso (Karst), it's not our fault; it's the Slavs' fault. It's not our doing, they tell us, if Italy is absent from the Balkans, if the railroad corridor to Kiev doesn't operate beyond Venice, if in Slovenia and Croatia, the Central European commercial presence is infinitely stronger than our own. It's not our responsibility that the Adriatic is a sea of mafias, that Bosnia is still a limbo where anything can happen, and that with regard to the sensitive issues of the post–World War II years, there is still no agreement because not all of the archives have been opened. It's the responsibility of the Slavic peoples, they tell us. Just as in 1914, evil still comes from the lands of the unquiet East.

An unknown star has poked through the sky over toward Saint Petersburg, on the horizon of the Gulf of Finland. She too is the first of this journey. She doesn't sparkle, she throbs. I'm walking in the fine sand under a row of flags jerked this way and that by the wind. I've missed the sea. Today has been a day full of blue visions, free thoughts that the hinterland had kept reined in. Memory: that's the key theme. If Germany has been able to pilot her expansion, it is in part because she has admitted her historical responsibilities, and this admission has made her light and less ambiguous, even in lands where she had committed the worst atrocities. Not Italy. Italy continues to pretend that it was not Fascist and that it won the war.

Instead, it was Fascist—and how!—and it lost the war right on the border where I grew up.

Germany has made her "days of memory" into a time of responsibility and repentance. For our part, the word *memory* almost always rhymes with self-absolution. I beg you, don't talk to me about "Italians, good people," because I live at the scene of the crime. In Trieste, Mussolini proclaimed the racial laws against the Jews, and that disgraceful choice had its prelude almost twenty years earlier with the political, economic, and linguistic oppression of the vast Slovene community. I know that during the war there were not only Nazi concentration camps, but also camps run by the Fascists, with thousands of deaths from hunger and privation. Why is there so little talk about that? Why do we keep on digging up the time of the atrocious postwar Yugoslavian vendettas as though they came out of nowhere? Italy has never had its Nuremberg. That's why it does not have the standing to ask its neighbors to do some cleaning up in their own memories. That's why a piece of my gulf is still outside of the European Community.

We have dinner at the seaside. On the other side of the restaurant's glass front, the sky is sporting green and orange stripes. We don't have the slightest idea how we're going to head south tomorrow. There aren't any trains. We've seen the station in Narva, as empty as a mortuary. Twenty years ago, the timetable had hundreds of departures for Warsaw, Berlin, and Prague. Today the traffic is limited to five half-empty trains: two from Moscow for Tallinn, two from Tallinn to Saint Petersburg, and one from Narva to the capital. Only east-west trains, and all of them—who knows why—in the middle of the night. During the day, only buses, but even they don't follow the main axis of our vertical Europe. "Nobody gets off in Narva," the ticket seller in Saint Petersburg had told us. We're beginning to understand why.

7. MIDDLE LANDS

"I'M GOING TO TARTU, south of here. Do you want a ride?"

Alexander Adamov, forty-five, a Russian-speaking Estonian citizen, sees us struggling with the extremely complicated bus schedules posted on a bulletin board in the main square of Narva and offers us two seats in his compact car in exchange for gas money. We go for it without a second thought, and here we are riding along amid cleared fields strewn with enormous rocks, left behind by Quaternary glaciers. This is the landscape—vaguely reminiscent of Brittany, or ancient Courland, one of the many mythological regions of Central Europe—that the collision of empires and the mobility of borders have erased from the maps.

With my swollen injured foot, this comfortable car ride seems like a priceless luxury. Plus, our driver is not taking the main road but skirting the coast of Lake Peipsi, one of the most mysterious places of the North, populated by a fascinating Orthodox minority, the Old Believers. Monika has already studied them in the Caucasus, Poland, and Romanian regions of Dobruja and Bukovina. We couldn't have asked for anything more. We Russianize our names for him with our patronymics: Monika Stanislavovna Bulaj, Pavel Petrovich Rumiz.

This is how things go when you travel light: stopovers generate encounters, and the encounters get the adventure rolling again. It works every time, even here in the green heartland of the taciturn Estonians. And so it is that between us and our providential Slavic-speaking chauffeur, a dialogue is initiated, there in the middle of those clearings, which is worth more than the reports of ten embassies on the situation on the Russo-Baltic border, one of the most delicate of the Union.

"So, how's life going, Mr. Adamov?"

"Badly, Pavel Petrovich. There's no work. If you don't speak Estonian, you can't find work."

"But how's that? Don't you know Estonian?"

"All I know how to say is 'bread.' I don't understand a damn thing."

"Excuse me, but how do you ask for directions when you're on the road?"

"Simple. I only ask Russians. Here on the frontier, we're the majority."

"You mean you can tell a Russian from an Estonian?"

"Sure—the Estonians' faces are rounder, they're better dressed, and they generally look down. And they walk differently."

"Differently how?"

"They're more awkward."

"For example, that guy over there who's hoeing his garden, what's he?"

"Estonian. No doubt about it."

"Shall we bet on it? I say he's Russian. Try pulling over, and we'll ask him something."

From the car window, we ask in Russian for directions to a village, but the man, courteous as can be, emits a stream of loud vocalic noises that sounds like a bellowing stag. *Aaaiiioooo*, followed by *uuueeeeeeooooo*. Pure Finno-Ugric. We thank him and get back on our way. Adamov was right.

"Sorry, but how did you know he was Estonian? That guy didn't have a round face."

"Right, but he had an English lawn. We'd never keep a lawn like that. We're more disorderly."

"Listen, why don't you just go ahead and learn the blessed Estonian?"

"They do everything they can to keep us from learning it. Friends of mine emigrated to England. They picked up the language in six months and now they're working. Here that's impossible. Why?"

"No, sorry. 'Why' is my question."

"Question of money. If you take an Estonian course in Tallinn, they reimburse you 90 percent of the cost. If you take the course in Narva, they reimburse 30 percent. It's simple. People on the frontier are discriminated against. They don't have money to pay for the courses, so they give up."

"And in the schools?"

"There it's free. And in fact, there it works. My children speak the language perfectly."

"Why don't you protest?"

"What a question. An EU passport is worth a lot more. If you have one, it's easier to emigrate and find work in the West."

"Why not emigrate to Russia?"

"No, no! I was born here, and for better or worse, this is my homeland. And you don't choose your homeland, just as you don't choose your parents." He tells us that the Estonians made him remove his patronymic from his identity papers. If it were up to him, his name would be Alexander Alexandreyevic, but today that's not allowed. Use of the father's name has been prohibited, banned, extirpated like a weed.

Be careful, I tell him. Before, you had Soviet homogenization; now you've got the EU brand.

On our right, we go past a sign for Sillamäet, the embarcadero for Helsinki. I have the sudden sensation of having been catapulted into the South. I look at my map. I'm nearing the midpoint of my journey.

I ask how relations are on the border.

"Terrible. Especially after the incident of the monument in Tallinn, the one to the unknown Russian soldier. They demolished it in April 2007. A disgrace. The Russians were enraged. They exhumed the bodies and took them back to Russia last summer. How could the Estonians do something like that? It's not only an affront to the dead soldiers. It's that history is history. What did those poor kids have to do with Stalin?"

"What's changed since then?"

"Everything. Crossing the border is harder. It's the worst of the three Baltic countries. Days of sitting in line to cross. Nobody has written that it's because of that monument, but everyone knows that's the way it is. All of Estonia is paying the price for that useless outrage."

We pass by some sort of hotel surrounded by walls and barbed wire. "It's a penitentiary," Adamov explains. "The prisoners are put up in double rooms with a private bath and TV. It costs six thousand krooni per person, double the average pension. What sense does that make? Here the poor can't afford to buy themselves a sandwich. The death penalty would make more sense."

We stop at a bar. It's full of well-mannered, round-faced Estonians, and the place is, obviously, silent as a tomb. A family is sitting at a table eating a quick lunch in perfect silence. I begin to understand Adamov. It's impossible to learn a language from people who never talk.

After sixty or seventy miles, the border turns into a lake. It's the immense Lake Peipsi, its shore lined with villages of Old Believers. They escaped here three centuries ago from the persecutions of the czar and sought refuge in the homeland of the tolerant Lutherans. Their Orthodox rigor rejected the modernization imposed by Moscow, which had massacred them for their legitimate disobedience. In their physical appearance, too, they seem like the Slavic version of the Amish, a perfect mix of Protestant rigor and Orthodox magic.

Their little wooden churches conserve the ancient traditions of a religion totally separated from temporal power, and their priests are elected by the people. Monika also searched for them in the labyrinths of the Danube Delta, one of their refuges, and she is happy to find them here, too, once again in a world of water and woods. They are a people of fishermen and farmers, and their relationship with the lake is still that of the New Testament. Their vegetable gardens, loomed over by spectacular gray-blue clouds, are the most beautiful in Europe. Little gardens of Eden.

Adamov has time, and because he has never seen the home of an Old Believer, he willingly accepts the detour. He realizes immediately that he has crossed over the frontier into another world. We pass by cemeteries where Orthodox, Lutherans, and Catholics coexist. Calm, cleanliness, agrarian enchantment. We ask for directions to an especially beautiful wooden church in a town called Raja, between Mustvee and Kallaste. It's Sunday and maybe we can attend the service. A farmer dressed in his Sunday best tries to help us, and immediately people come streaming out of neighboring houses to point out the best route to Raja. "You see?" Alexander says. "If we were in an Estonian village, nobody would have come out of the houses to talk to us!"

After a wooden church, Orthodox but with a Lutheran look, we come to a village so enchanting that Monika and I, exchanging a knowing glance, share the same resolution: not to reveal the name of this place. The names of the people we meet are enough— biblical and unusual names, such as Apalon, Salamania, Jelpindifor, Mercury. A vivacious woman by the name of Anphia invites us into her house, shows us her icons and her *pechka*, and then opens the door to her garden full of hydrangeas, on the edge of a rust-colored escarpment overlooking the lake. The long palisade is called Krasnaya Gora, and it's teeming with swallows' nests. Off the coast, in the middle of the horizonless blue-gray infinity, all I can see is a fishing boat. I'm no longer in Estonia but on the Sea of Galilee.

Not far off, Tatiana Pimenovna and Alexander Pimenovich, both in their eighties, are working the soil behind a little wooden church with an orange glint. As we approach, they emerge from the tilled earth like two soldiers coming out of a trench in the Great War, only they are incredibly clean. She has a wide face, high cheekbones, sky-blue eyes, and an amaranth handkerchief, tied like a pirate's bandanna around her still dark brown hair. Alexander is a handsome suntanned muzhik, and he is Tatiana's second husband. The first died twenty years ago in a storm on the lake. Their garden is a masterpiece of beauty as well as productivity. The tomatoes, almost inconceivable in these latitudes, are flourishing, the beneficiaries of some unknown devilish magic. Only the Walser were capable of such things, when they colonized prohibitive heights in the Alps. "Come to Pentecost," the old strapper exhorts us, "when we paint the eggs for the poor." "But our garden is nothing," Tatiana smiles in the midst of a forest of wrinkles. "The most beautiful place here is the cemetery." Now I understand why the Old Believers have always been offered hospitality in foreign lands. They are able to transform anything, even cemeteries, into gardens.

A distinguished gentleman goes by on a bicycle, gives Monika a perfect kiss of the hand, and one to me, too, hears of our interest in the religion of his people and offers to take us to the house of the batyushka, "little father," the priest elected by the community. Something that has very little to do with popes and archimandrites. The batyushka of the Old Believers is more like a rabbi, a sage entrusted with the task of talking with God and acting as a great father to families in search of the way of the Lord.

The sun is shining, and outside the house of Andrei Ivanovich, there are two women in bikinis immersed in the black earth up to their knees. One is his daughter, blond and tan; she's planting potatoes. The other is his wife, who lets go of the horse, throws on some clothes, and comes to prepare us a welcoming cup of tea. The batyushka has the face of a whaler from Nantucket, a well-kempt beard with no mustache, in the Protestant manner. He's confined to the house because he has recently had a slight heart attack, and he is happy to talk to us. He shows us a picture of a little boy baptized in an iron washtub, and explains that adults are baptized in a boat, in the middle of the lake, like the ancient Christians. He tells Monika that he's a self-taught priest. When his predecessor got too old, he realized that the community would soon be left without a guide, and so he went to have himself taught the trade. "He opened up the sacred texts for me, and then he blessed me."

He explains further: "I'm just a simple Christian," and as a simple Christian, he has to work to live. "There's the horse to take care of, the grass to mow, the potatoes to plant, the field to fertilize. I had the heart attack because of too much work." Another world compared to the Catholic hierarchy, celibacy, economic dependence on the state. He pours the tea, then takes from the credenza a New Testament from 1680, which is "a lot older than Czar Nicholas," and then a clandestine breviary (the books of the Old Believers were condemned to burning) written by hand by a certain Fyodor Sovotskin before the Great War.

"Three centuries ago, the people who came here from the Solovetsky Islands brought with them an icon with our whole calendar painted on it." I talk to him about the beauty of their wooden churches. He responds that they're not cold like the Catholic churches. "In our liturgy, it's not just the priest who prays, but the whole community. That's a big difference." Then he looks at Monika. "I can see from your eyes that your interest in us comes from the heart. Others come here as though they had come to the zoo to see exotic animals. Not you, your eyes have goodness in them. May God bless you. In the name of the Father, of the Son, and of the Holy Spirit. And now go in peace."

The next day my foot is in such bad shape that we have to rent a small car in Tartu. It's the only sensible thing to do if we want to get to Vilnius in some reasonable amount of time. There aren't any trains or buses that go south on the strip of terrain that interests us, the one closest to Russia. The rent-a-car place in Tartu is a realm of pharmaceutical cleanliness and has the tranquillity of a carpenter's workshop. The manager is a fledging woodsman who inundates me with friendly assurances. In Italy, rental car agencies are hotbeds of neurasthenia, devoured by haste. In Estonia, among the silent people, it's a totally different scene. After the angst of the initial contact, in response to our courtesy, the man of the North lavishes us with attention, becomes paternal, even loquacious. In the end, after watching us leave, he goes happily back into the office, almost trotting. I notice it by chance, looking into the rearview mirror.

Now the wavelength of the Baltic ups and downs begins to shorten compared to the area around Narva. The landscape is less planar, the curves more frequent, and with Latvia on the horizon, you start to feel the proximity of Poland. The air tastes of klezmer, Yiddish, Ashkenazim. In the copper-rimmed dark clouds, it's easy to imagine flying violinists, synagogues, and rabbis hunched over their Talmud, reading by candlelight. Chagall, Kandinsky. The dark wooden buildings in the countryside look like synagogues or sailboats lying belly-up in dry dock, and enkindled by the grazing yellow light of sunset, they stand out against the backdrop of immense clouds like a cubist painting. I glimpse the first redbrick houses, like the ones in Masuria and Prussia. The fantastic sky over our heads more than makes up for the monotony of the terrain. In the Mediterranean, the totalitarian azure vault of the sky crushes you. Here, on the Baltic, the sky offers constantly changing visions. Fat, bulging clouds, infused with black and Prussian blue, or white and light as fluttering banners. Sails flying incredibly high, wispy and puffed out by the wind. Or else anvils, galleons, lead-gray schools of sardines suspended in midair, in slow migration. And underneath them, perhaps, a hole, where the low sun shines through and fills every furrow in the firmament with a golden glow.

And so, just as I'm thinking that the people of the North have more sky than we do, I see two men at the bottom of one of the Estonian roller-coaster slopes, slender and dressed in black, or no, a man and a woman, standing on the side of the road waiting for a ride. As I approach, I keep changing my mind about them. Protestant black like the Pilgrim fathers; Jewish black, a couple of Hasidim on a pilgrimage to Israel; no, maybe it's the Orthodox black of a pope and his wife. Then I see that she has a black handkerchief covering her face and chin like a *hijab*, and for a second I think the Northern sky is home not only to flying Jewish violinists but also to Islamic imams, driven here from other latitudes. The man, black beard and slightly wild eyes, looks like a fanatical turbo-Islamist from the Wahhabi sect. But as soon as he opens his mouth to say he's Russian and that his name is Vadim, voilà, the mystery is solved. I am looking at ultraorthodox Russian pilgrims, headed for some unknown monastery in a foreign land.

She is frail, timid, submissive. She curls up in a corner of the backseat and lets her husband do the talking. He promptly explains that the veil she, Valentina, is wearing, is the result of a free choice of subjection to God, and obviously to her man.

A surreal dialogue has begun.

"You are Catholic. Convert. There is no salvation outside of Orthodoxy."

I respond with silence. I think, *You call it Orthodoxy, but it seems like Islam.* Not even in Pakistan had I heard such explicit demands to convert.

"Ecumenism is heresy; there is only one faith. The apostles' eighty-five rules have already been fixed in the Book. Your pope is an Antichrist." Vadim explains that it all began centuries ago, with the Catholics' decision to put the Son on the same level with the Father. "A single Latin word divides us: *filioque*."

I ask him if he was born a believer.

"I converted in 1992. Before, under Communism, I was controlled by unclean forces. My grandfather was an atheist, faithful to the party, and my father had to baptize me in secret. It was he who taught me that anyone can get to God, and if you get to Him passing through evil, so much the better."

I think back to the Old Believers of Lake Peipsi who welcomed me without proclaiming certainties and without attempting to convert me.

"We go from monastery to monastery, working a little here, a little there. We have just come from the Pechora River and from Sviritsa on Lake Ladoga. Everywhere the struggle is extremely hard. Even there, the forces of Satan are at work. The Satanists are always trying to get their hands on the holy relics."

"What relics, Vadim?"

"The relics of the saints. Orthodoxy is made of relics, of holy water, of incense, of candle wax that drips onto your hands. These are all blessed things that the Satanists want to destroy. Recently, some Communists and some Polish Catholics tried to get their hands on the remains of the saint who is buried in the monastery in Pechora, but they had been destroyed by fire. In Pechora even the birds praise God."

I decide to keep quiet. There is no sense in responding, and Vadim has no intention of stopping. He keeps on talking as though he's possessed.

"In the 1960s, Khrushchev's atheists decided to analyze one of these relics, and they determined that it was composed of molecules from another world, not explainable with reference to the periodic table of the elements. So Khrushchev ordered that they not be touched."

We're coming into the lake region. The sandy beaches are full of little gulls, bickering like mothers-in-law. Middle Europe is immersed in a fantastic lilac-hued light. When the two riders get out to make their way to a farm in the countryside, I thank them for their company in Russian, "*Spasibo*, Vadim."

But Vadim seizes on the opportunity to hold forth with another harangue. "*Spasibo*? That word doesn't exist! It is a perfidious manipulation of the Masonic Satanist Communists. Once, people used to say '*Spasi Bog*,' which means 'Save me, God.' And they also said '*Spasi Gospod*,' which is 'Save me, Lord,' but the forces of evil have extirpated the word God from the salutation."

We say good-bye to them from the car window as they embark on a path through the birch trees.

"Reform! You still have time. Rediscover the meaning of the word . . . the true faith . . . Orthodoxy."

Then his voice is lost in the wind.

The next day we take advantage of the car—the first exception to the public-transport rule adopted on this vertical journey—to take a look at the frontier at Võru, the southernmost and most difficult crossing in Estonia, on the most direct route between Warsaw and Saint Petersburg. We run into a line of trucks a mile and a half long, which in itself is nothing special. What's strange is that the trucks have been stopped here for three days, parked on the shoulder of the road. A lot of them are empty, pervaded by a haunting immobility. Their drivers have gone home or to a bar and left their keys with a colleague. We are faced with an immense linear bivouac, as though the Iron Curtain still existed and had only been moved six hundred miles farther east.

Monika spies an enormous Ukrainian truck driver, with brush-cut hair and keys hanging from his belt, who is shaving in front of a mirror that he's set up on the running board of the cab. She asks him how long he's been waiting and starts to take some pictures.

The guy doesn't shy away from the questions or from the camera. He can't believe he's getting the chance to talk. "Write it! Write that this crossing is a pile of shit. At Tehova, in Latvia, they go through thirty-five miles of trucks in two days."

"Whose fault is it?"

"The Russian customs officers stopped working six months ago. While you're sitting here waiting, they're watching TV, picking their noses, scratching their balls. Then they stamp your passport. They've received orders to behave this way. It all goes back to that damn monument in Tallinn."

Each question breaks down an already open door. I ask, "How do you pass the time?"

"This place is a shithole, an inglorious shithole. You got to do it in the woods, and the mosquitoes eat you alive. Swarms of mosquitoes on your ass. Look at all this crap on the side of the road, mountains of jars and cans and the smell of piss."

I point out to him that there are no signs with the name of the crossing.

"But no, look, it's called Miiisssooookuuulllaaaaa. I swear. That's the way the Estonians pronounce it. But woe to you if you make fun of them. They look at you with hate in their eyes. Come on, you try it now. Say it loud: Miiisssooookuuulllaaaaa."

He just can't stand them with that absurd language of theirs, and he keeps on bellowing at the woods like an elk, finishing his shave. I tell him that I need a razor, too, that I am on a long and difficult journey, like his, and that with all the abuse it's getting, my face looks as though it belongs to a beggar.

"Come on," he says, "what do you need a barber for? You don't look so bad. Besides, nobody can replace your real hair, not even the *salon krasoty*, the beauty salon."

I get back at him for the crack about my baldness. "That long blond braid of your [Yulia] Tymoshenko, is it real or not?"

"You wish it weren't, don't you? She unwraps it every now and again just to show that a prime minister can also allow herself to have real hair . . . not like your Berlusconi!" He laughs, his two-hundred pounds of belly bouncing up and down. Then he moves on to advice for the road.

"Rule number one: avoid truck drivers. There are a lot of wild men on the road and the wildest of them all are the Poles. Nobody drives worse than they do. They change lanes without signaling and suddenly you've got forty tons cutting you off. They're paid by the mile, and they never sleep." His map of Europe is totally different from mine. It's a leopard skin of off-limits zones, and his itineraries are designed to get around them. For example, "Don't ever stop in Lithuania; it's full of criminals. In Panevėžys it's 100 percent thieves. Once they stole all our gas and the spare tires while we were sleeping in the truck."

"And how is Russia?"

"Well, until Moscow it's not too bad. Then it's no-man's-land, like a combat zone. You have to pay the police and then the mafia, too, and if you don't pay, they burn you alive with your truck. If you pay, they put a sticker on your windshield, like EasyPass on the toll roads. But even then we've got to travel in groups to avoid ugly surprises."

I tell him that I haven't yet run into any criminals on my journey.

"Oh, you see fewer of them now because they've already made a lot of money. By now they've started investing, and they go to Italy to destroy the hotels. They all pay double the going rate because they don't know how to spend all the money they've stolen."

"But aren't things better under Putin compared to the past?"

"Putin? He commands everything inside the Moscow and Saint Petersburg beltways. Then it's every man for himself."

Back on the road, the new land is announced by electric-green fields of colza and a wall of towering clouds the color of tuna skin. We are all alone on the line of asphalt, like Charlie Chaplin and his belle in the final scene of *Modern Times*. Few encounters. A cow standing in the median strip, a stork, a hawk, a badger crossing the asphalt at a ferocious pace. The last human presence in the Estonian forest is a police patrol car with a radar gun that stops us in the middle of nowhere. Two young officers, shy and a little overarmed, explain the infraction to us blushing like teenage girls, incapable of relating to our relaxed calm. They stand there in their bulletproof vests, pointing at the digital display.

The reading is eighty-one miles per hour instead of fifty. That adds up to two hundred krooni. I tell them that's fine, but they want to know why I was going so fast. I tell them I don't know, I was distracted, I didn't see the sign. But they have to fill out a questionnaire thick with diaereses and double vowels, and the numbered boxes on the questionnaire do not contemplate the concept of distraction. So after some hesitation, they repeat the question, and I repeat, even more convinced, my response, so abysmally removed from their culture. I think how frustrating it must be for a Russian who lives in Estonia to have to deal with these mental pigeonholes on a daily basis. I sign the police report, receive detailed instructions on how to pay the fine, then get on my way, saying, "You are very fine people," which leaves both of them totally disoriented.

As the road skirts the Russian border, it becomes more complicated, zigzags between glacier-formed hills full of storks, little rivers, and prehistoric menhirs called *markalne* in the middle of the bushes. Then, on the only straightaway of this frontier labyrinth, a ghostlike kiosk appears, its door banging in the wind, streetlamps out, and what used to be a police guard box now become a shelter for the homeless. Is this the border crossing into Latvia? Yes, it is. The only surviving sign of sovereignty are the national flags alongside the star-spangled banner of the EU. There is no longer a bar between Estonia and Latvia, and so, too—they tell me—it will be between Latvia and Lithuania. Ephemeral frontiers: the Baltic statelets had only just inaugurated them with musical bands and solemn speeches to celebrate their triple independence from the USSR, but the Europe of the Schengen Agreement made them take them down, so today everything is as it was during the cursed times when Moscow was sovereign. The three Lilliputian states with their impossible languages (they can't even understand one another among themselves) have been forced to cohabit without the reassuring signs of sovereignty.

Forced to cohabit, I say, because they are so different. Leaving Estonia, just a few yards into Latvia, everything changes. Already in Alūksne, the first Latvian town, the flower bed nature and Protestant neatness are over, replaced by a creative disorder that is noticeably more Southern and indisputably more Catholic. Mud, puddles, terrain invaded by vegetation, marching music of the Middle European kind, the smell of sausage wafting out of the tavern on the square, the barbershop with its door open to the street. The sound of the language changes, too. The diaereses and Finnic vowels repeated to infinity fade away while "pipes" and cedillas contort themselves over and under the consonants. The spoken language is bastardized with German and Slavic words. And the people—finally—look you in the eye when they talk to you. Here we are, tumbling southward.

The unpaved road runs through the thrashing rain along the frontier with Russia. Guard towers, barbed-wire fences, light poles with storks. No more than one car every ten minutes. Bus stops forlorn on the plain, roofless, with people waiting patiently in the rain. It's raining, but the atmosphere is cheery. The woods are a symphony of chirps and tweets; the lines of rain look like vertical staves. The air itself is full of music. We are in one of the most musical nations on Earth, a place where the epic is taught in the form of song. No other country has as many choirs and as much production of traditional choral music. An old man from the Po Valley told me many years ago that on the plains, people sing in chorus because, unlike in the mountains, there is no echo that responds, so you need the group so you won't have to face the song all by yourself. The trees are full of insects that are tuning their instruments. Only in Greece have I heard similar choruses, with the cicadas that strike up at the first light of morning. We are in the Green Belt that runs along the border and turns into wilderness, especially here, where nobody ever comes.

When I first came to know Riga—which I found incomparably more beautiful than Stockholm—not long after Latvia's entry into the Union, it was about music, and not politics, that I spoke with Sandra Kalniete, the young EU commissioner in Brussels, born in a Siberian Gulag to her deported parents. This woman, whose life story is so novelesque, author of the best seller *With Dance Shoes in Siberian Snows*, told me that the Latvians are the Italians of the Baltic, for their temperament and their love of singing. They formed their identity from choral singing. "With song," she says, "we resisted Russification, with song we celebrated our independence, and with song we opened our arms to Europe." When I answered that Europe and Italy were singing less and less, she said that was all the more reason to persist. The singing of the Latvians, she said, was not the nucleus of a national identity but a universal heritage, recognized by UNESCO. It's something that "accompanies our lives from infancy to old age."

In Latvia, being the director of a chorus is a big deal. For at least a century, people here have been caring for and preserving this extraordinary intangible legacy. The Riga archives conserve some two million titles, from songs to folk tales, poetry and melodies. And the Latvians number two and a half million, so that's practically one title per person. One scholar alone, Krišjānis Barons, has classified five hundred thousand, the product of a life's research, which he left to the country gathered in a wooden chest—a mythical object that can be seen in a museum. Ms. Kalniete tells me, "We resisted the Communist Big Brother by singing. Our identity found shelter in music, in the art of allusion, in the slanted reading of the lyrics. The problem is that this mimetic endeavor absorbed enormous amounts of energy, which could have been used more freely in creative pursuits."

In the West, there are people who still confuse Slovenia and

Slovakia. Imagine how many there are who know the correct geo-graphic sequence of the three Baltic states. In the years of the big freeze, Latvia and her sisters disappeared from the maps, and now it is hard getting the flags back in the right place. You have to start by zooming out, explain that Estonia and Lithuania are between Saint Petersburg and Warsaw. When Ms. Kalniete was the ambas-sador in Paris, they were always asking her, "Where is Latvia?" and she had to say: "Think of Sweden. Now, we are on the opposite shore." Then they'd ask her, "You speak Russian, *n'est-ce pas*? And she would patiently respond that no, Russian was another thing altogether. It was really hard to explain that the Baltic states didn't have to enter Europe but simply remain there, because they had always been a part of the West. When Russian bureaucrats used to go there on vacation, they used to say with a wink, "Let's go to Europe." Already in the 1970s, there was a different atmosphere here compared to Russia. The coffee ritual, pastries, cleanliness. Everything was on a more human scale.

As soon as we return to our path on the edge of the Russian border, the melancholy returns: abandonment, barbed wire, guard towers. The forests sing, but the men on the frontier are silent. The terrain is scarred by train tracks overgrown with brush, useless, di-lapidated crossings, empty houses. Riga is far, far away. We're in the world of the forgotten, populated almost exclusively by Rus-sians. The trees give way to four six-story buildings, abandoned, with holes where the windows used to be, the facades pockmarked and eaten away as though by an army of termites. On the ground, ruins. Practically like Grozny, Chechnya, after the bombings in the nineties. A single living presence among the houses: a peasant woman in boots, obviously Russian, who is hoeing the garden and signals us to go into the shack where she keeps her tools. Her name is Vera and she immediately clarifies the mystery of the ghost town. "There used to be a Soviet ceramic factory; then independence came for Latvia and the company closed. That's when everybody left.

And they took everything with them, even the wallpaper. Only five of us stayed. They put us all in the last building down at the end. I used to live there on the third floor."

I walk among the empty windows like an insect in the eye sockets of a dead man. It must have all happened in a few days, like an evacuation. The only thing missing are bomb craters. The central heating has been turned off for fifteen years, and the houses that are still inhabited are outfitted with woodstoves whose chimney pipes punch through the surviving windows and blacken everything. Vera came here from Siberia forty years ago, and now she has no desire to go back. "Russia or Latvia, it doesn't matter to me. All I want is a piece of land." She laughingly insists that I chew on a piece of an herb called *ukrop*, which is good for "male potency"; then she recites a list of mushrooms and berries with incomprehensible names, her borderland sylvan treasures. She explains to Monika how to cook *boroviki* (porcini mushrooms) and *beryozov-ikiye mukhoviki* (mushroom-filled pastries) and shows us her tomatoes, potatoes, carrots, and strawberries. But she's worried about the fate of the forest. She's afraid it's all going to be taken away from her in the privatization wave. "They say there's a European project, but who's going to get all of this, we still don't know." From Murmansk to here, the anxiety I've heard about land going to seed has all been in the language of Tolstoy.

The musical merriment of Latvia explodes again in Rēzekne, which wakes up with sunlight and wind on market day. Geese, garlic braids, beets, and something in the air that's old and peaceful. There are no advertising billboards, and their absence highlights the beauty of the old stonework, aside from relieving the anxiety of consumption. At the top of the hill, on the main street, a statue of the Blessed Mother—equidistant from the Catholic church and the Orthodox one—bears the inscription UNITED FOR LATVIA. I read into it something ever harder to come by in this lame Europe: the acceptance of plurality, the sign of a well-functioning frontier.

The women out on the street are pretty, lively, the fertile fruit of bastardization. "*Gemischtes Blut ist das Beste,*" my old German teacher, expelled by the Sudetans in 1945, used to say. "Mixed blood is the best." She used to say that women are an infallible indicator of the bastard factor in Europe. Beauty emigrates from the monolithic ethnic groups in search of spaces where it can blend. Even back then, I had my own map of this feminine universe, tested in numerous journeys. I knew that the beauty of nations like France or Italy couldn't compete with the beauty expressed by melting pots like Belarus, Dalmatia, or Vojvodina, north of Belgrade.

In Latvia, the Jews and the Germans are still in the air. Their traces are everywhere. In the faces, in the houses, in the cuisine, and in the music. We happen upon a singing funeral, with the deceased taking his leave in a polyphony of notes that are soft, intimate, superbly rotund. The outdoor market is a fair of the contaminations forgotten by globalization. A triumph of the senses compared to the alimentary anemia of the West. Ah, *grohufka*, a hot soup of dried peas and chives, potatoes, carrots, and sour cream! And what to say about the cold borscht made from beet leaves and roots! And then the cherries, strawberries from the woods and mountains, and the candies made from milk and honey, as big as three normal candies and featuring the image of a cow, a jumbo-size sublimate of sweetness. The Latvian cow is worthy of a monument. She shows up on coins, too. That in itself is enough to make you love this country. Lithuania has a horse in harness with a warrior in the saddle; Russia, the magniloquent two-headed eagle of Byzantium; Estonia has three lions superimposed like English heraldic coats of arms; Poland, a crowned eagle with a cross between its paws. Latvia makes them all look ridiculous with its cow quietly grazing in a pasture, under an archipelago of migrating clouds.

The Chebureki Inn, next to the marketplace, has a counter that looks like an iconostasis, a redbrick wall that separates the dining room from the kitchen as the church from the altar. In the middle of the wall there is an opening where, instead of the pope, there is a buxom woman intent on squeezing beer from the tap. On the sides, it has two symmetrical doors where, in place of the beardless deacons busying themselves with incense, florid blond waitresses come and go, carrying trays loaded with all God's bounty. Even at the tables, the women are a clear majority, almost all of them vendors, taking a break from the market to have a bowl of soup. Estonian silence? The freezing cold wind of the Gulf of Finland? The blushing of the silent people of the North? Now distant planets. Here it is a triumph of chattering, shout-outs, greetings. The challenge is not striking up a conversation but keeping to yourself.

In comes a blond saleswoman by the name of Nelly. She sees that I'm writing and, curious, she comes right up to me and sticks her eyes on my notebook, shooting into my nostrils her entire hormonal code and the aromas of the open-air market. Strawberries, milk, chives, potatoes, and spicy salami. She starts in on me in Russian and gives life to a dialogue that in Tallinn would have been inconceivable, with Monika acting as interpreter and trying not to laugh.

I tell her about the journey we're making. I say, "This place of yours is magnificent, it nourishes the soul."

But Nelly cuts to the chase. She replies, "You're a handsome fellow," and it's as though she had said, "This Italian rooster is mine for the plucking."

I respond that I'm an old codger with a two-week-old beard and that I'm in urgent need of a barber so I can go out in public.

Nelly: "What barber? Come to my house in the country, and I'll take care of your beard." Monika translates, undaunted.

Next comes a friend of Nelly's, as brigandesque as she. Her name is Janna. Nelly calls out to her and says, "Come here, come here, this guy's Italian."

So Janna takes the field, too. "What do you do for work?"

"I'm a writer," I reply.

The two look at each other surprised. Up to now, they've met only rich wholesalers or chain-store reps. Who knows, they wonder, how rich a writer is.

Janna, decisively: "Come out to our ranch. We can milk the cows together, and then drink the warm milk."

Nelly: "Come on, I'll teach you how to milk; you'll see how easy it is."

Janna draws a map on my notebook of how to get to their town and writes down her name and phone number. She continues: "I've got a special tie to Italy. A dear friend of mine is married to a Sardinian."

I tell them that Italy is beautiful, but we like the countryside of the Baltic countries. The smells, the people.

Nelly won't let up. "We can spend a wonderful day together. Come to our place. Tomorrow is not a market day."

There's no escape. I keep repeating my *we*, but the two of them go right on with the singular *you*. They're in the market for an Italian chicken. They look at Monika as though she's a secretary/interpreter, and it's easy to understand why, because such is the usual companion of the Italian man traveling on business. Telling them that we have our own work deadlines is useless, so we don't have any choice. We're forced to get out of the fix in English, making a false promise of an appointment for the next day. With all best wishes to Janna, Nelly, and their milk and honey candies.

We have arranged a meeting at a café in the center of town with a Latvian Pole, an attractive, distinguished-looking woman named Regina. She explains to us that Rēzekne is actually part of one of the many cross-border regions that were broken up by the empires and consequently erased from the maps. "Here we are in Latgale," she explains, "a place of Lutherans, Orthodox, Catholics, and Jews, whose plurality is a headache for the Latvians of Riga." Russian has been the lingua franca here for centuries. The Soviet occupation has very little to do with it. "It was full of Germans here, and Hitler saw those Teutonic advance guards as the prototype of the new Aryan race, cold colonizers."

It's not easy to explain this complicated place, and Regina has to help herself with a drawing. She tears out a page from my notebook and draws a Baltic space that is totally new, where the nation-states are absent but historical regions crop up on all sides. Jutland, Livonia, Latgale, and then, in Polish, lands whose untranslatable names sound more or less like Kizensky, Zenigalsky, Rizensky, Vizensky. They are the territories of the "Deluge," swept away by the Polish-Swedish War, a disaster that destroyed Poland like a "plague of locusts" between 1600 and 1629. The drawing is thick with annotations and important dates: 1553, 1583, 1722, 1795, arrows indicating the movements of the armies, lines representing roads but more often borders, occupations, liberations. Looking at this brown-haired woman bending over her map, I realize that Latvia is the center of my journey. That paper is a cornerstone, the frame of the squeaking front door to old Europe. A Sarajevo of the North.

Ludza—yet again the shadow of the frontier. Clouds swirling above lakes and forests, over the maternal dome of the Orthodox church and the spire of the Catholic one, like a meringue. Once the country's population was 50 percent Jewish, and it is said that in 1906, when a pogrom was ordered from outside, the local Christian population rebelled and proudly saved their Jews. Today the people of the synagogue have vanished, and Russians have taken their place. Forgotten by the central government in Riga, they are the new "strangers." We arrive in town on the day of the Latvian national holiday, on which it is obligatory to display the flag. A scowling Russian is in the process of lowering his flag at twilight and says, "I have to show the flag; if not, they hit you with a fine." Like everyone who is part of the ex-Soviet minority, he too is under special surveillance. We have a lot of good reasons to explore the lake.

Already at seven thirty the streets are deserted. The only open store is the alcohol-and-sweets shop across the street from the

Orthodox church. It's a curfew that cannot be explained simply by the lake being so near to Russia. This is the void left by a heavy absence, and it is surely the absence of the Jews. Monika strikes up a conversation with Anna Sergeyevna, who is looking out the window of her ground-floor apartment together with her grand-daughter Viktoria and a six-month-old dog. There's only one Jew left, she says. His name is Bernacki and he is a lovely person. He lives two blocks from her house, on the way to the country. "The others have all gone. They come back every now and again just to visit their dead in the cemetery." But for a lot of the dead Jews, as we know, there is not even a tomb; after the Holocaust, all that's left of them is a name on a plaque. But when did the last Jews leave? In the early 1990s, as soon as the Communist regime fell and it was easier to get a visa. And the synagogue? Where was the synagogue? Anna Sergeyevna points the way. It's about three hundred yards toward the lake. It was right under our noses and we hadn't even noticed.

The void—that's the sensation of the curfew in Ludza. A recent void, unfilled and perhaps unfillable. The Jews did not disappear in the Hitler years, as we had thought, but fifty years later. The break is recent, perhaps irreparable, in this all-Russian ghetto where Latvians would rather not live. But there's the synagogue. In the style of the 1700s, in dark wood, with a roof that looks like the upside-down hull of a galleon, alone on the edge of the lake populated by ducks. Before we left on our journey, Monika had showed me a book on wooden Jewish houses of worship in Eastern Europe (*The Doors of Heaven*) and now I am looking at one of those forgotten masterpieces here in Ludza, where Mount Zion seems to have wedded the forests of the North. Through the basement windows, we can see that the books are still there. Nothing but the wind has touched them. Abandonment, not devastation. Until 1991, we are told by people in the neighboring houses, you could still see the lights shining on the first floor.

The ground floor is bolted shut, but we're able to get inside through the women's gallery by way of a shaky external stair. From up top, you can see everything: the ark, the side benches under the large windows, the octagonal elevated platform for the reading of the Torah, the ceiling like the keel of a ship, on which something may have been painted. Under the gallery, a collection of closets, old books still open, ornaments that shine in the half-light of the evening.

It's striking to feel like an archaeologist of an era that ended less than thirty years ago. We go out to look at the lake in the twilight. Water the color of bronze, the sky almost green, two semicapsized boats, a small monument to the Jews exterminated by the Nazis. The splash of a jumping fish that breaks the silence. Amid the many flourishing trees, there is only one that's black and dried up. On one of its branches, two crows as black as the tree seem to be listening and eager to tell us something. Then we are swallowed by the night, the first really dark night of our journey. We go to bed without saying another word.

The next day we go back there. Monika has a sense that there's something more. There's a house that has an air of mystery about it. It looks like a puzzle, as though in just a few years not one but five or six eras had superimposed themselves in it, inside and outside of the perimeter walls. In the garden there is an old woman hoeing. She too is clearly Russian, and her name is Rita. "Yes, the Jews used to pray here, too," she says with a wide smile, and she explains that the synagogue was transformed into a barn by some beastly men in uniform. Those animals declared the people that prayed there "aliens," killed them, and buried them in the woods. One day, however, the barn again hosted pious men and became a place of celebration, music, and joy. But since in the lives of mankind, the dark times and the joyous times inevitably alternate, one day the house again became a place of sadness, the last refuge of people labeled "aliens" by a heartless Europe.

This is the story of Rita and Volodya, old Russians trapped in Latvia by the latest shift of the moving frontiers, an unimaginable story of forgotten Europeans, third-class passengers, hidden like something to be ashamed of in the last cars of the luxurious train of the "community."

"This was a synagogue," Rita explains, "but in 1941, Hitler kept his soldiers' horses here. You know what happened next. Thousands of Jews murdered, even here on the lake. Then we came, in 1946. Come on in, dear friends. I'll show you what it's like on the inside." She goes in the house, lifts up a carpet, opens a trapdoor and shows us a cement drainage hole. "The Nazis built this to drain off into the lake the water they used to wash their horses."

Inside the walls are wood slats; the arcades have been shortened and turned into windows.

"In the beginning, a lot of Jews came back. God only knows from where. Auntie Gyela, Auntie Fruma . . . dear people, we called them aunt and uncle. And then Boris Gansen, Jasko Moissev, Doctor Schmutze, old lady Zagoria. Today there's hardly anybody. They either died or went to Israel."

I ask where she was born and her surname.

She pulls out her passport, shows me something printed in Latvian: *Nepsilona Pase*. Just underneath, the English translation: Alien's Passport. An alien, a nonperson, someone who can't vote even in local elections.

"What do you want? I'm not Latvian enough, I'm no longer Russian, and my first identity card was Soviet. There are a thousand of us here in town. We're supposed to pass a language exam and a national loyalty test, but what can you do? I'm too old to learn Latvian. You know, in the beginning I felt really bad, but today I don't even think about it."

I listen to her, ashamed. I'd like to become an alien myself, cry out against this well-mannered fascism that is invading Europe, Italy included.

The pendulum beats out five o'clock. Rita's husband, Volodya, who has suffered a hemiparesis, is lying on the couch and limits himself to a formal hello.

I ask Rita if she feels any strange presences in the house.

"My granddaughter says she hears whispering, but I tell her that's stupid, impossible. We are protected by this holy place. In the USSR, the Jews were treated well. We were all happy, poor and equal. If you were a lazy bum, they got you right away and sent you off to work. Today we're all unequal and unhappy."

Now Volodya wakes up, nods his head to say yes. He's never seen anyone pay attention to his life like these two strangers who by chance have come to visit his house. He gets up, takes a case out of a closet, and opens it. "Here, this is our whole story."

He takes out some old pictures and starts narrating. "The Jews were incredible musicians. Arkadi Kovnatar was a great accordion player. He died just a while ago. Davidoff was another phenomenon. And this here in the photograph is the People's Wind Orchestra. They were the best in all of Latvia. They didn't play Jewish music, but four out of five were Jews. Look here: from the left, Karotkin, then Moissev, Kovnatar, and Davidoff. The only non-Jew is the fourth, and he's also the only one who is still alive. Take a good look at him. Who is it? Why, it's me, Vladimir Dirbenyov," and with a glint in his eye, he does a half bow toward an audience that's not there.

"People used to dance until they were ready to keel over. We played at weddings and funerals; everybody wanted us. Our years with the Jews were our best. When they left, in the early 1990s, everything turned sad."

Rita: "Who knows which of them are still alive. Ah, *zhizn proshla*, life has passed by, my dear. But how nice it is to be with you two. We're people, aren't we? And people were made to meet one another. Do you want some tea?"

I say that I'd rather hear some accordion. I can tell that Volodya is dying to take it up again. It's been two years now that nobody has asked him to play. I exhort him, and he doesn't back away. He gets up and picks up his case. The instrument is really heavy. He rubs his fingers over the keyboard; the emotion is strong, and his hands are stiff from his illness. He makes an enormous effort and tries to play "Come Back to Sorrento." He struggles with the rusted body, his face is tense, his fingers search for the notes, but slowly the melody takes shape, the bellows swells in search of more difficult notes, and it succeeds. Volodya relaxes and smiles.

Joy has retaken possession of the house of the spirits. "Come on, Volodya, sing for us!" But Volodya shakes his head no and keeps on playing.

We insist, and he looks sly. "Give me a hundred grams and I'll sing." "A hundred grams" is the Russian way to say "a little glass," and a little glass is never denied in the presence of guests.

So Rita brings in the carafe, brandy made from fermented barley—called *samogon*, "homemade." Golden yellow, excellent aroma. She explains how it's made: a kilo of barley, two liters of water left to soak in a bucket with three kilos of sugar. Then you put it on the stove to boil. When the water starts to diminish, you add two hundred grams of yeast, and in two days, the yeast does its job. Another day to let it cool, and in the end, there's your *samogon*, nice and ready.

Rita: "There, now you know our secret. Volodya knows how to do the same thing with wheat. When he went to work in Kazakhstan, he learned that procedure as well."

Volodya confirms and stamps his foot. "Drinking is fine, but what are we going to eat?" By now it's clear, our dropping in has been transformed into an invitation to dinner.

On the little table between the couch and the armchair arrives some homemade bread, homemade butter, smoked fish caught by Volodya in the nearby lake, and fresh greens grown by Rita in the greenhouse out back. A triumph of the zero-mile diet. I think that when the great food crisis comes, the Russians will survive, but

Europe won't. The aliens and the uprooted, whom we have forced to learn the art of survival, will survive, too. Like the Jews.

We toast one another and take a sip.

"Good," says he, satisfied. Now I'll sing for you, Nekrasov. He concentrates, swells the veins of his neck, his vocal cords, his lungs and then lets go and sings, moving from whispering to thundering, he carries us away like the carpet of *The Master and Margarita*, in flight into the great Slavic night that surrounds us. The occasional false notes from the long-unused instrument make the singing even more soulful. It's the duende, sung of by García Lorca—the spirit that possesses a man when he renounces cold perfectionism and performance anxiety.

I can feel that I am in the heart of my journey. It's all here: Slavic culture, the Jews, uprootedness, the frontier, the return of fascism, the goodness of the least of us. And this Latvian sky that sums up the North and South of my continent.

Rita: "Come on, sing 'Voyennaya pesnya.' I want to cry a little. It's good for me."

He starts in: "There's an old tree on the edge of the woods." She follows, and now they're singing together, sweet octogenarians. In the refrain I hear *Miliy moy Andrei*, "My sweet Andrew." Andrea, like my son. Our mutual longings go searching together.

He grumbles: "My voice is fine; it's my fingers that can't hack it. But give me another hundred grams, my friend."

Rita happily fills his glass, then recites Pushkin: "This is how things go." Volodya rebuts: "Pushkin was Pushkin, but Lermontov was better." And there goes another poem, "Now I no longer die of love, even if at night my heart runs free." Then Rita says, "Listen to that. There is no love like that anymore. Today it's all vulgarity, banality, bodies for sale," and her eyes are as ardent as a thirty-year-old's.

"Ah, literature. Once there were lines to buy books. You remember, Rita? We had to reserve our place in line so we wouldn't miss the best ones. Today our books aren't any good to anyone. Nobody reads anymore. Not even our children. We have to throw them away after loving them for so long. They've become toilet paper."

Monika translates, and I notice that she's joined us on our little trip without buying a ticket, that is, without drinking even a drop of *samogon*. That's her specialty; she becomes a member of a group by the power of self-suggestion. She becomes an Afghan among the Afghans, a Jew among Jews, a Russian among Russians. That's why people let themselves be photographed so easily by her. Now she sings a Polish song, then an Italian one with me, and finally a Triestian song that speaks of wind and the Mediterranean, to tell Rita and Volodya something of our world. She's in the duende, too.

Volodya accompanies me to take a piss in the outhouse in the middle of the garden. He takes the lock off the door, waits for me, then walks me out to the lake. I can't understand how we can manage to walk straight. We're happy, on the periphery of this shtetl still full of old nobility. The wind whistling through the reed beds, little ducks cleaning their feather coats, a purple sky. I don't feel worthy of what I've seen and heard. What little there is left of the soul of Europe lives here, among the forgotten—the Russians, the Slavs, the Jews who aren't here anymore, the Gypsies perhaps.

A full moon is rising. I had forgotten about the moon in the low skies of the North, where the anemic night isn't able to light up the planet. Now it's huge, the color of parchment; rising slowly behind the trees, it illuminates the little obelisk in memory of the Jews killed by the Nazis in that exact place. As the wind turns the anemones inside out like enormous frog-mouth helmets, I empty my pockets and, in one machine-gun-like burst, throw all of my Latvian pennies into the lake, begging fate to bind me to this place forever. A dog barks, alarmed by the noise of that brief hailstorm in the silence, another answers him from beyond the wood, and it is as though all of the dogs on the twenty-eighth meridian were calling out to one another all the way to the Dnieper, Istanbul, and Smyrna. Time stops.

Ludza is my center of Europe.

The next day, as we are leaving for Lithuania, we go out to say good-bye to the couple in the synagogue. It's also a sort of checkup visit. I feel well despite the drunk, but I'm worried about the effects of the alcohol on Volodya. When we get there, we find him standing in the door to the house. His eyes are shining with happiness.

"How did you sleep, Volodya?"

"*Normalno*," he laughs, and adds, "never so well." Then, worried, "And you, old friend?"

Hugs, addresses, telephone numbers, exchanges of small gifts.

Rita: "Come back. It was one of the most beautiful days of my life."

Volodya: "Be careful with the Lithuanian police. They give the highest fines in Europe." And he laughs again. He looks like a new man.

Before we get to the Lithuanian frontier, the spires of the Catholic shrine at Aglona call out to us from the woods, but the church and grounds are a disappointment, like the Croatian Medjugorje, which I visited during the war in Bosnia. I see an architecture of power and image, a tourist attraction with little or no soul, with strange athletic priests, strange black cars, strange hotels and campgrounds, perfectly empty among the fir trees. We're getting closer to the land of Wojtyla, Poland, and the Vatican already appears to be a mega–travel agency, a multinational of pilgrimages with branches all over the world. Maybe I'm too quick to judge; mine is not a journey of deep investigation. But I've learned to trust my instinct and my first impressions. They are rarely off the mark.

I've never loved triumphant religions. I prefer the minor ones and the losers, the catacombs, the peripheries or the advance guards where the hierarchies don't stick their noses in, and power struggles are nonexistent. Maybe that's why I felt God's presence more in the abandoned synagogue in Ludza than before the vaguely tomblike marbles of Aglona. In the same manner, Catholicism glistens more intensely on the high plateaus of Peru than in Rome or in Ratzinger's Bavaria. But there's something else disturbing about Aglona. Maybe it's the gloomier woods, maybe the nearly vanished birch trees, replaced by the needles of the evergreens, as shady as the ones in Grimm's fairy tales. Maybe it's the ever more visible signs of the void left by the Jews, too hurriedly refilled.

We stop to have a bite to eat in a forest blue with blueberries and green with comfortable cushions of moss. Under trees whispering with the pallid colors of Klimt, there unfolds on a tablecloth a very Slavic menu of chives, buttermilk, cucumbers, brown bread, garlic, salami, and radishes. For the first time since Murmansk, my ankles sink into the underbrush; I notice that digging is easy. After the permafrost of the Arctic lands and after the polished granite of Karelia, the soil is sandy, marked by slight swellings like little knolls. Not always are they morainic residues of glaciers. Here, everyone knows that every rise and fall might be a common grave. From the Baltic to Ukraine, Europe is one big necropolis, still to be discovered.

Even more than Rēzekne, Daugavpils is characterized by the redbrick houses of their old tenants, wiped out by the Holocaust. We drive through it in a hurry. On the streets, children with their heads shaved, as in Italy during the war. In a bar, less than reputable types, muscular refrigerators just hopped out from a big-engine car; it's black, too, like their clothes. Then comes the border with Lithuania, in total abandonment, green buildings falling apart, the trailer once a currency exchange office now a shelter for the homeless, the floor covered with broken glass and two-liter plastic beer bottles. A moth-eaten border crossing that looks even older than the one with Russia. But nature triumphs. On the road to Vilnius, colossal linden trees tower over the landscape, maybe the biggest ones I've seen in my whole life.

On the outskirts of the little town of Sventa, on the road to Vilnius, pan Eduard, Mr. Edward, is sitting in his garden shed with two Russian friends, Yevgeny and Grigori. Lithuanian, born in 1930, and a face dripping with irony, he's smoking a cigarette and weaving wicker nets for catching lake fish. Between the two World Wars, Lithuania was part of Poland, and today Mr. Edward lives in the house of a Polish official who escaped in 1939, right after the Ribbentrop-Molotov Pact, which had decided the partitioning of his country. "He was a despot," he tells us. "Eight families worked for him. He had twenty-five cows and six horses, and he rode around on his horse to inspect the hay harvest, carrying a club. If he didn't like something he saw, he would point the club at someone and say: you don't work for me anymore."

The lesser Polish nobility didn't make itself loved around these parts, but today its absence is noticeable. Mr. Edward's hay is mowed very badly. With the passing of the club-wielding lords and the passing of Communism, life has been reduced to small things. It is spent fishing, smoking a cigarette, sipping a beer. "Ours," he says, offering me a glass, "you absolutely have to taste it. Since independence it has gotten much better." Yevgeny weighs in on the subject. He wants to know how much beer and vodka cost in France, Italy, and Poland. His geography is all alcoholic. He writes down scrupulously with pencil and paper the Italian prices. Mr. Edward: "Things have gotten better. The stores are full. You used to have to get in line for meat, and when you got to the head of the line, the meat was all gone. To buy something decent you had to be a friend of the store manager." Grigori laughs. "Today the stores have everything. The only thing lacking is money."

Yevgeny tells us that after independence in 1992, he got in his car and started heading west nonstop. "I put it in first, second, third, fourth, and I kept going, going, going. Without stopping, without sleeping. Poland. Germany. Just about all I saw was gas stations, but I was hungry for space, I was euphoric like an escapee. I wanted to go all the way to the Atlantic. But in France, they stopped me. The police said to me, 'Monsieur, your tires are bald. You can't drive like this.' So I spent all my money on new tires, and I came home." I ask if things have gotten better since 1992. "The country is emptying out. At the time of the USSR, there were two hundred kids here in the elementary school. Today less than half. People aren't having children—the cost of living is too high. Private businesses do whatever they want; they're buying up everything. They tell me it's like that in Russia, too."

Monika asks if there used to be Jews around there. Grigori: "Sure there were. They were rich and poor, like us, but people hated them. And when the Germans came in 1941, the Lithuanians turned into animals. The Germans gave the signal and then they just stood and watched. Meanwhile, the Lithuanians slaughtered the Jews and the Gypsies with whatever weapons they could get their hands on. Saws, hammers, clubs." Mr. Edward has finished weaving his wicker cage for the catfish. "There's a place on the river, twelve miles from here, where before they killed them, they forced them to dig a common grave with their own hands. People were drunk with blood. Svincane is the name of the place. It's a huge cemetery like the one in Ponare, the old quarries just outside of Vilnius." I ask him if the old owners of his house have ever come back. "One day a woman came, maybe the daughter. She didn't do anything. She looked around, didn't say hello to anyone, and then she left."

After the Neris River, we give a lift to Artur and Derek, two cheerful twenty-five-year-olds who are hitchhiking to Vilnius. Only one of the two has a girlfriend there, but they're traveling together. The stuff of days gone by. Their dream is to work in the West because in Lithuania "it's all a fraud." Derek tells us that he's a bricklayer who used to be paid €1,200 a month, and now he gets €300. "The Germans are the only ones who pay for the work you do."

Artur works as a carpenter and a welder, but now he's unemployed. "My last job was building a church. The priest got some funding from the EU and came up with the idea of a nave in the form of an overturned boat. I made him the vaulting ribs to hold up the roof." Monika whispers to me: "He's the modern version of Väinämöinen, or maybe the latest version of Hephaestus." But anyway, the onion spires of Vilnius, lit up at night, come into view on a horizon of hilltops.

The legendary city of Judaism and of Catholic Poland begins with our first Italian tourists, in front of the station, where we drop off our rental car. They are three men from Puglia, judging from their accent, obviously on the hunt for women. One is obese, one skinny as a rail, and the other incredibly nervous in what looks like a bulletproof vest. A scene from a comedy. They think they've arrived in the Third World, that they should be able to go to the airport by taxi for a euro and seventy cents. An enraged taxi driver explains that the closest place where they can buy something for a euro seventy is Ulan Bator, in Mongolia. They play the tough guys, bother a few more cabdrivers with their arrogant behavior, but in the end they retreat. They're behind the eight ball. They've got all the cabbies against them, and they don't know what to do. They consider taking a bus, but they don't speak English, let alone Lithuanian. So they go back humiliated to Canossa and get in the first cab at the head of the line.

The cabdrivers in Vilnius are phenomenal. They talk loud, bicker, argue continuously, and make you feel that you're definitely in the South. The world of the mute Finno-Ugrics is gone forever. Lithuania is the southern Italy of the Baltics. The driver who picks me up at the station is upset with himself because he can't guess my nationality. "You are surely not Lithuanian, surely not Russian, and surely not Polish." I keep him in suspense for a while. My Istrian-Balkan-Mitteleuropean face is tough to figure out. His, on the other hand, is unmistakably Mongol. Eyes wide apart and small, nose minimal and pug like a boxer's, face wide like a nocturnal bird's, cheeks enormous and bony. "I'm Italian, but a little Slav and a little German," I tell him. And he, proudly pointing to himself: "Polish surname, Russian language, Tartar mug." And to say "mug," he uses the Polish word *morda*, disparaging, animalesque, and frankly untranslatable in Italian.

To seal his friendship with his bastard cousin from Italy with his aquiline profile, he takes his hands off the wheel and, without stopping the cab, turns around to shake my right hand vigorously. The car swerves but imperceptibly. When I notice that he's controlling the gear shift with his knee, I understand that I am hostage to a grandson of the Golden Horde, the band of knights from the steppe. He's certainly one of them. Once quartered in Poland, in the time when Poland also included Lithuania and ample slices of Ukraine and Belarus, they—Muslims—put themselves in the service of the Catholic king and became the most feared defenders of the realm. It was they who brought about the overwhelming victory of Jan Sobieski against the Turks, outside the walls of Vienna, they who galloped against the Soviets in the Russo-Polish war of 1920, and they yet again who launched themselves with their swords drawn in the charge against Hitler's panzers. That's why my cabdriver is beating the steering wheel as though it were the halter of a horse, making it move in a terrifying manner, herky-jerky, braking on the curves, accelerating wildly, cursing, furiously denying the right of way to all comers.

Ah, Vilnius, the Vilnius of the Jews, wellspring of kabbalah and culture, how you sparkle today with fast-food chains. You've already become an amusement park. In just a few years, you, Athens of the Baltic, seem already to have lost much of that fascinating nineteenth-century mold that during the terrible time of the Soviets, you had somehow managed to conserve.

By now it's dark, and tired as I am, I'm not ready to go exploring. But Monika, who as a Pole knows each of the city's stones one by one, won't give in. She takes aim at the hill, sniffs out some tracks on the old pavement, and thus meets Mr. Jan Pogrzelski. He's a Greek Catholic, a member, that is, of that Orthodox confraternity that, to get out from under the repression of the Kremlin, subjected itself to the pope of Rome. A mild-mannered man, polite, well dressed and subtly possessed by his religious persuasion. He accompanies us up the hill to show us the church that once conserved the relics of a certain Saint Jouzapatas (something similar to Jehoshaphat), which were in danger of being "deported" to Moscow in the eighteenth century—and he underlines several times the term *deported*, as though he were talking about a living person.

Jan tells us stories of battles and massacres, and everything he says could be summarized by the single concept: "Yes, it's possible to stay together, Westerners and Orthodox." It's not hard for me to sympathize. I'm a frontier Catholic who goes to Mass in the church of the Greeks on his own turf. But then comes the apocalypse. His discourse turns into a list of martyrdoms and betrayals, of sacraments denied and crypts of relics kissed for the last time by believers condemned to death. He evokes the emergence of a late Christianity erected on a base of tenacious paganism, child of the forest and the long nights of the North. And it's always Moscow, the East, the czar, the great Antichrist. "For Russia, I am a renegade, all of us Greek Catholics are." And then, returning to his Jehoshaphat: "Peter the Great ordered his corpse to be burned, but the monks hid it so well that it was conserved here. And when the time of the Soviets came, Moscow again tried to appropriate itself of the relics, but the Ukrainian cardinal Slipyj succeeded in moving them to Saint Peter's. That body was not to be left in Muscovite hands. Only when Ukraine became independent was he returned to Lviv, his hometown."

The obsession with relics: I had heard it with this force only from the Greeks in the temple of the Holy Sepulcher. The body, the body, the heart of the problem. The body that becomes mummy and the mummy that turns into the holiest of icons. "Jehoshaphat had his head broken open with a hatchet because already in the 1600s, three centuries before Wojtyla, he wanted to champion ecumenical ideas. Then they threw his body into the river. But that body was so pure that it shone in the night and, like the body of Casimir, patron saint of Lithuania, it showed no signs of decomposition. So it was brought here, and when Peter the Great conquered the Grand Duchy of Poland and Lithuania, then celebrated the victory for three days in Vilnius, he entered this church drunk and asked whose was the body contained in the case. The monks said, it's the body of a saint. Then Peter killed them all. In the beginning the massacre was covered up, but later the truth came out." Night has now fallen in the city of the spirits.

"'Vilne shtot fun gaist un tmimes, Vilne yidishlech fartracht.' Vilnius, city of spirit and innocence, where silent prayers are murmured, soundless secrets of the night . . . I often see you in my dreams, my Vilnius, woods, mountains, and valleys of Vilnius, Vilnius that was the first to raise the flag of freedom. . . . 'Vilnius, Vilnius, under heimshtot,' city of our birth." What's left of the myth after the tabula rasa of Nazism, the nullity of Communism, and now the final storm of the market on the ruins of a glorious epoch of spirit and innocence? Maybe there is nothing left for me except this heartrending song in Yiddish that my friend Salamone Ovadia sang to me, many years ago, well before this frontier journey, which he was the very one to suggest that I take. I sing it to myself as I'm digging, exhausted, in the deep of the night after all that light in the North.

But in the midst of this darkness, Monika is searching; I can see her eyes shining like spotlights on the "soundless secrets of the night," until Vilnius presents her with still another gift, the surprise of a rabbi, black of beard and jacket, who is coming toward her on the sidewalk. There he is, strangely responding to her greeting. I say strangely because an observant Jew, I've been told, is not supposed to communicate with a woman in a public place. The shade goes on its way and vanishes, but a little later there he is, reemerging from the labyrinth of the old city, and he bumps into us at the corner of a house. We introduce ourselves. The Jew is Samuel Jakob Pfeffer, he looks to be fifty or so, with wild hair. He is a rabbi who observes the rule of the *gaon* (genius) of Vilnius, Elijah ben Shlomo Zalman Kremer, luminary of the Talmud, who in the eighteenth century declared war on the mystics of the long curls called the Hasidim.

He's American, Rabbi Pfeffer; that's why he so nonchalantly responded to the feminine greeting. It's as though he had been expecting us. He just about takes us by the hand and leads us in front of his synagogue, showing us proudly the date of its construction, 1906, and an inscription beside the Star of David. The words announce the prohibition of entry by the followers of the Hasidic heresy. We ask him, what has been the fate in Lithuania of the mystics who disobeyed the ancient rules? and he answers, "Gone." And the other Jews, what do they do? "They are few; what's more, they're timid." And from his lips, as from the lips of the Greek Catholic Jan Pogrzelski, comes another story of martyrdom: the story of Count Valentin Potocki, burned alive for having converted to Judaism. "The *gaon* of Vilnius wanted to save him," the American tells us, "but the count said no, because he wanted his death to be his testimony of his discovery of the true faith."

Rabbi Pfeffer gestures to us and takes us to see what's left of the Vilnius of the Jews. He looks like a great nocturnal bird, and he does nothing to fit in. "The atmosphere is not healthy," he confirms. "A lot of people shout at me: Jew! And what else can I do but look them in the face and ask them if they've got a problem? Why should I lower myself to their level and shout back?" He talks about a big Jewish cemetery, five hundred years old, which the Lithuanians would like to transform into a shopping center. "The situation is very dangerous for all religions. By now, money rules over all; the sacred is in pieces. Tell me, how can you do business over the bones of the dead? How can anyone think that something like that can bring good fortune? How can we construct a cohabitation by abusing memory in this way? How can we forget what happened here under Nazism?"

Somebody has torn down the street sign for the Street of the Jews, and someone has painted a swastika on the base of the bust dedicated to the *gaon* of Vilnius. The Zavln Synagogue on Gėlių Street has remained as it was seventy years ago, burned inside and out, and it seems that the land will be sold. Suddenly Pfeffer's shadow lengthens and grows larger on the pavement by effect of the only streetlamp on the edge of a public park, which is shining on him from thirty yards away. It happens only to his shadow, not ours, even though we're fairly close to him. Monika plays with these effects, freezing on film the owl eyes of the Jew and his black hair inflamed by the neon signs of the bars. We sit down in the square, at the open-air tables. Samuel Jakob drinks calmly as though in a saloon; the American in him conflicts with his rabbinical role, with Vilnius itself. Then he starts back in on his gloomy prophecy: "Many communities will be extinguished, maybe even mine. But it is important that something remain, because this was a central place."

8. K TOWN

RIDING HIGH on its Siberian antisnow heels, the Moscow–Kaliningrad—a snake made of twenty illuminated cars—is rolling along in the early morning light. To board it, at three in the morning, I had to show my passport, visa, and ticket to a sleepy-eyed cop shut inside a glass booth under platform ten in the underground passageway of the Vilnius train station—the only one, surrounded by barriers and guarded by police. On its sides there is a double railing a little bit longer than the train, outfitted with video cameras. I'm on a Russian train going to Russia, but Kaliningrad is an enclave detached from the fatherland. In order to get there, you have to cross Lithuania, part of the European Union, and the Lithuanians have to make sure that nobody tries to sneak off the train along the way. Maybe even the two of us, with our Muscovite visas, are under special surveillance.

At platform ten of the Vilnius station, the problem is not boarding but getting off, because this is the corridor that connects the two Russias. It feels as though we were at Tempelhof Airport during the Cold War, when it was the only transport facility that kept Berlin in contact with the West. This border crossing for Kaliningrad is exactly the kind of frontier I've been looking for, a tough frontier, one of those old-fashioned borders that, since the Schengen Accords, we are no longer used to crossing. There are only two stations, both highly guarded, between the Lithuanian capital and the Russian territory on the Baltic, but just the same, some clever daredevils occasionally manage to get by the police. All that has to happen is for the train to slow down to around thirty miles an hour, and some shadowy figures start slipping out through the windows. That is why, I'm told, the tracks are constantly checked and repaired: to leave no alibis for unscheduled stops or slowdowns.

I can see my shadow projected as though by a magic lantern from the still-illuminated window out toward the thick of the woods. The train is painted green and flaming red, like those pretty czarist uniforms in the film *War and Peace*. With their immaculate sheets and mothering female conductors, Russian trains coddle and reassure, even here on the road to Königsberg, the city of Kant, now a place for submarines, contraband, and secret services. I have arrived here without touching either Tallinn or Riga, too far from my border-skirting itinerary. But now, for the journey to be complete, I have to make a long detour and go to K Town. I couldn't miss Kaliningrad, the island of the recluses, surrounded by fortress Europe. In order to get there, I had to procure for myself, not without some difficulty, a double entry visa stamped on my passport.

I ask the conductress for a tea, and I buy a packet of Bolshevik cookies, in a red and yellow wrapper. Everybody on board is snoring. The corridor is empty except for one woman, on her feet, watching the sun come up between the Baltic clouds, nibbling on a chocolate bar. She says to Monika, "The others are sleeping, but I can't. Lithuania makes me anxious. There is a strange relationship between the two police forces. They help each other out, and they always know where to look." She tells us that at the border station between Belarus and Vilnius, the police went directly to wake up a young guy, who was sleeping like a rock. Only him. Then they threw him off the train. Some days ago, they caught a man with fifty pounds of amber, and his was the only bag they opened in the whole compartment.

In Nesterov, lost in the mountains ninety miles east of Kaliningrad, the customs officers search under the train with a mirror. Then at the border, there's a general mobilization. Railroad security, tax police, army. The Lithuanians come aboard with a wolf-dog, then with a strange team of men who go looking for something with a magnifying glass. Then it's the Russians' turn. A policewoman with a long blond braid scrutinizes our documents with another magnifying glass and then again with a sensor. Finally she spells our surnames into her walkie-talkie. Twenty seconds later, from the other end, crystal clear, maybe even from Moscow itself, there arrives a blunt *nyet*. There is nothing negative in our records, and I can feel that K Town is already capturing us like an insect inside a drop of amber. Then once again, we're off, in the rain, toward the Baltic and the former East Prussia.

"Kaliningrad, Kaliningrad Station, prepare to detrain," the conductress notifies us, as she comes by to collect the last sheets and pillowcases. Just outside the station, decorated with marble and fountains, K Town announces itself with fantastic visions. Submarines in the rain, sandhills, Prussian spires, a sky brewing like a kettle of ink. An elegantly refined old couple—he, bow tie; she, a silver pagoda hairdo; both in cream-colored suits, shoes included—who disappear inside an enormous black Volga. Young pallid women striding long and briskly into the wind. My bloodred hands, from the overripe strawberries purchased from a peasant woman, and the station with a huge clock displaying the hour of the lord and master, Moscow. We could be in 1950s Monte Carlo if it weren't for a certain odor of herring and this Jewish sky out of *Fiddler on the Roof*.

What a surprise. The recluse island is not at all a desperate relic of the Khrushchev era. Detached from Mother Russia, surrounded on all sides by the star-spangled banner of the EU, it shows no traces of claustrophobia, despite the vexations of the Lithuanians, who have imposed a transit visa even on those Russians who, to reach it by land, must cross the territory of the EU without getting off the train. We've never seen as many stretch limousines as here, as many shopping centers, ATMs. This western outpost of the former empire, Putin's favorite city, is living the easy life. The chief of the new Russia found his wife here, invests his rubles here, and here he has decided to play out his hand by dropping his strongest card: a military base in the middle of the West, like the eye in the huge head of a whale.

Let's decline it then, the consonant of destiny. K as in Königsberg, to start with. Its old Baltic name, perfumed with sailing ships and merchandise. K as in Kaliningrad, today's Soviet name, stuck on in 1945 to immortalize Comrade Mikhail Kalinin, who never visited it and became president of the USSR by vaunting his merit in having let his wife die in a Gulag. K as in Królewiec, the name given by the Poles to the most closed city in Europe, capital of the only piece of Russia detached from the Great Mother. An armor-plated planet sealed off from the world, half the size of Belgium, which the enlargement of the European Union has isolated even more than in the times of Leonid Brezhnev.

But K is also for *Krieg*, the war, the Second World War, which exterminated the Baltic Jews, forced the Prussians to escape, and reduced the cities to rubble. K is Kommunismus, the big freeze, which completed the job begun by the Allied bombers, deported the region's inhabitants, militarized the territory, swept away its memory. Yet again, K as in Koka-Kola, symbol of the capital that today governs an enclave where everything is bought and sold: women, oil, nuclear warheads. Finally, K as in Kant. Immanuel Kant, founding father of modern thought and quintessence of German rigor. The philosopher is back in vogue in this advance outpost of the ex-USSR. He can be resuscitated partly because his memory has never truly been banned. Lenin did not fail to appreciate the German philosopher, and Stalin—having conquered the city—saved his tomb from demolition. Today, his shadow is reemerging, becoming a symbol of the West, perhaps the only one possible in a city deprived of its history. He is becoming a symbol partly because of the children of the population that was forced to immigrate here after the eviction of the natives. New-generation kids, like Lyudmila Putin, born here to a family of "alien" immigrants.

Today the newlyweds of Kaliningrad place flowers on the red granite stone that covers the remains of the great sage, behind an old redbrick Protestant church. Kant didn't spend much time in churches. He contemplated the starry skies above him, and this caused him problems with the bigoted king of Prussia. Today there are those who come here to touch his death mask as though it were a good luck charm, not knowing that it is only a copy of the original, conserved in the University of Tartu, in Estonia. But that doesn't much matter. Few people here have read a line of *The Critique of Pure Reason*, but that's not important, either. Kant is an immanent thought, a shade who oversees the fascinating and terrible destiny of his city.

But K is also for Kristina, a twenty-year-old woman who invites us to stay at her house and picks us up at the station with a friend. She studies international relations (her friend, design), has an apartment with a bay window in the "good" part of the city, dreams of the great wide world, and flies to Berlin for weekends. She has a father who sails, a mother who works in the finance industry, a sister who lives with her and passes the time playing video games. I'm astounded. My mental categories are in pieces. I'm looking at a Russia that has been totally Westernized. The frontier? No problem for Kristina; on the contrary, she experiences it as a resource, with the same "let the good times roll" spirit of New Orleans in the Prohibition era. She's got other problems: building speculation, the dominance of the Muscovites, drugs and prostitution, the highest incidence of AIDS in Europe. Kristina is sure that her city, left free to attract investments, would become a Switzerland of the North.

She says, "The Muscovites are rich; they come to the seaside here, but they build concrete monsters that nobody will ever live in, eliminate parks and squares; the identity of the place is in danger."

To get a better understanding, we hop on a tram to the center of town, the first one that comes by. The food market is a people's place, full of onions and smoked fish, where Kristina, accustomed to the restaurants of Berlin, would never go. An immense market, four times as big as the one in Budapest and much more authentic. In Budapest, you get only Hungary. At the market in Kaliningrad, you get the whole Soviet Union. Apricots from Uzbekistan. Cossack honey, sold by Cossacks. Smoked Baltic fish brought from Saint Petersburg. Crisp, crunchy bread from Azerbaijan. Throngs of peasants with blueberries and currants. Folk cures for tuberculosis and old age, such as bear fat, badger fat, and even dog fat, sealed under glass and lined up on the counter next to the sausage. Here you don't get the bland blend of the global, but rather the succulent plurality of an empire.

In the pavilions, the pavement is a paste of dust, grease, and sugar that sticks to your shoes. All around, there are strange-looking types checking out everything, more often than not bristly Caucasians with eyes flashing like knives. One of them, attracted by my notebook, comes over to listen to the questions I pose to a meek pensioner who is selling dried fish and complaining about the prices. Nikolai Semyonovich, eighty-two, war vet, one functioning eye, asks how much somebody like him makes in Italy. The intruder listens, acting as if he belongs there. A while ago, he would have been a spy; today he is the guard for the gang that oversees the deals, gets rid of nose pokers, and makes sure there aren't any thieves hanging around. I suddenly realize that in my entire trip through Russia I have never encountered a police officer.

I'm hungry. My stomach is whining like an untuned violin. There is an Azerbaijani tavern called Osyag that's emitting irresistible smells of food and deals. I worm my way in. At a nearby table, three more bristly types are eating, answering their cell phones, and ostentatiously counting out wads of hundred-thousand-ruble notes. They're doing everything possible to be seen, and so we strike up a conversation. I ask them how life is in Kaliningrad, and the most bristly of the three smiles radiantly, puts three fingers of his right hand over his mouth, kisses them with a smack of his lips, and replies, "Awesome." Then he adds, "Life is easy. It's a sweet place, and there are lots of deals to be made."

A loaf of braided bread arrives, kefir with wild herbs, and exquisite dolmas stuffed with meat. Three gelid blond guys also arrive, Putin wannabes, and sit at the table of the Azerbaijanis. The ethnic division of the business couldn't be clearer. The blond guys are the bosses of the territory, and they've come to pick up their percentage. A brief sotto voce chat, a meeting of the minds, and the blue wads of hundred-thousand notes change hands right under my nose. An enormous figure; to eyeball it, something like €300,000. A handshake, as it was done by the Sicilian clans in New York a century ago.

Outside of the Arcimboldian teeming masses, the surprises keep adding up. Money machines that distribute, besides rubles, dollars in big and small denominations. Black megacylinder limos, ten or twelve yards long, with tinted windows, transporting to the town hall white-dressed brides and men in cream-colored suits. It's the trendy color on the Baltic, the same color worn by the old couple I'd seen at the train station. The women are almost always stunning. The men are divided into two varieties: businessmen around forty, boxer builds, with horrible-looking bodyguards; or handsome, slender young men with passionate eyes, fired by an ardor unknown in the West. Monika slips into courtyards, snapping pictures in a light that changes by the minute, teetering between sunlight and rain.

Iosip, Georgian taxi driver: "This is my second fatherland. I came here twenty years ago, and it was all gray. Today, it's upbeat, and above all, there's no risk of war. Life is good. And tell me, where is it written that the frontier is a downer?" No-man's-land, a rarefied space of the imagination, Kaliningrad is a fantastic nonplace like Trieste and Odessa, a city of illusions and intrigues, comparable to postwar Vienna, an ideal setting for Bogart films. Maybe to understand the city—its billionaire smugglers and its pockets of poverty, its military installations and its depressive psychoses—you really do need the philosophy of Kant, the man who, without knowing it, laid the groundwork for modern psychiatry, sanctioning the unknowability of reality with his historic distinction between "das Ding für mich" and "das Ding für sich," the thing as it appears to me and the thing in itself.

"Who knows what the German thinker would say about the Russified Königsberg of today?" The city's postmodern intellectual circles amuse themselves with such questions. When the Russians routed Prussia and occupied the Baltic port from 1758 to 1762, Professor K didn't have a bad time of it. The man by whose afternoon walks the city set its clocks turned out to be an accomplished dispenser of salon witticisms and an excellent pool player, and thanks to the czar of Saint Petersburg, he even had an academic career. The historian Manfred Kühn recalls that Kant greeted with pleasure the new Slavic air that had enlivened the small Prussian world, too methodical and predictable, too dour-faced from Protestant piety and regimented by a dynasty of sergeant-kings.

We have an appointment with Kristina and her girlfriends at the Plaza shopping center, a concrete and glass giant surveilled by more gorillas, not far from the Prussian cathedral rebuilt with German capital. The terrace restaurant is pure America: boom-boom music, giant screens with soccer games, a vacuous horror dripping even from the hyperdecorated walls of the restrooms, vocal communication absolutely impossible without shouting. A friend of Kristina's explains that the punitive system of the Lithuanian visas discriminates against the poor, who cannot afford to fly. "And if we go from Moscow to Kaliningrad carrying Russian medicines, the

Lithuanians seize them because, they say, they're not in conformity with the regulations. They consider them addiction-inducing narcotics. But it's just plain old protectionism. In Klaipėda, there was a nice market for Russian medicines; today there's nothing."

When I go out onto the terrace to get a breath of fresh air and enjoy the view of the boulevards and the former Palace of the Soviet, now an abandoned ghost, the waiter runs out to get me because staying outside is prohibited. It seems that one day someone was thrown off the terrace to the ground below. I escape again to people-watch. On a tram, I encounter a Mongol woman of breathtaking beauty and a troubled-eyed Slav with a braid as thick as a rope. On a bus, there's a Georgian gang that ogles my notebook and forces me into an escape in English. At the zoo, guarded by two matrons at the ticket booth, I'm left bewildered, watching a clearly crazed sea lion swimming in an undersize pool, not far from a melancholy giraffe, immobile under the Northern sky.

Leopold Baranowski, ex-submarine officer in charge of the torpedoes, takes me to visit the B-413 submarine parked at the dock. He traveled underwater for more than twenty years, from 1960 to 1982, in all the seas of the world. "I've seen your hometown, too, through the periscope," he says to me about Trieste. "Your defenses were excellent," he continues, but complains that Western films about Russian submarines are all nonsense. "Even the Russian films are all lies. The only realistic one that I've seen is German, entitled *Das Boot*." I ask him how long he used to go without seeing the sunlight. "Up to six months." How did you do it? "Today, I ask myself that same question." While we're in the wardroom, two steps away from the periscope, we hear a ticking sound like a pounding rain that takes possession of the hull. "It's nothing," Leopold smiles, "it's just another ship passing nearby." Kaliningrad by itself is worth a journey.

In the square with the monument to the fallen of 1941–45, there's Andrei, twenty-two, just named midshipman, in a white uniform and dress sword, who waves a bunch of fuchsia-colored flowers in our faces to invite us to drink *shampanskoye* with his friends. He has just disembarked in Murmansk from the missile launcher *Peter the Great*, where he put his studies of ballistics to use, and he is celebrating his promotion with a group of young aspiring officers. I tell him that I have a son by the same name. Then I add that my father was also an officer. Right away he asks me if my father fought on Hitler's side, a question that is as naive as you like, but unavoidable. "*Da*," I reply. Yes. "Sometimes," I explain, "it happens that you fight on the wrong side. But he was an officer and a gentleman. And in any case, he was a good father."

Sorry to have embarrassed me, the young man in uniform whispers sweetly, "I understand." Then he raises his glass again and proclaims to his friends, to us, to the city: "I love you. I love you, and I carry you in my heart." I'm not sure any Western soldier would say something like that, especially in the presence of strangers. Meanwhile, at the base at Baltiysk, eighteen miles from the city, on this side of the big sand dune that closes the Baltic, Putin's nuclear submarines, lined up like glistening mackerel on a fish stand, put the West on notice that the Bear never sleeps.

I've already talked about the marvel of Russian trains, the small strawberry- or pistachio-colored stations where they stop in the middle of the forest, their steaming samovars, the original geometry of their bunks, and the endless, orderly picnics that are consumed on board long-distance runs under the watchful eyes of a maternal hostess who takes everyone and everything under her wing.

What I haven't mentioned yet is the magnificence of their tickets, decorated like banknotes, solemnly titled Travel Document, sheathed in a multicolored sleeve, perfect souvenirs with your revered name in Cyrillic, departure and arrival times, your passport number, and a plethora of data that make them irreplaceable documents of your life. Nothing can compare to them except perhaps the stamps applied to your visa. They are so baroquely beautiful that I have gathered them all in a case, which I keep in the stationery compartment of my pack. The ticket purchased for the ride from Petrozavodsk to Saint Petersburg–Ladozkaya, along the border strip with Finland, is a light primrose pink, with a pompous script RELEASE near the top in perfectly matched brown Cyrillic, and on the lower right, the signature of the ticket vendor, rich with Victorian swirls. The route from Olenegorsk to Kyem, the embarcadero for the Solovetsky Islands, is represented by a prune-colored card with flaming red decorations, and on the left a golden yellow icon, like a coin, bearing an image of the locomotive of the new Russia, racing toward the future. The sleeve of the tickets issued at the central station in Kaliningrad features a map of Russia with a radiant sun in the center, and it changes color progressively from one side to the other with all the shades of the rainbow. It's as though all the pride of the nation were concentrated in these pieces of paper.

But the tickets are nothing compared to the ticket booths of the former Soviet empire. In Russia, a ticket vendor—more often than not a woman—is a ranking public official to whom you must address yourself with respect. The people's deferential attitude in front of a ticket window is one of the most interesting things to be seen around these parts. Already in Murmansk, Olenegorsk, and Saint Petersburg, the lines had taught me a different—much slower—dimension of time, with flexible working hours interrupted by microintervals for union breaks (one every forty-five minutes). But it wasn't until Kaliningrad that I understood their complex operations.

We go to the station to buy two tickets to Warsaw, and we get into one of the five lines in front of five open ticket windows. Right away, the woman in front of us politely explains that she is in line for six other persons and so we should evaluate our waiting time accordingly. Then, without any preliminaries, she offers to wait on line for me too and explains that if I, by getting into another line, were to save a place for her and the others, she would be infinitely grateful. Monika, who understands the language, immediately agrees to take part in the game, and invites me to do the same. Instantly, the mechanism is revealed. In front of the ticket windows, a strategy of "one for all, all for one" has developed in response to the uncertainty of the pee-pee breaks of the ticket vendor.

A rugby scrum could not play out any better. The five lines are processed in perfect order as though they were only one. Nobody tries to sneak in front of anybody else. I don't know what generates this solidarity. Maybe a compassion born of a great shared pain, the suffering of a people that has experienced a century of horrors, which have left their mark on the soul. The fact remains that even the ticket vendor, faced with a stammering foreigner, me, is moved and does everything she can to help me. "Departure is at 6:30 p.m., but that is Moscow time, so you have to be here by 5:30." And then, with a maternal gaze, "Be sure to have your passports ready, the train is on platform six."

<hr />

When I see it, I can't believe it. The train for Poland sitting on platform six—the Kaliningrad–Gdynia–Berlin with a change in Malbork for Warsaw—is not the usual interminable procession of cars with which I crossed the tundra and the boreal taiga to get to the Baltic. It's a sort of commuter train, small and half empty, that quickly heads toward the coastal dunes emanating terrifying noises—barks, snarls, howls, and trombone toots, a kind of concert of ghosts, a wailing of the dead that drifts across immense fields of grain, whizzes by freight yards, mountains of coal, barbed-wire fences, towers, searchlights, control bridges, and finally the windswept dunes of the Baltic, and it seems to be taking us to the ends of the Earth.

I don't realize right away that this is a train for small-time smugglers. But when we come into the station at Braniewo—classic Prussian red brick—and the Polish customs police erupt into the car with electric screwdrivers to dismantle the bulkheads above the baggage racks and the passenger seats, I understand that this is hardball. It's not just a customs check; it's a face-to-face stare-down between cultures. The Russian rail personnel and the Polish police each know the language of the other, know it perfectly, but there's no way they'll speak it. At this checkpoint along the "wall" of united Europe, maybe they both know that they're going through the motions to nab chicken stealers while leaving untouched the most dangerous mafia in the world.

Meanwhile, as cartons of cigarettes are popping out, even from under my seat, there begins a sequester of food. Because all food products not labeled EU are considered "impure," sandwiches, hams, sweets, and salamis—all homemade—have to be eaten right there or thrown into a dump outside the train. Obviously, the passengers all eat as much as they can, and the car is transformed into a frantic picnic, to which the Russians invite me, too, so as not to throw away their God-given bounty. The smell of onion and cheese and the sounds of unfolding paper and munching jaws fill the train. The Polish soldiers perform this odious part of their duty with ascetic professionalism. No insults, at least, unlike when Albanians arrive in Italy and are treated like pack animals.

"Ma'am, the salami," insists a young man in uniform to a Muscovite who won't resign herself to giving up her treasure.

"Please, I've come from Moscow; I'll never do it again. Let me keep half at least."

"I can't, Ma'am."

"If you knew how good it is . . . you can't get salami this good where you live. This is the best and the most expensive."

Out of her bag comes a huge cylinder, at least three kilos of salami, and a matching smell of garlic. "Alright, I'll give it to you."

"Ma'am, I'm not allowed to touch it. You have to carry it outside yourself." So the Russian woman gets up and goes out, under escort, to the Dumpster of shame. Welcome to Euroland, mesdames et messieurs.

By now the train has been stopped for an hour and a half, all for a few cartons of cigarettes and some salamis. Apparently it's that way every time. The conductor goes to complain to the Poles. "Do your job, but please don't say anything to the railroad people in Kaliningrad, or I'll get fired." He claims he's the victim of a trap. In the meantime, one of the passengers, a Polish man, is taken into custody by the police and escorted off the train.

Now two hours have gone by. The entire car has been dismantled and the sun is going down behind the stupendous Prussian station at Braniewo. The passengers limit themselves to complaining sotto voce, emanating the infinite Russian patience. The woman whose salami was seized has also calmed down and she tells me about the magnificence of the Saint Petersburg cathedral. Even the guy who was taken off the train is released and comes back on board.

The train leaves again after dark, and right away the incredible happens. Voicing an elegant apology, the passenger hauled off the train by the police and then put back on board starts opening, one by one, the upholstery of the uninspected seats. He rapidly pulls out the remaining cigarette cartons and puts them in a sack. Just like that, right in front of everybody. In Italy, he would have been skinned alive. Not here. The passengers—force-fed like geese, beleaguered by the seizure of their food, and punished on his account by an apocalyptic delay—discover their fellow feeling for this chicken stealer, who has to, poor guy, feed a family. "Excuse me, just for a second, get up, I have to look under here, too." He asks me to move just like the others, and from my seat, too, cartons of king-size American cigarettes come sliding out. "It's even worse in Poland," a woman from Danzig tells me. "My country is the best place in the world for thieves. They kill someone to steal twenty euros, and they get off scot-free."

9. VISTULA

THE LITTLE TRAIN heading southwest from Kaliningrad is cutting through countryside labeled with new names invented in 1945 after the defeat of Hitler in order to conceal the Prussian spirit of the places. It's the revolution of the toponyms, adopted from the Baltic to the western half of Poland—west of the Vistula—the former German Saxony, where Halbau has become Iłowa; Naumburg am Bober, Nowogród; Sorau has been transformed into Żary, and Görlitz has sprouted Zgorzelec, on the other side of the river Neisse. The landscape, however, is magnificent—cows grazing in an azure fog, storks' nests silhouetted against the pink sky. Nature doesn't say that millions of Germans were forced to evacuate from here between 1944 and 1950[6] and were replaced by others, Poles driven from their homes in the heart of the East, from lands that are now Belarus, Lithuania, and Ukraine, in a double exportation to the West.

What does Europe know about the wounds inflicted here? What history book in Italy tells about this tragedy, as large as the Istrian exodus multiplied by thirty, yet which is still nothing compared to the deportations in Russia? In 1945, after the concentration camps and the Stalinist deportations, the engineers of ethnic cleansing were still at work. From the eastern territories ceded to Russia, the party brought to this place waves of Poles terrorized by the bloodthirsty hate of the Ukrainians for their former masters. With horrific symmetry, it sent eastward millions of Ukrainians who had been trapped inside the new borders, to die of winter in a Ukraine stripped of its population by the Nazi war and by Stalinism's siege of hunger against the peasants.

But there was still room in the immense void left by the expulsion of the Germans, and so in 1947 Operation Vistula was launched by the Communist government of Poland. The southern frontier needed to be "purified." The minorities near Czechoslovakia—innocent peoples, mountaineers like the Lemkos and the Boykos, or people without a homeland, like the Gypsies (to whom Monika has dedicated years of work)—came to be judged as ethnically suspect. They were forcibly deported with barely two hours' notice, and sprinkled about in the villages of western Poland already inhabited by the first wave of refugees from the East, to die of homesickness in camps with no horizons, where the wind encountered no obstacles and froze their souls as well as their bodies.

They were in a land of refugees, but since they were the last to arrive, they were more refugee than the others. They were called *przwitrzeni*, those carried by the wind. People were afraid of them. The police had spread panic before they arrived. "The bandits are coming," said the police officers in charge of the deportation. They spread fear because distrust among exiles was useful to the regime and kept the people in submission. But it wasn't over. The last wave of Stalinist terror was unleashed in Ukraine and the Poles who were still there also escaped to the west. When all the moving was done, nine million people had changed countries between 1945 and 1956.

Janina, Monika's aunt born in 1940, today a lawyer in Wroclaw, escaped from Ukraine when she was six, with her mother, two suitcases, and her six-month-old baby brother. It was the winter of 1946, and her father was still missing in action in Germany. They put her on a train, on the same line and in the same freight cars that had transported Jews to Treblinka. It took them two months to go from Lviv to Lublin. Sixty days to go 120 miles. She adds: "They parked us on dead tracks, in the middle of the snow. The Soviet soldiers came and robbed us." During that same winter, Janina's father tried to make his way home on foot from the German concentration camp where he had been locked up, and the only way to find his family was to wait at the border, on the train tracks. He waited for weeks for the great move to the East to be completed, until the right train came by and the family was reunited. Then they were offered a house that used to belong to Germans, in former Silesia, near Wroclaw. It sounds like a novel by Pasternak, but everyone in Poland, says Monika, has stories like that.

Today, the Poles from the east, like Janina, live in western Poland, where the great void left by the Germans weighs on their souls like the Jewish void in Latvia, Ukraine, and along the Danube. It is a land of ghosts and the uprooted, where still today the question asked in order to get to know someone is not "Where do you live?" but "Where are you from?" and where the biggest hidden fear is the fear of the return of the old masters, the Germans. In the meantime, in Berlin, the German exile lobby starts to put pressure on again. National public television hammers away with reports on the newly admitted EU member countries to the east, talks about "Germans and Poles deported due to 'no fault of their own,'" the latter to the homes of the former. But behind the equanimity hides the trap of revisionism. "I don't like what they're saying," Monika explains. "The Germans have their responsibility, and then some. We, on the other hand, didn't wage war; we only suffered its consequences."

The train jolts up and down with a clanging of hardware on the boards of the bridge over the eastern branch of the Vistula, and stops in the dark in front of the magnificent station in Malbork, intact in its Prussian red brick, the ghost of a lost Europe. The train will continue to Berlin, but this is where we get off to catch our connecting train to Warsaw and also where we see, given that we're here, the famous castle of the Teutonic Knights, the border monument that many Poles look upon as an advance guard of the Nazi invasion of 1939. At the Panorama Restaurant, on the main road, girls in low necklines are generously showing themselves off at the billiard table while a group of young lads, ignoring the women in action, are watching a soccer match shown on three plasma TV screens, and a DJ is blasting a deafening sample of techno music. At midnight, thanks to an accommodating taxi driver, we find a place to sleep at an inn next to the castle, in which the West is present in the form of one of its immaculate icons: the bidet, the first of our journey.

The night sky is quiet, full of stars. The Vistula is murmuring a hundred yards from the balcony, and the castle's big windows, like those in the kremlin on the Solovetsky Islands, look like eye sockets. I am lighthearted, with little pangs in my heart from the sense I have of the distance we've traveled. I've just read a map from 1695, signed by Gerardus Mercator, which reconstructs the *Tabulae geographicae orbis terrarum* (Geographical Tables of the Circle of Lands Known to the Ancients) by Ptolemy, and I found our journey there. Sarmaticus Oceanus, the Baltic; Chrones, the Neman River; Montes Pencini, the Carpathians. The Gulf of Finland, Karelia, and the Kola Peninsula are still terra incognita, like the land beyond the Tanais and the Montes Hyperborei, that is, the Don and the Urals. What I find unsettling is the sense of the mobile frontiers of this Poland, which in 1945 shifted 120 miles west, just like that, because of a distracted mark made by the Great Powers on the map of Europe. Danzig, Stettin, Masuria. Swedish, Mongol, Russian, and German armies. Peter the Great, Hindenburg's mustache. There is absolutely nothing that indicates the boundaries of this flat country, nor the boundary of the West.

The next day treats us to brilliant sunlight. Already at dawn, the sky billowed out like a spinnaker over the dunes of the Baltic.

Nonetheless, Malbork still manages to fill us with anguish. It's immobile as a watchdog, an inanimate golem on the edge of the river. This city was the departure point for a campaign of Christianization by the blade of a sword, and centuries later came the apocalypse. The church, deprived of its roof by the Russian bombardment and re-covered with a cement ceiling, still has at the end of the apse the pulpit and throne of the grand master. The statues of the evangelists, at the base of what remains of the vault, are decapitated or missing their jawbones. Wooden statues crushed by the bombs, trapdoors, secret passages. The signs of the Wehrmacht, with its headquarters in communication with Hitler's Wolf's Lair to the southeast. The echo of German boots in the corridors and on the stairs of the bell tower. The white mantels with their black crosses, the gray pewters, the red bricks, the deep green of the linden trees. The blue-gray of the Vistula and the train pulling out toward the belly of Poland.

After the thrust onto the shores of the Baltic to see Kaliningrad, we're heading east again, finally without obstacles, smugglers, or police. In Warsaw, we'll try to get our visas for Belarus and maybe get back the car that we left there before leaving for the North. We've been told that from there to Odessa, the border-skirting journey we'd planned to make with public transportation is a desperate enterprise, especially for someone with a limp, like me, so we have left ourselves this way out. Meanwhile the train cuts like a knife through a buttery landscape, reemerges, and dives back in again without a tunnel. It seems like a submarine piercing the long waves of the ocean. Wheat, barley, poppies. Tannenberg, the Masuri Lakes, stories of the Great War. At Narew, at the sandy confluence of the Bug and the Vistula, swimmers lying in the sun. Then the arrival, painfully slow, creaking, at the station in Praga, the part of Warsaw on the left bank of the river. Where in 1944 the Red Army waited for five months while the Nazis finished slaughtering the Polish patriots, who were seen as troublesome by Stalin.

Unyielding with chicken stealers, the border of the EU suddenly turns warmly welcoming for the brigands, bandits, and scoundrels of the globe-trotting elite. That's what I find in Warsaw, after the surreal adventure on the train from Kaliningrad, fleeced of its salamis and cigarettes by Polish customs. The city is crawling with tourists, and to find a room I'm forced to turn—against my principles—to a hotel for the rich on Grzybowska Street. I get off to a bad start. Because of my backpack and long beard, they frisk me at the entrance, and only the sudden appearance of my credit card manages to force a smile from the mug of the bouncer who is patting my jacket and then saccharine welcomes in English from the people working the reception desk.

Then, taking the elevator up to my room, I happen to find myself next to two enormous Russian gorillas with shaved heads, impeccable gray suits, and spiral-wire earphones sticking out next to their jugular veins, blood-swollen like a turkey's. Both are obviously packing heat, their jackets bulging with holstered guns. I can't contain myself. I go back down to the reception desk without unpacking my bag and tell them I don't want to stay in a hotel where they frisk ordinary customers but don't frisk gangsters. I provide the embarrassed management with information on where they can find the two head-shaven monsters, but since nothing happens, I return my key and leave, not without declaiming, in a loud voice in the lobby, my sacrosanct reasons for doing so.

But Western Europe immediately bids me welcome with still other unpleasant episodes. The pack on my aging back becomes the object of thinly veiled commiseration, and interpersonal communication on public transport diminishes sensibly, while the incidence of indifference and boredom soars. But above all, time. It is consumed with the anguishing velocity of a candle. I have a vaguely fixed appointment with a Greek Catholic priest outside of Warsaw, who is very familiar with the Kaliningrad border, a priest who organizes folk festivals and trains combat dogs. But when I phone him to say I'm on my way, the reverend responds icily that I was supposed to confirm the appointment earlier and he won't be able to see me. "I'm sorry," he tells me, "but I haven't got time." And he adds, with a touch of venom, "Since we've joined the European Union, there's no time anymore."

The city I have loved and visited many times suddenly seems to have been sucked into the void. Bermuda shorts, ice cream cones, rude tourists, a square invaded by multicolored papier-mâché bears on their hind legs with their forelegs raised in the air like fools. The analgesic illusionism of the West appears to me in all of its dementia. After just one day, I'm exhausted. Where is it written that traveling is wearisome? Three hours in an overheated Internet café tire me out more than the five Russian trains I had to ride to circumnavigate Lake Ladoga. Even Monika, who is at home here, is in a state of crisis after three successive lines at the Belarus Embassy to request a visa. Maybe the unfriendly priest is right: in the countries of the EU, time is consumed in senseless acts. Beyond the frontier, there may be Europe's last Communist dictatorship and its toughest police, but that doesn't matter to us. We want to return to the East. Our biorhythms have changed.

But then old Warsaw redeems itself. The bookstores are better stocked and more crowded than in my illiterate Italy, where they've been ruined by television and mobile phones. At a book sale in the Rynek, the market square, there is a line thirty yards long outside the door, as at a film premier. The theater marquees are more interesting than those in Rome. And my spirits are also raised by the map store in John Paul II Street, where the best show of all, as Ryszard Kapuściński told me one day when we went in there to get out of the snow, is seeing "the people hungry for the world," browsing the shelves. The great Polish journalist was to die two years later, and I had the sensation then that he was like a nomad shut into a space that was too small for him.

His life, too, I must confess, was consumed in repetitive acts, which clipped his traveler's wings. He was restless, seemed to be chasing after something in a blizzard. "Time," he would say, "I need more time, and time is a luxury for me. They besiege me: honorary degrees, lectures, letters, prefaces. Ah, how happy I was when nobody knew me!" The memory of that phrase has never left me, and now it surfaces again, clear as a bell, in the heart of this journey where the return to the West signals a speedup like the ones in silent movies. Kapuściński said, "How wonderful it was way back when. All I had to do was get on a train, listen, and take notes. I enjoyed anonymity, which is the basic requirement for a reporter. Today that's all over. If I could at least write about Poland, but by now they know me too well. As soon as I enter a town, out pops the mayor, then the bishop invites me to lunch, and I've already stopped working."

His notebooks had filled up with stories of the pueblos of Central America, of aurorae boreales and monsoon rains, but after all that traveling, his pen couldn't manage to stop anything anymore. I now had the same impression: Warsaw was already a different place compared to two years ago, and what I had written then was already archaeology. Kapuściński said: "If I return to Latin America or India, I can't recognize places I've only just been to. It's devastating. Every second gets consumed as though it were the last, and then news inflation hits and we're totally disoriented." He was starved for slowness and simplicity, for old hotels, for shoes to dirty. He didn't use taxis but streetcars, shuffled along in the slush toward food stands to buy beets and cabbages, noted like a foxhound every detail of store windows, grumbled about multinational hotel chains that were "too expensive." I once saw him help an old woman who had slipped in the slush, until an impetuous snowplow passing through a puddle soaked us both to the bone in Grzybowska Street.

In the evening, we go to the house of Jacek Kopciński, a friend of Monika's, to pick up my old car with the intention of going as far as Odessa on four wheels. We had discussed it for what seemed like an eternity, and in the end we decided that traveling by car in Belarus and Ukraine was the only way to get deep into the lives of those two countries. After all those trains, stations, waits in the wind, I discover myself dreaming of my old compact, and the idea of unloading my backpack after three weeks as a globe-trotter seems like an incredible luxury. We've got everything we need: insurance, international driver's license, visa. Even a small supply of Italian food to use in what we fear will be the Lenten fast of Belarus. Thus outfitted, for a moment it seems that the journey to the Black Sea is going to be a breeze.

But the unpredictable happens. When Monika's friend takes us to the car parked in his yard, the journey by car suddenly appears to us to be perfectly insane. The trunk and the backseat are crammed with stuff that three weeks ago I had judged indispensable and today seems the fruit of some delirium, aside from being utterly superfluous: books I would never have the time to read, an Italian espresso maker that I would never use, clothes that I would never want to wash or even wear. Even two pillows, in case we ended up sleeping in the car. Away, away with it all; traveling light has changed us. Kapuściński is right. We can't turn back the clock; we have to win back our time. And so, in front of a bowl of beet soup, we formalize our change of plan by giving the car keys back to our stupefied friend.

Jacek is beside himself. "The journey takes care of itself," we have told him, to justify our change of plan, and now he wants to enter into our philosophy. He asks, "What is it that moves you to go? Empathy? Compassion? Images that have attracted your attention?" He forces himself to rationalize an instinct, dooming himself to be wrong from the outset. "I don't even know myself what makes me go," I tell him. "All I know is that when the season changes, I have to go. I clean my flight feathers like a bird preparing for the big move. It's a thing that ornithologists know well: it's called migratory restlessness." We put down in black and white a few basic equations of travel. For example, less weight equals more encounters. Pace equals metrics equals story. And above all: the greater the difficulty, the more stories to tell. And who cares if we end up trying to hitch a ride in the middle of the Carpathians? We'll have more things to remember.

But we still haven't solved the problem of the Belarus visas. We can ask for a tourist visa, but everyone rushes to warn us not to be too clever, because the Minsk police are implacable. On the other hand, we're not going to Belarus to conduct an investigation but simply to travel, and what's more, by the most "transparent" means of all, the train. So we decide to declare ourselves journalist and photographer but also to write the word *tourism* in the box asking the purpose of our visit. Last precaution: for fear—which will prove to have been exaggerated—that my notes might be seized, I photocopy them page by page and send them to my address in Italy. Then I hand over my car to a young woman named Ola who is planning to come to Italy in a month with a friend. Meanwhile, with a little wheedling and a lot of patience, Monika succeeds in getting the visas. The road is clear.

The next day we're back at the Warsawa Centralna station waiting for the train to Belarus. We're feeling euphoric again. After giving up on the car, our journey seems to have acquired greater awareness. Right there on the threshold of the last dictatorship in Europe, we realize that we are free and that slowness allows us to ransom our occupations—photography and journalism—which have become embroiled in the race for profits and the allure of the virtual. We are also replacing investigation with the simple sampling of the territory, casual encounters instead of appointments. Warsawa Centralna is comfortable. The TV screens do not show a succession of commercials, as they do in Italian stations, but news, and it's news from the border. Arrests for smuggling in Zamość, drug traffic in Lublin, cross-border tourism between Poland and Lithuania.

In the waiting room, I see people who are starved for space like us. Young people with backpacks, families with children who are reading in anxious anticipation. Children reading—there's another thing that's disappeared where I live. I'm in the midst of a people of travelers. Being constantly on the move was an obsession for Pope John Paul II, and nomadism is a Polish national illness. It's not only the desire for freedom after the fall of Communism. It's also the reflection of an ancient claustrophobia, born of the sensation of being crushed between two cumbersome neighbors, Russia and Germany. So cheers for Warsaw, cheers for Kapuściński's shoes. Into my fifteen-pound backpack, I have slipped an old edition of *Journey to Poland* by Alfred Döblin, the only luxury extracted from my car. The adventure begins again.

Even the name of the train is propitious: *Niemen*, variant of Neman, one of Middle Europe's great rivers, maybe the most legendary. In Poland, every child knows its name from a historical novel about the country's peasant origins. Napoléon crossed it with his Grand Armée at the start of his Russian campaign. It happens that the spirit of places seeks refuge in minor rivers. In the Drina and the Tibiscus (Timiş), for example, rather than in the Danube, which they flow into. The Drina marks a still visible cultural frontier between the empire of the East and the empire of the West; in Serbia you can read about it in elementary-school books. For Hungarians, on the other hand, their Timiş signals the beginning of the great open spaces to the east, the endless horizons beyond the elbow of the Carpathians.

My mind grinds together sleepiness and thoughts, and in the meantime the train crosses the Bug, wide and brown in the midst of an absolute flatness covered with woods. The map says Treblinka is just a few miles away. As we're nearing Czyżew, the flash of an image: a shack in the middle of the forest with a thirty-foot white limousine out front. Next to us, on the window side, a couple of peasants in their seventies, sturdy as trees. They've both taken their shoes off, and she has put her feet between his legs on the seat. They don't smile. They don't read. They speak only rarely, in the low voice of the confessional, and when they do, it's all a *shishing* of Polish *s*'s. Monika's language sweetens everything, even death (*śmierć* compared to the sour *smrt* of the Serbs), but it has the defect of revealing itself immediately with its excess of softened consonants that sound like a pair of shuffling slippers in an empty house. With a language like that, you can't gossip, conspire, or even prompt, because it's a dead giveaway.

10. NEMAN

AT BIALYSTOK, near the frontier, we change for White Russia. Waiting for us is a little brown local. The flatness of the landscape and the consequent absence of curves account for the small gap between the cars, which is less than two feet. Instead of the accordion connector of normal trains, passage between cars is by way of a simple open gangway as on the trains of the Old West. Because there are no doors, looking back from the first car behind the engine, I can see all the way to the last one, at the end of a straight line of Euclidean perfection. One police officer can keep watch over the whole train without moving, and I can see a crowd of women spilling out from the compartments—small-time smugglers—loaded with all kinds of packages and bags. I haven't seen anything like it since the 1970s, when Yugoslavs returned home from Trieste wearing four pairs of jeans. Bedlam.

"Tanya, give me a hand here," and there goes a pack of DVDs, vanished inside her bra. "Natasha, help me out," and a roll of Scotch tape does a circumnavigation of a thigh, attaching a pair of iPods as an electronic garter. If the Kaliningrad–Berlin was transformed into a picnic area in response to customs checks, the Bialystok–Grodno turns into a dressing room, for the same reason. The acoustics are dominated by the zips with which four, even five dresses are shimmied into place over female flanks, by the ripping of adhesive tape, the unwrapping of packages, and the scrunching of cellophane. Hundreds of CDs vanish into old books, shiny new gym shoes are filled by delicate feminine feet. Robust women are in the minority; contraband is dominated by the slender, who have more useful room under their skirts and jackets.

The train leaves the station at a snail's pace toward the Belarus barbed wire. It never bends, despite the ups and downs of some occasional hills. The fields grow wilder, trees appear that are older and stouter than the trees in Poland. On board, the frenzy grows instead of diminishing, and the re-dressing and concealment manages to emanate, despite the rushing, its own sort of professional nobility. When the women, having noticed my notebook, fall into a fearful silence, I decide to delegate the scene to memory and put my notebook back in my pack. I make a conciliatory gesture with my hand. In response come smiles of complicity, sighs of relief, the final adjustments of skirts and jackets. Then out come the spray deodorants, to hide the cellophane smell of newly purchased goods. The final touch of clandestine professionalism.

A half-hour stop in the middle of fields. I offer a sampling of Polish cherries. The pretty smugglers accept and begin eating ostentatiously as the police are checking passports. This too is a masking operation. Eating is a sign of a clear conscience. Two police officers have come on board, with a wolf-dog, an official, and the train conductor—an attractive brunette in fishnet stockings. They are satisfied just to stamp passports and don't show much interest in the goods. The train pulls out again into the underbrush, and fifteen minutes later, it slows down, rumbling into the station in Grodno. The luggage check, it's clear by now, will be done on the ground.

I barely have time to get up when the doors open and the women, overloaded with shopping bags, hampered by pants stuffed with new purchases and three-ply overlaid outfits, are off their marks like sprinters, covering in just a few seconds, under the amused eyes of the customs agents, the distance between the platform and the customs office inside the station. Nobody shows any amazement, but I've never seen people fly like that except in Chagall paintings. Why the rush? I don't know. Maybe to be the first to get to the local market with the goods. Maybe to be able to take the next train back to Poland, or to avoid the most annoying checks, which are often saved for those at the end. Or maybe to make it to the black market faster. It all goes by in a flash, and there's no one left of whom I can ask the question.

We are the last to pass through the checkpoint with our tourist visas. Monika explains that, yes, we are a photographer and a journalist, but we travel with the people. The agent understands immediately: a man on a train with a backpack cannot be a troublemaker.

The dark green current of the Neman meanders on its way in the night, emanating a great sense of calm among the wooded slopes of Grodno, city of churches and synagogues near the Polish border. Neman, a name like a lullaby, the portal of a labyrinth of streams leading to other legendary rivers of Middle Europe: the Bug, the Dniester, the Pripet, the Western Berezina. They spring from no mountain, ice over in the winter, wander through a no-man's-land of rolling hills, and it seems that it would take only the slightest change in slope to push them to empty themselves into the Baltic instead of the Black Sea.

This frontier is perhaps the most arcane and the least legible of those we've encountered so far. The first impact with the only Communist country in Europe is even reassuring: an absolute green that dominates everything, an agrarian landscape dotted with excellently preserved wooden houses, geese running free around the villages. And then this Grodno, Polish until 1939, a shopwindow city of Austrian tidiness, now a beehive of gentrifying restoration, baroque like Vilnius and old Bialystok, full of young people, swallows, and stunning women.

But very quickly it starts to not add up. The old and the new clash without mediation. The Belarus Hotel, where I find a room, is a monument to Brezhnevian grayness, but its rooms are full of horny Sinhalese—in town for a fair—who will be trafficking all night in the hallways trying to find some women for hire. At the bar I see Russian *shampanskoye* next to five-star Greek Metaxa. A doctor makes €150 a month, but in the restaurants, the prices are higher than in Poland. And then the inflation: at the change office in the station, they give me, in exchange for €100, a wad of bills as thick as my fist. So many and so equally gray that I have to divide them between two pockets. The under-fifty bills in the lower right and the fifty-and-over bills in the upper left. I haven't seen paper money with that many zeroes since the time of the war in Yugoslavia.

"Welcome to the country of millionaires," cracks a passerby, watching me fumble with all that paper. On the train to Bialystok, I read that Belarus is broke and that next winter it won't be able to pay for its Russian gas. But then where does all the money come from for all these restaurants? Who was able to finance this gigantic real estate development operation? I pose this question to two old women sitting in front of the door of a redbrick house. They respond without hesitation: "The *gosudarstvo*," the government. Those people let the old houses fall into ruin, make the inhabitants move out, and then they speculate on the land. And if I ask how they found all that money to build new things, the answer is: "Simple, they don't pay people who work. Here, life is good only for people who don't work." In the station, Alexei, a retired army officer, told me, in no uncertain terms, "They steal. It's disgusting. And one day they'll find the red star up their ass."

In Poland, they told me to be careful, because Belarus is full of police in plainclothes. They may be right, but here nobody is afraid to talk. In an hour, all I hear are merciless critiques of the regime. A former army officer who makes a living driving a taxi tells how he denounced corruption and he was thrown out of the army because of it. "They made me blow up the balloon to demonstrate that I was drunk. But the balloon didn't change color. So they put me in a mental institution, but General Grizikin had me released for meritorious service. So they discharged me without a pension." Thin and hyperkinetic, the former Soviet officer shows me the restaurants with violins for the rich and the houses of the poor with old women wrapped in miserable dressing gowns. "A revolution is going to break out," he sniggers, and he takes me to see three paddy wagons of the militia ready to intervene, hidden in an alley behind the Catholic curia and the church of the Poles.

In a meadow overlooking the river, some young people are sitting on the grass at sunset passing a hookah as the Neman Valley is submersed in the warm colors of the stories of Bruno Schulz. Tanya, red hair enkindled by the sunlight and a star-of-David earring, says that "Grodno isn't Minsk; it's a real city, old, with its own history," and that's why she loves it. Her friends are also proud of their "city of Europe," and they say that the West begins here. They point to a nearby synagogue, lit up by the sunset, and on the other side of the river, the Church of Saints Boris and Gleb, almost a thousand years old, all alone, a belvedere amid centuries-old maple trees. Then they show me the Gradnicanka, the palisade of the lovers that slopes down in terraces to a tributary of the Neman. They offer us their hookah, point out to us the lights of the city. "We like Grodno; the Poles call it 'little Switzerland.'"

Another extraordinary thing: at seven in the evening, the elderly and adult population dissolves into nothingness. On the street, on the benches, in the squares, or along the river walk by the Neman, only young people with potato chips and cans of beer. I don't know whom to talk to; there's no one who gives me the impression of being able to talk about the history of the place. In an hour of exploration in the city center, I observe that I am the only adult human in circulation. It's as though in Grodno, and perhaps in all of Belarus, there had been an extermination of sixty-year-olds, as though yellow fever or the Spanish flu had eliminated the elderly. Alcoholism, rampant in these parts, is not enough to explain this demographic earthquake. There has to be something else. I feel that I am in a country that's teetering on the edge, vulnerable, divided among orthodox Communism, crude capitalism, and an ingenuous age-old agrarian civilization in danger of extinction. There is supposed to be a bronze statue of Lenin in the heart of Belarus, but here all you can feel is a single superhuman presence: the market.

The next day is Saturday, and we go to the synagogue to see the service. There are only ten survivors of the once numerous community. I feel again the void that I sensed in Latvia and northern Poland, and the Jews are only the most conspicuous absence. Not only have they disappeared, but also the Poles, the Lithuanians, the Germans, the Ukrainians, and the Armenians. A century of pogroms, deportations, and exterminations has created an ethnically simplified Central Europe by destroying its transnational fabric. "Adonai," "Elohim," the old people chant in the otherwise empty synagogue, and everything seems to be hanging on the thread of these ancient words, which ensure the continuity of the world. But that is what is really scary. When they are not heard by anyone anymore, then Europe will have definitively lost itself. You realize that already, when the silence returns to the choral space, heavy with nostalgia for a chant that is no longer.

"The French Jewish banks are eating up everything we have." Those were the words I'd heard the night before from an old woman waiting to be evicted from her home. But here in Grodno, there were seventeen places of Jewish worship, and now there is only one. The name written on the outside, GRAND CHORAL SYNAGOGUE, is the sign of a building designed especially for song. It was designed and built in 1853 in pure Persian style by an architect brought in especially from Italy. Mariya, the old custodian, is a former Russian Orthodox converted to Judaism, but her faith is a hybrid of the two religions. She says, with feverish eyes, "Everyone is waiting for the coming of the Messiah. He will come when everyone takes up arms against Israel. Then the heavens will open up and He will go to her aid. It will be the second coming of Christ. The time will come soon; so it is written in the Torah. Then the Jews will believe in Him. Jesus will bless them, and Israel will be the first among peoples."

They tell us that there is an old Jewish cemetery on the other side of the river. A taxi driver drops us off in front of a wall of overgrown brush and says, "You can pass through there." There is a path between the thorns and, at the end of it, an infinity of tombstones made crooked by the roots of the birch trees. We also have to climb over a crumbling wall covered with thistle. On the other side, the stone of Polyakov Abram Lazarevich. Then comes Rosenzweig David Bulfovich. The tombs with the star of David rise up out of the vegetation like menhirs, covered with gray and mustard-yellow lichens. Some of them have a red star. Over everything shines the fiery light of sunset. Thousands of dead among the blueberry bushes, and they are the minority. The others were burned in the ovens.

Amid the thorns and brush, a woman in a poppy-red dress is sweeping off a grave. She looks like a vision, a mirage. With her is a little boy who is helping her. Not far off, a man is cutting the underbrush with a sickle. The name of the woman in red is Lilja, and she tells an extraordinary story. "My husband and I are Orthodox, but we have adopted this place. Since we retired, we clean one grave every day. I live in that house back there, next to the perimeter wall, and for years, I've been struggling to keep this place from decaying. I know all of the people who inhabit it." She says "inhabit," because she speaks about her tenants as though they were still alive.

The man: "In 1969 confessional cemeteries were abolished and no one could be buried here anymore. Today, it is allowed again, but there are almost no Jews left." He tells us about his losing battle against the underbrush and the tree roots. "The law prohibits cutting down trees, so I spend my life pruning. But by now the tombstones are one on top of the other and you can't make heads or tails of them." I ask him why it is that there are no Jews helping him. "I knew a lot of these dead people, and they fought together with me so this place wouldn't decay." He tells us there was also another cemetery, but they built a stadium on top of it. "A terrible thing."

Littler Igor says to Monika, "Come with me, I'll take you to see the tomb of a saint," and climbs onto the base of a pyramid covered with Hebrew characters. "He was a rabbi. Lots of people come to visit his grave. They always ask him something."

They have two wolf dogs. They are the guards of Lilja's house. Once they smelled some strangers outside the gate. Lilja saw some boys trying to get in. She screamed, threatened them, and scared them off.

"Vandals! They ruined some tombs in the Orthodox cemetery too. They come here to drink; they smoke, make a mess, screw. A lot of times at night there are ill-intentioned thugs who come around, and we get scared. That's why we have the dogs. But I say to myself, with all the drunken hoodlums that there are around here, why in the world doesn't the city government send a custodian here to clean the place up?"

I ask why she has chosen to do this work.

"I love the Jews. They are extraordinary people. So many of them were killed, and so many have gone away. The big exodus was in the 1990s, and now we feel even more alone."

But doesn't the cemetery make you sad?

"I don't live with the dead. I live with the living and for the living. For the ones who come back, and there are lots of them. This pastime gives my life meaning. And it keeps my husband in good shape."

We go back to the city. The moon has risen over the Neman. The church of the Poles, the former lords of Grodno, is full of women and resounds with shrill vespertine chants, charged with national more than religious ardor. In front of the Orthodox church of the Mother of God, at the end of the service, women with handkerchiefs around their necks are exiting tumultuously and rapidly from the nave, which is full of lighted candles. Are they running away? No, they're just making a run up to a final twirl to face the church and make the sign of the cross. Christian prayer in the Slavic world is highly corporal, much more forceful than the distracted gestures of Roman Catholics. The final twirl morphs into a bow and the bow into an elevation. Their entire bodies arch upward to allow the right hand to make a long vertical parabola and then the transverse movement, which together trace against the backdrop of the stars the sign of the cross and—why not?—the coordinates of my journey along the frontier.

Endless fields, snowlike frost backlit by the morning sun, and then land, land, grain tall enough to dive into, to swim across. Spaces that would go to the head of any farmer, or any general in the mood for conquest. Belarus, green heart of Europe. A four-lane highway, empty as a takeoff runway, cuts across it without a curve, with interminable ups and downs. Road signs indicate the beginning and end of towns that aren't there. There's nothing between one sign and the next; the inhabited area is far away, reachable by side roads between woods and birch stands. In the twenty-five days since the Kola Peninsula, we have gone from winter to midsummer. Forests and sky. Sky and forests. With nothing in between.

I look for the remains of the uncontaminated peasant world that Primo Levi, liberated from Auschwitz, discovered and loved during his railroad saga all the way to the Dnieper and on to Romania. A happy world whose epicenter was in Belarus, in a village known as

Stariya Darohi, Ancient Roads. It is exactly those ancient roads that we have decided to travel, for just one day, renting a taxi to take us as far as Baranovichi, in the belly of the country, where our train for Ukraine leaves from. There are no train lines that run along the border; before we go south, we have to go east. Horizontal Europe blocks our route more frequently now, and we have to resign ourselves to proceed in a zigzag fashion, like a sailboat tacking into the wind. To get to Baranovichi there is no alternative to the automobile. The bus network is too complicated and too slow; the magnetism of Minsk is too strong. All the roads converge on the capital, and it's hard to escape its web without independent means.

It's six in the morning and the taxi driver is grumbling. He doesn't want to get his Volga dirty, but we stubbornly seek out dirt roads, villages, geese, rivers. We are crazy about this blinding sunlight, sharp, already southern. The towns are Swiss tidy, the roads without a single pothole. If the Russian countryside is falling apart, here the entire country seems to be committed to and involved in a conservation and maintenance program. Wooden houses, blue and mustard yellow. In a wood, lovely girls in two-piece outfits walk barefoot with baskets of strawberries. Very few *matryoshka* figures; even in the countryside the female beauty is radiant. In Žaludok begins the *chernozyom*, the legendary black soil that goes all the way to the river Don. In Pieskavce, fields covered with dew, spiderwebs woven between birch limbs, crosses adorned with flowers at the intersections. Sailboats in dry dock. The Neman.

Two down-and-out types are fishing on the convex side of the bend in the river. They smoke overlooking little whirlpools like hieroglyphics and a patrol of barn swallows diving into the current. The fishermen drag on their cigarettes until they burn their lips. They're suspicious as otters and respond rudely to our attempt to break the ice. No, this is decidedly not Russia. The people here avoid us; they're afraid. If I then take out my notebook, they run away even if I don't ask them any questions. I don't ask questions because I respect the rules. I'm here on a tourist visa, not to work as a reporter. I look, say hello, listen, and note down. That's it. But looking and listening are more than enough to understand. With 450,000 police officers for its 10,000,000 inhabitants, Belarus is one scared country.

Three pigs behind a wooden fence. Rooting through the kitchen leftovers, they don't smell as bad as ours. Without multinational feed even pig shit is different. "How's it going?" I ask a woman in the vegetable garden. Response: "All right, but our men are dying like flies." She doesn't say that the cause is alcohol. She doesn't say that it's the reason why masses of women run off to the West. I'd like to stay here; Pieskavce is enchanting and I could spend a week here, just fishing and writing. Places like this are to be lived right now before the global gets here and settles in with transgenic grain and supermarkets. But instead, it's onward again, in the midst of clearings that open up between fairy-tale forests, teeming with birdsong. In one field, I see some girls in bikinis hunting for wild berries. Triumphant verdure, orderliness, brilliant sunlight, intense heat. It's unimaginable that in the winter, temperatures go down to forty below zero.

In Dziatlava, over a Catholic altar, God is painted with a wizard's hat. He looks like the bard Väinämöinen encountered in the legend of Kalevala, up there in Karelia. In the shadows of an Orthodox church in another town, I encounter the reassuring eyes of Saint Nicholas. In Italy, we don't know that gaze and that beard, everyone's ideal grandfather. To understand it, we have to pass the frontier that divides us from Eastern Christianity. In another church, dedicated to saints Boris and Gleb, there is a catafalque covered in green velvet with a big cross and a wooden skull. In that semidarkness you can breathe in all of the silent lethargy of expectation, the same expectation that explodes in Orthodox churches on Easter Saturday night, from Greece all the way to Saint Petersburg and Vladivostok, with the shout: "He is risen!"

In Novogrudok there is a market with all of God's bounty: straw-berries, birch juice, and elderly women with colored bows on their heads. The Slav woman, Monika explains, tries to be pleasing even on the edge of the grave. The countryside captures us. Chernobyl is only 120 miles from here, but it seems far, far away. In Karelichy, the farmers milk their cows in the open air, in the middle of the countryside. They invite us to stay over; the pig market is tomor-row. "Come!" they invite us joyously, but we can't. We have to get the train at dawn in Baranovichi. Time, here too, time is short. I'd like to stay, like Primo Levi in Stariya Darohi. I should have planned a shorter journey. In Turzhets I get lost amid dirt roads and skeins of geese waddling back home to their barnyards. Horses ride into the violet sky, reflected in small lakes of the same color. They all have a name; here as in Poland they are seen as friends of man, and butchering them is viewed as a barbarous act. I think intensely of Mario Rigoni Stern, who died only recently. He loved this world, which welcomed him fraternally in 1943–44, even though he was a soldier on the opposite side in the war.

In Mir, next to a seventeenth-century castle restored to look like an ice cream cake, a rock concert is about to begin. Patrols of girls are arriving from every direction, but where are the males? Ah, there they are; there's only a handful of them, and they look lost. At dusk, the old men vanish, too. As in Grodno, there's a curfew for adults. At the hotel Gorizont (horizon) in Baranovichi, where the taxi driver, fed up with our aimless wandering, drops us off with a gruff good-bye, I notice that I'm the only man in the dining room. On one side, a table of lovely forty-year-olds, maybe a graduation anniversary. On the other, a group of newly licensed hairdressers, celebrating the end of their training course. Phenoms with tower-ing high heels, miniskirts, hot pants, sky-blue tulle wedding veils, leopard-skin leotards. They come in all together, in a line, with long, catwalk strides. They plunk down bottles of vodka on the table al-ready laid out with sausages, cucumbers, and tomatoes, and then they start to dance. I'm in a feminine universe; even with my eyes closed, I would realize it from the smell.

The orchestra strikes up a samba and the hairdressers go wild. They're into it, they're sweating, they're happy to be there in the company of women. They don't need men. The local fauna is depressing. Every so often, two or three men stop in front of a side door to have a look. Glassy-eyed, big-bellied boozers, half drunk, vanilla or mouse-gray shoes and white socks. Stalinist ruins. They don't dare come in to the bacchanal; they walk off with their tails between their legs. Incredible the ferment in the Communist provinces. We leave after a half hour of ear-splitting uproar.

The square is full of young people. Twelve-year-old girls go by in high heels, tanga panties in plain view, and heavy makeup. Everybody looks us over: we're aliens, idiots who come looking in the East instead of staying comfortable in the West. There's an Internet café. I go in. A smart aleck with a face that's asking to be slapped slips me a keyboard with illegible letters. I've got Net time until 10:00, but at 9:52 my connection goes down when I'm writing to my son. I ask Slap-My-Face if he's the one who unplugged me. He says yes. I respond that it's not 10:00 yet. He says it is. I respond that even if it is, you don't cut someone off without notice. He looks at me as though I'm a microbe; other young people give me the microbe look, too. I'm a sixty-year-old who has defied the curfew. Maybe even a dirty old man who wants to steal their women.

I leave, without even looking for the police. In a country that has a police officer for every twenty inhabitants, the police are unnecessary if you already have alcohol and the void promoted by unbridled consumption. A thunderstorm hits, and Baranovichi sinks into catacombal darkness. The streetlights go off at 11:00 to save energy. Poor country, I worry that it will sell itself for under market value, end up in the hands of unscrupulous merchants, with all of its sweet, endless countryside, its rivers, its fishing swallows. So we make our escape in a taxi in the middle of the night, through suburbs full of water and darkness, toward the central station, which awaits us amid thunder and lightning with the train from Saint Petersburg to Lviv already in position at the rain-soaked platform, impregnated by the smell of patient humanity in transit.

The train for Lviv, heading for the Ukraine border. Night, rain, and swamps. For three hours, the glowing caterpillar penetrates like a submarine in a world of water. Everything is so monotonous that it would be easy to miss your station. That's what happens to a woman and her child. As soon as she realizes that she hasn't gotten off at the right stop, she screams desperately, "Disaster, disaster!" but the whole car laughs heartily at the scene, only to then shower her with advice. Day is dawning, the sky opens up over the bridge on the Pripet River, much wider than the Po. We are in the heart of Polesye, another of the mythical shadow regions on this journey. Kapuściński was born here, the unforgettable maestro of my journeying.

"As a kid," he writes about that place, "I had sandals made of tree bark, that's how poor we were." Ah, shoes, the pleasure of putting on a good pair, of traveling with them for thousands of miles. The desire to travel was born in him then, in this most loved homeland. He spoke to me about it with nostalgia in his eyes and accompanied me with his story in the fluvial labyrinth of his eastern Poland, which became Belarus after the war. He wanted to write about it, but he ran out of time. His Tartar eyes burned bright, blue under bushy gray eyebrows. "Vast forests, villages reachable only by water, dirt-poor peasants. We were the poorest of Europe's poor. We lived on fish, mushrooms, and berries. There were Lithuanians, Jews, Poles, Belarusians, Germans, Tartars. That's where I learned to understand the Other and the world of the least among us."

Years ago, I flew over this piece of Europe, on a flight from Kiev to Warsaw, on a cloudless day. There were no cities or even mountains. No reference points. The land was covered by a tangled labyrinth of waterways. I was over the least perceptible watershed in Europe, a place where all it takes is a gust of wind to make a stream flow toward the Baltic instead of the Black Sea. Now I'm seeing it close-up. The water doesn't fall, it overflows. From Polesye, the maestro used to say, you can reach the whole world by boat. Now I realize that the key to this journey is not land but water. That's why Väinämöinen has followed me everywhere.

The West has not only run out of time, which keeps slipping through its fingers; it has also lost the reassuring company of water. It no longer burbles, roars, or lulls. The turbocracy has won across the board. But here, the song of the first element follows me and invites me. The Bug, the Vistula, the Berezina, the Dniester. I think back to the frozen black lakes of Lapland, the silver torrents among the mines of Kola, the Narva loomed over by lead-gray rival castles, and yet again to the shores of the Onega with the *chaika* staring into the wind, and to the Latvian lake next to the lost synagogue, where I threw my coins of remembrance. Water, without a doubt, has been my great companion. A formation of wild geese flies overhead. Meanwhile, the sky's cloudy apparel has changed. The inky black bubbles of the Baltic have disappeared; now it is the vaporous whites that dominate. The sun comes out; swamps and lakes shine like zinc. To the southwest, a glimpse of periwinkle blue. The frontier.

11. CARPATHIANS

THE UKRAINIAN POLICE OFFICER, white shirt and lavender perfume, opens the door for us to the world where a visa is no longer necessary. Then here comes a gigantic woman selling dolls and teddy bears, overflowing with goods and flesh. "Ah, our Gypsy has arrived." The conductor laughs, and meanwhile the train fills up with what sounds like Serbian music. I hear phrases like "my Ukraine," "my sweetness," and "heart of mine." I'm plunging into the South. The language becomes more modular; the chitchat rises in volume, and the convivial Slavic warmth—momentarily gone into hibernation in Belarus—reexplodes. I recognize pieces of the journey that we've already done: a mother from Murmansk with two children, traveling for seventy-two hours. When she left, it was still winter, and here it's already insufferably hot.

What a metamorphosis! The men who come aboard are less suspicious and the women more robust, suntanned like farmhands. The frequency of pale, slender Baltic beauty tapers off. The train is heading southwest, toward Lviv, in a world that's more vigorous, sunny, Gypsyesque. Towns are not as well kept, apparently poorer, but the fields are fertile, with grazing horses and geese, as in a Soviet documentary from the 1950s. The cemeteries, joyously colorful with fresh flowers, are not enclosed; they grow up spontaneously by gemmation. The deep green of Belarus has been tinged with yellow, maybe it's a prelude to the steppe. Saddled horses, dust, riding boots. There's an air of Middle Eastern caravan, and yet—how strange—I'm getting closer to home. The map says that the elbow of the Carpathians and Hungary are right next door.

My map of wonders indicates that this is the area of the Russian gas pipelines that supply Europe. The stability of the world depends on their spigots. That would be a great journey! Follow the pipe from your very own kitchen stove all the way to Siberia. An epic. I note down words like *Klondike, Putinian power.* Monika fires me up, talking about the legend of the Rachmani, a subterranean people of fire carriers. The train continues southwest, but now my imagination is galloping northeast, across the Don with the Italian troops at the front in 1942, over the steppes of Oryol and Kursk, where the last open-field battle of history was fought in 1943, to the headquarters of Gazprom in Moscow, the Kremlin. Then the great mother Volga; Kazan, the city of towers on the rivers; the end of Europe and the hyperborean mountains, the Urals.

What a grandiose terrain, unexplored and current. An investigation and at the same time an exploration. Beyond the Urals, toward the oil fields trapped under the permafrost—there you have it, the world's biggest swamp, an endless horizon of mosquitoes and migratory birds. I see the Ob, monosyllabic river, the Po of the great North, which the icebreakers just barely break open at the end of April, to the tune of dynamite blasts. Siberian stories, the tundra, the Gulags, the Arctic railways built by convicts, mammoths under the frozen ground. Novy Urengoy, the city of Utopia, reachable only by plane; the land where fire is born. Yamal, the last peninsula, the reindeer, the Arctic people threatened with extinction. The frozen Arctic Ocean, and again the madness of the midnight sun. The spaces whence we have come.

The train shoots into long valleys, imperceptible, the first change in the lay of the land since lacustrine Polesye. Until 1918, this is where Austrian Galicia began. Outside there are signs of a different aesthetic, of a different order. A new *limes*, a new sign of the mobile frontiers that have determined the fate of millions of people. The ethnicities mix. At Brody a blond with a Greek profile comes aboard. She looks as though she just got off a horse, a mythic Amazon. In the back of the car, Monika has found a Gypsy of savage beauty whose eyes invite her on the road to the Carpathians.

The bus for the South is dancing wildly like a crazed tarantist, but the driver is a jelly-bellied jolly guy who sings and accelerates through the potholes because that's the only way to get by them. The bus is jam-packed, a crowd of farmers who engage in animated conversation, eat, and sing with the windows thrown open, in an amazing vortex of spinning air. The road to Murmansk was a different music. The same potholes, but a leaden silence behind the wheel. Tinted windows hermetically sealed and a bleak gloom among the passengers. Like a paddy wagon full of detainees.

It's amid this chaotic earthquake that the Vision appears. Beyond the clamor of the confabulating passengers, the fields of grain, the villages with their onion-domed bell towers, beyond the yellow and blue Ukrainian flags fluttering in the wind and the bus's orange curtains, rumpled and torn by the current, there appears a black line, as wide as the entire horizon, regular as a breaker that rises up following the reflux of the surf. Mountains! The black line of the mountains! It's not a serrated crest like the Alps, but a barrier with a soft silhouette like a tidal wave. Barrier is the right word because the Carpathians are standing there like a dam, after thousands of miles at zero altitude, amid minimal hills, sand dunes, forests, and vast clearings.

Having a terrestrial limit to hold on to is a blessed thing, and I'm immediately overcome by a rush of good cheer that breaks the dam of reserve between me and my fellow passengers. I offer my neighbors some Uzbek apricots and Bulgarian almonds purchased in Kaliningrad. They thank me and return the favor with pumpkin seeds (another sign of the South!), laugh with a full display of teeth in their bony, caravanesque faces. Who are they? Alans? Sarmatians? Dacians? The legendary Scythians, who ensnared and defeated the Persians on the endless plains? They're also asking who we are, with our long thin faces and blue-green eyes staring out at the long wave of the last horizon.

Let me try to recapitulate how I ended up in the middle of these people. It all happened in a flash. Outside the train station in Lviv we hopped on the first bus directed toward the Carpathians, to throw ourselves into that frontier "entanglement" where Poland, Slovakia, Hungary, and Ukraine all touch each other. "Run, run, and you might make it," they told me at the ticket booth, pointing at a bus with its motor running in the middle of a hundred or so motor coaches haphazardly parked in front of the station. If I had stopped in Lviv, I would have lost myself in the city. Too much fascination in that city-bazaar, Gothic, Slav, and Jewish, so Northern for those who come there from the South and so Southern for those who arrive from the North. For the Italian soldiers on their way to the Don, Lviv was the place of their disillusionment. They saw emaciated Jews on the train tracks, pushed and shoved by German soldiers with whips, and they realized what a heinous cause they were going to fight for.

The bus starts to climb and enters the first tunnel on its route, crosses the newborn Dniester, and everything changes again. The Ukrainian neglectfulness ends together with the plain and is replaced by valleys of Alpine tidiness, sprinkled with pagoda-roofed wooden churches. Another frontier between cultures. What to do? The place is worthy of a stopover, but should I get off here? Are there hotels? Inns? Try looking in Turka, they tell me, maybe you'll find something there. We get off in Turka, but there's not even the shadow of a bed, and night is about to fall. Poland is right next door, and the border is a tough one. They told me in Warsaw that the Chechen mafia makes money from smuggling across that mountainous border.

The Dnieper Inn emanates an excellent aroma of soup and welcomes us like shipwreck survivors. We order dinner and ask for information, but the waitress knows nothing; she's not from here. Just as in Italy, the young people have lost a consciousness of place. So I try my luck with a merry table of customers at the bar, three women and four men.

"Why don't you have a car?" they ask us immediately, looking at our backpacks.

I shoot back, "Because we're crazy."

They burst out laughing, followed by a round of vodka.

I ask if there are really Chechens in these mountains.

Another laugh with the reply that those are just Polish fables. "But you two," they ask, "what are you doing here?"

I tell them about my vertical Europe, about Murmansk still covered in snow and about the EU frontier. They're left with their mouths agape. "Then you really *are* crazy!"

But the conclusion is fated: "You did well to come here. In the Carpathians we have open minds." Meanwhile, the second round of vodka arrives, and the dinner companions open up. The most talkative is the mayor of Turka, Yevstaky Ivanovich. The second is Ivan, a rascal police officer. The third is Bogdan, a friend of the group who offers to take us to a motel and, the next morning, on a tour of the nearby villages.

"You can trust Bogdan," says the mayor, "the important thing is that you don't trust the police officer. The police always lie." More laughter. One of the women at the table explains that the mayor won the election with good humor. Like this, telling jokes.

"Is that right, Yevstaky Ivanovich?" I ask him.

"I'm a Boyko, and you can say whatever you like." The Boykos are one of the ethnic minorities of the Carpathians. Monika knows them well.

I ask if there are Jews in Turka.

"There were lots of them. Today there is only one left. But he . . . is careful not to tell anyone." More laughter, this time with mouths closed. Yevstaky urges me on like a Cossack: "Drink up, have one for your horse, too!" They had warned me: careful of the Carpathians; they'll drown you with vodka and hospitality. Confirmation arrives promptly.

We head for the longed-for hotel in an indescribable sunset, apple green and apricot, outlined by the serrated profile of the pine groves, amid meadows covered with pale blue fog. In the distance, a lighted train makes a wide, slow curve in ascent. It brilliantly overcomes the steep slope with endless turns and switchbacks. "That's the Elektrichna," Bogdan explains, "the Austrians built the line in 1905." The whistle train that goes up and down the valley and connects with the Trans-Carpathian, toward Hungary, along the watershed that was one of the bloodiest fronts of the Great War. That's how we're going to continue our journey.

In the motel, crowded with hyperexcited excursionists, the only available place is over the sauna, and in the room—all in flammable wood—it is at least 100°. But that's no problem, I'm carried off by a leaden sleep. But at two in the morning, the temperature goes up to 120°, and from underneath me comes a concert of thumps, barbaric grunts, and female whoops. Pandemonium, with the flame from the sauna crackling distinctly just inches under my bed. The room is full of smoke even though the windows are wide open. I go outside to breathe some fresh air, and I realize that this incendiary earthquake is the only hotbed of noise in the boundless silence of the Carpathians.

The next day, they take us to a wooden church near the source of the Dniester. The nave breathes, creaks, hisses, resonates like the bottom of a boat. The pope sings the Lord's Prayer with just two notes, repeats ad infinitum the word *Gospod*, Lord, and the women respond in chorus. Candles around the icons, children serious as soldiers, in white shirts. It's a mixture of Baroque Austria and Orthodox Russia, Rome and Byzantium, all smelling of resin and decorated with lighted candles like Christmas. Monika has been traveling in Central Europe for twenty years, away from the centers of power and the delirium of ideologies. In places like the Carpathians, you understand clearly that in church what is celebrated is the community, and the sense of limits that looms over it.

Out on the street, a grandmother, with a red handkerchief, and a little girl, her granddaughter, dressed as a bride. She is dressed like that for her mother's birthday, but her mother has nine children and can't afford to keep her at home. So she lives with her old Osipa, Josephine. "They gave me my name because I was born on Christmas," she explains, and recounts that she was once a telephone operator and then the letter carrier for the town. "I went around on a bicycle, even in the snow. A hard job but nice, because you get to talk with everyone."

Osipa has a serene face and lots of tragedies behind her. Here the whole peasant world seems to be suffering unspeakably, even in these towns with genteel names like Strawberry or Apple. Just a while ago, in another church, we heard the pope cry out that "the devil has entered our community" and something had to be done. People were arguing heatedly, the parish was being attacked, and the enemy could have but one name, Satan. Josephine tells us atrocious things: a son of hers was burned alive—she repeats "burned alive"—by a madman. The other son was taken from her at age twenty-five by cancer. And her daughter isn't able to bring up all those children by herself, so she has to give her a hand with the produce from her vegetable garden. She makes us a present of a liter and a half of fresh goat's milk that we would drink later, sitting between a sheaf of wheat and a stream.

That evening, the proprietor of the hotel, after moving me out of the infernal room and giving me another, tells me that the hotel was a kolkhoz, of which only the walls were left because everything else had been robbed after the fall of the Soviet Union. "I bought the stones and spent ten thousand dollars to make a hotel out of them. But I have to fight with those damn plants that you see outside there." He takes us outside and shows us gigantic flowers, ten feet high, that besiege the grounds. "They were planted by the kolkhoz, to feed them to the cows so they would make more milk. They come from Siberia, and they are so happy to be here that they've become monsters. Now there are no more cows, but they are still here; they've invaded the mountains. You can't get rid of them even with a flamethrower, and they're poisonous for people."

Who knows, maybe the devil that's tormenting the Carpathians has taken cover in this killer plant. Already, on the Arctic Ocean, I've met a giant killer crab from the depths, brought there from Asia in the name of progress. Maybe the demon is globalism, which has made its nest here, too. It's hard to sleep in these mountains. The Austrian train goes by in the middle of the night.

In the mountain range where the vampires live, local trains come and go, to and from various heads of the line, with nonexistent connections. Especially in Ukraine. But that's the nice thing about it. It happens that you get off in a place called Yablunka (Apple Tree), in a countryside resounding with cackling hens, and you have three hours to wait for the next train, which might take you only twelve miles farther. But the stop-off offers you the opportunity to meet the signalman, drink a tea together, and see a group of young people on horseback, bareback like Andalusians, riding alongside the tracks. You can't understand the Carpathians without the syncopated rhythm of the train known as Elektrichna.

At Turka, I stop in for a beer at the blue shack that hosts the Klub for Afghanistan vets. In Syanki, a Ukrainian soldier stops us. We are the only passengers to get off the train with bags, and those bags indicate that we are engaged in a long journey on a train that is used only by local passengers. The man in uniform wants to understand.

"Where are you going?"

We reply, "To Uzhgorod."

"The next train is the right one."

"We know that," I respond, "but we want to see the border. That's what we're here for."

"There is nothing to see here. And above all there is nothing to photograph."

I explain that I'm interested in this place because my grandfather fought here in 1914, against the Russians.

"Passport, please."

We give him our documents, and the soldier gets even more upset. The importance of our visas, together with the poverty of our clothing, confounds him. He can't figure us out.

"You can't see the border. There's a cordon here."

"What cordon?"

"The frontier cordon. The security strip."

I ask him how wide it is.

"Eighteen miles."

We try to buy some time in a tavern frequented by Gypsies, smugglers, and the forgotten. The store is interred, has no windows, and no ventilation. Outside, a groaning of engines, wind, dust. Inside, beer, cheese, bread, cigarettes, and turbo–folk music that sounds Dalmatian and gives me once again the false sensation of being around the corner from home. Instead, I'm very far away, trapped in the damned Carpathian elbow, which inscrutable powers have decided to turn into a dead track. Monika asks the customers how it was under the USSR. "Nothing has changed. The barbed wire fences are still the same ones." An old man is even more pessimistic: "Today, it's even worse, the cordon is much wider." I notice that even civilians are wearing camouflage. Since 1914, history hasn't unloaded anything here except armies and uniforms.

At Uzhok, among bales of fresh hay, we encounter a freight train pulled by four gigantic engines, and as we wait for the next passenger train, we chat with the signalman, in a black uniform, red beret, and a wig. There is always a guardian angel, even in the most out-of-the-way place, and the signalman, having heard about our plan to skirt the Romanian border all the way to Odessa, gets upset and warns us that the train lines along the Tibiscus are called "desire." And, anyway, if our destination is Odessa, "you have to go back to Lviv." But he underestimates our stubbornness, and he watches us desolated as we head for the pass. We climb some more, where there is a monument to the fallen Russians and Austro-Germans of the Great War. Another frontier or, better, another front. The one where my grandfather, wearing an Austrian uniform, fought against the Russians of the czar.

The diesel engine bites into the slope, a barefoot grandma in a meadow waves her handkerchief, mountaineers run down from the villages to catch it. The Elektrichna has cars with wooden benches and it carries children, customs officers, lovers, and peasants. It whistles, shakes, creaks, whines, winds around itself, flirts with Poland, and shows you outside the window the Schengen Area guard huts and barbed wire, as solid as the Soviet ones. At Minjova, the station is a small building ten feet away from the barbed wire, but behind it is a Lilliputian world of little houses, chimneys, people, cows, and tunnels like the plastic villages of model trains. Everywhere you look, people intent on mowing the hay.

On the sliding door at the end of the car, a poster: under a pair of lenses with, reflected inside, two little boys in tears, the words DON'T PUT ON THE ROSE-COLORED GLASSES OF WORK ABROAD. It's the first sign of a country dramatically depopulated by emigration. I ask the ticket taker how many miles it is to Uzhgorod. She answers, "Sixty-one." I ask how long it will take. "Four hours." Why so long? "But it's sixty-one miles!" she replies, her gaze darkening. And we're already descending toward Uzhgorod, toward Hungary, in a rain forest heavy with vapors, swarming with microscopic, implacable mosquitoes.

                                                  ———

Pannonia[7] is very close; the Balkans, too. Like a stork, I can feel growing inside me the migratory instinct to fly directly south, following the meridian, toward Belgrade and Greece. But it is right here that the vertical border of fortress Europe makes a brusque turn to the east to outline Romania all the way to the Black Sea.

The faces on board have changed again; they're pointier. This is the world of the Ruthenians, another minority that has been shaking its fists after the fall of Soviet homogenization. Here's Nykola, eighty-three, a former orchestra director, from Lviv, thick white hair and deep eyes of someone who has seen it all. He spent his adolescence in Siberia, then in Kazakhstan, manufacturing bullets for the Red Army at the front. But in the meantime, he had already formed a chorus. "The Russians," he grumbles, "didn't bring us anything good." I say that up to now in Russia, we have only met good people. "Well, sure," he says. "On their home turf they're fine." And how is life in Lviv? "Worse. It's in a state of total anarchy. And the oligarchs have got their hands into everything." I explain our journey to him, and his eyes pop out. "You could have gone by plane." I reply that if I hadn't taken a train, I wouldn't have met him. He smiles. Then he sings an aria from *Der Rosenkavalier*.

Ferns, fog, mineral-water springs, paleosocialist factories in the rain. An old man climbs aboard with a pail full of porcini mushrooms to sell. He's wearing short pants and rain boots. Outside it's hot; inside it's a sauna. The train keeps getting more crowded. Nykola: "If you knew how much I love traditional Italian songs . . . and then, ah, Verdi!" He intones "Catarì," then "Il soldato innamorato," and then "O sole mio." He explains that the Slavs—"we Slavs," he underlines, including the Russians now, too—adore this kind of music. He writes down meticulously on a sheet of paper his address in Lviv and offers it to us. "Come. It's really not so far from Italy."

The station in Uzhgorod is a little jewel with a mausoleum inside in commemoration of a famous assassination victim: Georgyi Kirpa, a former Ukrainian minister, done in, they say, by pro-Russian militants. In the middle of the waiting room, there is a case with his clothes and some tablets with the story of his martyrdom. The hostility toward Moscow is palpable. At ticket window number five, a shrew refuses to respond in the language that I've been using now for a month without any problems, even in the Baltic republics. Her nationalism immediately sends blood rushing to my head, because it demonizes the people rather than the criminals who govern them. I send her to hell in Italian and change to window number three, where my vendetta is promptly served up. Two Slovaks, despite knowing how to speak Ukrainian, speak English with the woman behind the glass just to highlight their membership in the club of the rich. She doesn't understand, but they keep it up, refusing to make themselves understood even though they understand perfectly.

I look for a good hotel. I'm sick of scalding-hot rooms with saunas and discotheques on the floor below, and I find right away that in Uzhgorod everything works. The roads of five nations converge here; there is no lack of business and money. The English language shows up again at the hotel, lobster and Caesar salad on the menu, as well as, naturally, air-conditioning. But superimposed on the slipshod Soviet construction is the costly and marbled nullity of capitalism. And while all of a sudden everything works, just as suddenly there are no stories to tell. The West is the place where the yawn reigns supreme. The equation constructed by my friend Jacek in Warsaw is confirmed: "Difficulty equals story."

Luckily, there are the Pannonian mosquitoes. The meanest, sliest, most ferocious, and hardest to snag of my entire life. Lying in wait behind the minifridge, hidden in the folds of the drapes, dug in like Vietcong in the darkest corners of the bathroom, they emerge one by one in the middle of the night to prevent us from sleeping and provide us at last with something to recount. I'm too tired for big-game hunting, and I take cover under the sheet. In the darkness, I'm reminded that one day on a comfy and punctual Swiss train, a woman said to me—I swear—that she loved Italian trains because they didn't work and therefore, "there was at least something to talk about." Obviously she was a snob and regarded these little inconveniences as the only surprises capable of interrupting her incommensurate boredom.

The next day. New train, to Chop, on the border with Slovakia and Hungary. The idea is to go up the Tibiscus to its source back in the Carpathians, not far from the stomping grounds of Count Dracula. My map indicates a line that goes up the entire valley and then runs down toward the Dniester near the city of Chernivtsi, from where I'll leave to go down to Odessa. We are traveling full of hope through the desolate flatlands of Pannonia. And Chop isn't a city; it's a gigantic terminal full of fog, high-tension electric towers, gas pipelines, networks of tracks, immobile freight trains shiny with rain; and further still, ramps, warehouses, luggage trolleys in the scrub under a forest of electric wires. Long fields, typically Hungarian, on triennial rotation. The banks of the Tibiscus are no more than two or three hundred yards away, covered with tall yellow flowers. On board, the dark faces of Gypsies.

We bend toward the east to outline Romania. The sun comes out; vine-covered hills appear; the Tibiscus River valley begins, and the most legendary of the Danube's tributaries appears, solitary and wild, under the southern slope of the Carpathians. Meanwhile, I discover that the train has no toilets. "It's logical," the ticket checker explains, "it's a train for people who get on and off for short rides, like a bus." At Khust, we discover that the train ends there, because the old Austrian line goes only about thirty miles on the Romanian side of the river. The fragmentation of the old Soviet world and then the wall of fortress Europe have destroyed most of the old transnational connections. Nobody will ever persuade me to abandon the conviction that Europe was more European a century ago, when my grandmother traveled by train in one day from Trieste to Transylvania.

In Khust there's nothing that can't be bought and sold. The main square is a little bazaar. To continue on our way, we can choose a bus or a car with a driver, which comes at a more reasonable rate than in Belarus—€80 ($110) as far as Rakhiv, sixty miles. Our driver for the trip is Mikhail, a former building engineer with years of emigration behind him. He sings as he drives, loves his country, and has no intention of emigrating. He drives us through a magnificent valley dotted with the houses of emigrants who have prospered, but their houses are nightmare concoctions: medieval-style castles with towers topped with blue plastic roof tiles. The aesthetic model of independent Ukraine is Disneyland. Moscow may be even farther away than it was, and at ticket windows, they may speak only Ukrainian, but nevertheless the centuries-old knowledge of building materials has been lost and the identity of place along with it.

Unreachable on the opposite shore, the Romanian side, is the much more authentic beauty of Maramureş, which I saw years ago, with its wooden churches and its cemeteries adorned with paintings of laughing angels. Beyond the river and the trees, I see the bell tower of Săpânţa, one of the jewels of old Europe. It would be magnificent to go over there, but it's not possible. The border crossing at Teresva has been closed for two years. But it's all show—"*reklama* [advertisement]," Mikhail says more precisely—because here, too, smugglers come and go as they please. "Plus, for three thousand euros (five thousand dollars) you can buy a Schengen visa with no problems." I take a good look at the river. Swimming across it would be a joke. I don't understand. Why is there an eighteen-mile "cordon" on the border with Poland, and here there's nothing?

What a put-on, this frontier. Mikhail confirms that during the Cold War, it was worse. No sense of Communist brotherhood; if you swam across, Ceauşescu's Romanians filled you with lead. We turn north. Now both banks are in Ukraine. Tributaries of the Tibiscus flow down the slopes swollen with clear water between fields of corn and tobacco. Grape arbors in front of the houses, heaps of watermelons for sale under the linden trees, rafts for rent for whitewater river excursions. Then the valley narrows, and right there, treacherously outside the borders of the European Union, an old Austrian plaque marks what late-eighteenth-century geographers identified as the center of Europe—as if to say that the heart of the continent beat in the old empire much more than it does in the European Union.

I find a place to stay in Rakhiv, in a cabin on the river, while in a nearby house, they're slaughtering a pig, and the poor thing's squeals are echoing up and down the whole valley. Above us is the roof of the Carpathians, Mount Hoverla, 6,760 feet. I look up at the slopes of the mountains. They're full of people going up and down. It's a world that you can discover only on foot. The mountains are populated, high up and on the high meadows, even at dusk; it's a constant up and down of farmhands at work with hay and herds. There's a farmhand who's piling up hay in a typical Carpathian hayrack. "Working on the *klatki*, you age well," he tells me, referring to the scaffolding. He has ten children, twenty grandchildren, and he's as slim as a herring. In the immense silence of the evening, I drink a beer with my feet soaking in the river and a dog by the name of Uaciata sitting next to me, come down to greet me from the house next door. Her name, so tender, means "sketch."

Stars. Dinner of cured ham and cheese by the hearth in the inn. Above it, the room looks out on the river; that's the only sound I can hear. The ideal place for a good rest, but I can't get to sleep. Monika is sleeping so deeply, it seems she's on another planet. I, on the other hand, suddenly feel crushed under the weight of all the things we've seen. Too many. I have no idea why this is happening to me here and now, at the center of the continent. It's as though all the notes I've taken in the last month have fallen on me at once. A month as long as a year. Six full notebooks. How will I manage to decipher them after all this time? I've never made a journey so dense with encounters, and all that lived experience turns into weight, ballast. I've been working meticulously, maybe too much, like a botanist or an entomologist, gathering, recording, reproducing, investigating with a magnifying glass.

Just before six, just to pass the time, I start rummaging through my pack and discover that my rigid blue notebook that I've been filling with drawings isn't there. I look again; nothing. Nothing, nothing. A month's work up in smoke. I'd drawn the little Belarusian houses, Lithuanian beer labels, Norwegian road signs, the Cyrillic menus from the inns in Murmansk. I curse, dripping with sweat. The idea of going back up into the mountains above Lviv without a car is simply crazy; plus, I don't have enough time left for such a long detour. I'm desperate. But just as I'm getting ready to resign myself, out comes the damn thing from a side pocket as dark as night, and for a second, its seventy drawings seem to shine in the semidarkness like the figures of a magic lantern.

"LA-LA-LAAA, / It won't bring us luck / This stolen night. . . ."

The descent from the Carpathians to the plains stretching south to the Black Sea begins on a bus full of sleeping peasants and angelic children, with OUR FATHER printed large in Cyrillic on top of the first aid kit and a Slavic sound track capable of killing you with a fatal attack of nostalgia.

"You can't build / Your happiness / On the suffering of others. . . ."

Behind the wheel is a stocky driver in a muscle shirt who identifies me right away as Italian and tells me that he picked fruit in the fields of the Po Valley near Brescia.

"Did they pay you well?"

"So-so. Four euros (six dollars) an hour. Lot of work, not a lot of pay."

"And now?"

"Now, driver. Now also not a lot of pay . . . but at least I'm home."

We start into a series of shallow, parallel valleys, made from the slightest of rising slopes and separated by small rivers, where the dominant colors are the yellow of the wheat and the red of the poppies. In the scorching-hot clouds of dust, the bus stations turn into caravanserais. The one in Kolomyia looks like the round heart of a daisy whose petals are the shelters, shooting buses out in every direction. The food kiosks are the European outposts of the bazaar, with an irresistible aroma of *burek*, the thin, flaky pastry filled with cheese that I discovered in the Balkans. My gluttony won't allow me not to bring back on board a greasy paper bag full of them, and good manners oblige me to share them with my neighbors.

But the wonder of wonders is the bus station in Chernivtsi, the Czernowitz of the Yiddish world, the world capital of klezmer music. Around the bulldozed lot, buzzing with the whirling fan belts of hundreds of buses, is an endless series of kiosks whose pots are simmering with *zurek*, the local soup, bubbling over with mountains of green peppers, onions, and poultry from the valley of the Prut, the river that runs southeast to form the border between Romania and Moldova. Amid the fragmentation of its borders, it appears that the bus is the only means of transport able to hold together the pieces of what used to be the Soviet Union. At the head of the line, my bus empties out in the blazing heat of midday: the passengers come from distant places, but they know exactly where to go, what to buy, and from whom.

Chernivtsi is an interchange of cultures, food, and music populated by mild-mannered people at peace with the world. Among the merchants and the chickens, a pope walks arm in arm with his wife. He is satisfied in his yellow-gray tunic, ponytail, black beard, and vest. She's happy in her chaste long skirt and coquettish long-sleeved blouse. All around are Cossack butchers with cascading mustaches, buxom Moldovian farm women, vociferous Romanians selling strings of braided onions, bony-faced Carpathian natives with baskets of mountain herbs and greens. The only missing player in this chaotic scene is the Hasidic Jew with his wide-brimmed black hat, black long coat, and curls down to his shoulders. He's no longer present. But something of his presence has remained in the air, permeating the market with a special kind of meekness.

In Chernivtsi, we're supposed to get the train for Moldova in an attempt to cross it and head to Odessa. But the schedules are impossible, and we run the risk of missing the ferry for Istanbul. After the fall of the USSR, the train lines have been shortened, and the waiting times between trains would discourage even the most stubborn of slow travelers. So we look for a bus that will take us to Kamianets-Podilskyi, a jewel of a city we have heard great things about in Warsaw and where we could connect with the train line for the Black Sea.

We have two hours before departure, and because—as always—it's during stopovers that things happen, we end up being part of an unforgettable scene. There is a restaurant on the edge of the market, with tables outside under the plane trees. We're the only customers. The waitress passes the time sitting at another table with a muscle-bound guy with a shaved head in a white T-shirt. While we're waiting for our food, two cars drive up and stop right in front of the door, next to a bus stop. A stocky forty-year-old with the face of a boxer gets out of the first car. The guy sitting next to the waitress gets up and goes over to join him on the other side of the street. They sit down on a bench in the shade of a tree and launch into an animated discussion in low voices.

Suddenly, fists are flying and the two fall to the ground under a billboard advertising the modular kitchens by Burzhua—bourgeois—the word condemned by communism. The older man is stronger; he must be an ex-boxer. He gets ahold of the kid, puts him back down on the bench in an almost fatherly manner, and tries to get him to listen to reason, holding him still with his knee as a sign of domination. Things seems to have calmed down, but appearances are deceiving. The guy with the boxer's face is not a father. He's a boss. And he suddenly lets fly a punch out of nowhere, a professional blow, landing just above the left eye of the other guy, whose face becomes a mask of blood.

Just then, his partner gets out of the second car to check things out, but the partner who's busy settling accounts orders him to get back in the car. He's not worried at all about being seen; he's the boss of the territory. People go by and act as though everything's normal. Even the waitress, blanched with fear, doesn't do a thing for her boyfriend. So I get up and move closer to them to see if they'll stop. I sit on a bench ten feet away, but they just keep at it as if I don't exist. They talk and I can distinguish every word. If I knew Ukrainian I would understand everything. The scene continues as though it were a film. After a while the bloodied young man calms down, and with a half grimace, he shakes the hand of the older man, who gets back in his car and leaves, followed by the second car. Only then does the beaten man get up, take off his white T-shirt, use it as a bandage to stop the bleeding, and then go off to a side street to lick his wounds.

I go back to the table and ask the waitress if she saw what I saw. She says yes. I ask her why she didn't call the police, and she shrugs her shoulders, her eyes open wide, then she serves me a bowl of soup and a salad. At that point, the young man with the cut over his eye comes back, picks up his car keys that he'd left on the table, and walks over to a taxi, his, and leaves. Two minutes go by, and an enormous car pulls up, a four-wheel-drive Japanese SUV, black, naturally, with, naturally, dark tinted windows. The door opens and a shaved-headed guy with a scowl on his face gets out, takes a long look at what's written in my notebook, enters the restaurant, and comes out again in a few minutes after pocketing the protection money. End of story.

I had observed something emblematic—not so much for the violence itself as for its flagrance. The whole thing happened right before my eyes; even worse, it was purposely thrown in my face. The message was: we're in command here, not the police, not the state, and certainly not the new independent Ukraine.

I start to understand why millions of people have decided to emigrate from this meek country. I have not seen such an open exhibition of criminal hegemony anywhere else outside of the small towns around Naples. One time in Acerra, for example, a guy walked right up to the front of a long line at the post office window and a naive customer protested. The bully flattened him with a punch to the nose and then went back to the window to complete his transaction, in the most surreal silence.

Once we're on the bus, Monika recounts the incident to the peasant woman who is sitting next to her. She's not surprised and tells us, "Dear friends, twenty years ago it was worse; the gangs had shootouts in the streets. And in the 1960s it was even worse. Then there was the Topor Gang. . . . They were animals. They played cards, not for money but for their lives. And if one day they got the idea to kill everyone dressed in blue, they did it. Then it was the turn of people dressed in red. Today things are better. The criminals are all involved in finance." Sergei, on his way to Kamianets-Podilskyi, also evokes the horror of the "bad old days," when his parents were arrested for "anti-Soviet resistance" six years after the end of the conflict in which the incident was supposed to have taken place. They were sent to Siberia from 1952 to 1975, and that's where they met.

We still have ten minutes before departure, and a Gypsy comes aboard, the sweetest and best-mannered Gypsy I've ever seen. She offers blessings for the journey and asks for something in exchange, but without even a trace of importunity. I'm amazed; people offer her the equivalent of one or two euros, which is a lot of money here, a sign that the woman's work is considered important and reliable. Some people instead give a tomato, a sweet, a piece of cheese, and the Gypsy—who knows this—holds out two hats, one for money and the other for food. After each donation, she closes her eyes to make contact with God. This is her recognized occupation. Concentrating deeply, she mumbles something incomprehensible. When she's finished, she gets off, and the old bus, comforted by the Gypsy-style exorcism, is ready to leave, bouncing along toward the granary of Europe.

France is sweet, but Podolia is even sweeter. You've never heard of it? No problem; go there. It's in Ukraine, beyond the Carpathians.

It is one of the many regions lost in the great simplification enacted in Central Europe in the first half of the twentieth century. You'll see an endless sea of wheat, and fortresses and palisades along the rivers, where at a certain hour, there springs forth from the ravines, as though from a fountain, a prune-colored liquid shade that fills every dip and basin and spreads out over the hills. In France and Italy, evening descends from the sky; in Podolia it rises from the earth.

The Loire is glorious, and the Rhine is too, but looking out over the Dniester literally takes your breath away. It has the primordial meanderings of the Po but without the wearisome flatness. It flows in a sunken bed, and its castles regard it from on high with the glowering eyes of Cossack warriors. The Loire is a sleeping beauty. The Dniester, on the other hand, has the vital potency of a *limes*, a place where armies, caravans, horses, and camels come to drink, where the pealing of church bells clashes violently with the chant of the muezzin. If there exists a frontier, this is it.

Before coming to Ukraine, I didn't believe there could be anything more formidable than the fortress in Petrovaradin, high above the Danube, built by the Austrians north of Belgrade as a bastion against the Turks. Now I'm looking at the massive towers of Khotyn as they stretch out their shadows over the Dniester, and I'm forced to change my mind. Around its walls in the seventeenth century, thirty-five thousand Poles and forty thousand Cossacks stopped two hundred thousand Turks, and the clash was so powerful that the sky itself caught on fire and the walls shook from the cannon volleys. This is where King Jan III Sobieski and his cavalry overcame their ancestral fear of the Turks, whom they would then go on to defeat definitively under the walls of Vienna.

I look out over the river flowing in the night. The northwest wind swells it and pushes it toward the sea as it would a sailboat in a mistral, carries the smell of stubble from the sea of grain all around, holds up two storks suspended in air like gliders, blows into the half-empty bottle of Sarmat beer—what a name!—that I'm holding and makes it sing like a flute. A sailboat goes by, the Dniester turns silver, the sky purple, and the riverbanks seem still to be echoing with the shouts of soldiers, merchants, and customs officers.

Kamianets-Podilskyi is a place unique in all the world: a natural fortress city. They built it on the Smotrych River, a left tributary of the Dniester that forms large bends and cuts a canyon through the limestone table of Podolia. At the point where the river does an almost complete switchback and seems to have decided to go back where it came from, forming a sort of omega, a city grew up that is naturally defended by the river and watched over at its only point of contact with the right bank by a formidable castle. With its huge perimeter walls and a dizzyingly high bridge, the bastion controls access to the city and, in the gorge fifty yards below it, passage on the river, navigable until very recently.

When the river is in spate, the channel above the bend and the channel below the bend, separated by a narrow, rocky interspace presided over by a hydroelectric power station, can be connected directly. A perfect system, which the Turks—in the twenty-seven years of their dominion—not only didn't destroy, but improved. In Kamianets, it is said that the Ottomans, when they were forced to leave, buried a hidden treasure in the riverbed and that some years ago scientists in Kiev organized a secret expedition to search for the sultan's gold.

The upper city is a world unto itself, where the seventeenth and eighteenth centuries suffered almost no changes during the Communist regime. Next to the Baroque church of the Dominican monastery, the Turks built a minaret, transforming the building into a mosque. When the Christians came back, rather than demolish the tower of prayer erected by the infidels, they put a stunning statue of the Madonna on the top, which today can still be seen from afar like a lighthouse in the sea of grain of Ukraine. Neither the Turks nor the Poles destroyed the religious symbols of their predecessors. They limited themselves to inhabiting them, wisely recognizing that the god of the others was the same as their own.

It wasn't only a matter of respect, but also of economics and common sense. There was no point in destroying a place of worship in excellent condition. In the Dominican church in Kamianets, the *qibla*—the superb niche topped by a shell (a single piece of white marble!) that indicates the direction of Mecca—was not removed or modified but ably integrated into a staircase made of the same marble, where the words of the prophet are decorated with gesticulating chubby little angels and meringue-like Baroque swirls. Cultural conflict already had inflamed Europe back then, but the opposing parties—contrary to today—did everything possible to know each other.

Confirmation of this arrives on the padded stairs of the little hotel where we have found a room. They are inhabited by oil portraits of armed men who appear to be modeled on the stereotype of the cutthroat Turk. But as soon as I read the labels on the frames, I discover that they portray instead the most ardent adversaries of the Sublime Porte, the Cossacks. The faces looking at me are those of their historical leaders: the hetmans—the bald Severyn Nalyvaiko, the grim Maxym Zalizniak, the one-eyed Danylo Apostol. Beyond the landing, I'm ogled by the fat Pavlo Polubotok and the proud Bogdan Khmelnytsky, the most famous of all. As on other European frontiers—Croatia and Poland, for example—the defenders of the nation seem as though they try their damnedest to resemble their worst enemies.

We walk into the sunset on a stone stairway that leads down to the river toward a small wooden Orthodox church flanked by majestic trees. Kamianets is still aflame in sunlight, a Greek sunlight. But down by the river there is shade and cool air. On the banks, a dozen houses surrounded by greenery and a great swooping of swallows. This is the neighborhood called Karavasari, because once, many years ago—as the locals tell it—a Jewish woman named Sara lived here and turned it into a stopping place for caravans. Over time, the two words were joined together, and Karavan, joined with Sara, became Karavasari.

An elderly couple is relaxing on the grass, enjoying the cool air. He rolls himself a cigarette and plays with some white doves that he has just liberated from a dovecote. She has a crutch, a cane, and three thin ropes with which, standing still as though at the center of a spiderweb, she manages to govern the grazing of three kid goats whose collars are attached to the ropes. Above the two, way high up, the battlements of the fortress tinted orange. They are Viktor and Lyuba, next-door neighbors, born and raised in Karavasari.

All it takes is a "Good evening" from Monika, and they start talking to us as though that was all they had been waiting for. They start with the genesis of the place. All elderly Russians begin their stories from way back when.

Viktor points out the vertical rocks that stand way over our heads, a bit like the cave dwellings of Matera or of Chaco Canyon in Navajo country, rimmed by the last orange glow of sunset.

"Look, that used to be sea. . . . Genesis doesn't lie; the Flood did all this. It fashioned the white rocks from which the city was built, its walls, its cathedral, its castle."

"The ships on the Dniester came up this far; the river was much deeper then," Lyuba recounts, hobbling over toward the river on her crutch. The vertical rocks between the castle and the river form a natural amphitheater, and her voice carries, full and round, in the perfect acoustics of the place. Flowing water, screeching swallows, legions of croaking frogs. In the distance, barking dogs and shouting children multiplied by the echo of the cliffs. On the other side of the river, a group of men is fixing the bridge over the mouth of a torrent. I can hear their laughter. Chimneys are smoking. The smell of soup is carried on the breeze.

Lyuba: "A hundred and fifty thousand Jews passed over that bridge up there, holding hands, surrounded by Germans. I even saw Byela, sweet Byela, who sold candy to children. We shouted to them: 'Rise up! There are a lot of you! You can kill them!' But they answered, 'God will help us.'"

Viktor: "They killed them in a village not far from here, called Mikraion. The ground was red with blood."

I ask if anyone was left alive after the German retreat in 1944. They tell me yes, but the last ones left twelve years later, in 1956, after Stalin died. At the time of the revolt in Hungary.

Viktor searches in his memory: "I remember Arkhip . . . Lyuba, Harik, who drove a taxi . . . Lonka, who had a mobile cinema and showed me the world when I was a kid."

"There was also a Jewish market, here on the right side of the bridge," Lyuba adds, "they sold some excellent cured meats."

Monika listens, asks, translates, and takes pictures, all at the same time, without interruption. I don't know how she does it. She's captivated by this world, by what she calls "the people of God," the creeds and the simple souls of the Other Europe to whom she has dedicated twenty years of her life. She passes her enchantment on to me.

"There's goodness in your eyes," the little lady with the goats tells her. She offers her some berries. "Eat them, they're good for your heart. And drink from this spring here, the water is exquisite. Drink with your hands; don't be afraid. Water is life." It's an invitation to both baptism and the Eucharist; an ancient ritual is carried out through her.

Karavasari, sunken in the shade, seems to be in touch with the profound. I feel as though I can hear the ancient voice of the earth. A drum, a slow pulsing. Lyuba herself is the earth, the black earth of the granary of Europe.

"The young don't appreciate the countryside. They don't make it fruitful, don't make it live. That's why Ukraine is poor. Look at the fields all around us. They could feed half the world . . . and instead they're full of weeds. Who knows, maybe one day things will get better, but I won't be around to see it."

And Chernobyl?

"It changed everything. More and more people are dying of cancer. It didn't used to be that way. Do lots of people die from cancer in Italy, too?"

"Yes, a lot of people die from cancer there, too." We ask her how things were before, during Communism.

"With the USSR, there was more order. Sure, we were poor, but it was paradise here. Now it's a mess. Everybody drinks too much, even the women. Morality has gone way down, and opportunities for work, too. Everyone thinks only about themselves. I like living on Earth with the others . . . the Earth belongs to everyone . . . What do you think? Am I wrong?"

No, Lyuba, you've got it right.

"I don't know the world, but I know enough to understand that God gave us a wonderful Earth. Here there is so much land. All you have to do is take it and use it. It's an immense gift, especially in times like these, when young people can't find work. But land is hard work, and today nobody wants to work hard."

Land and water—*zemlya* and *voda*—Lyuba repeats the two key words like a litany. They are the origin of everything, the genesis and the regeneration.

Monika asks Lyuba if she lives alone.

"Yes, I live alone. My daughter comes every now and again to bring me bread and semolina. Everything else I get from the garden. And my goats."

What did you do for work?

"I was a schoolteacher for thirty years, then a custodian. But at school they didn't know where to put the children—there were so many of them. Now the schools are closing because there aren't enough. We've got eight million emigrants, the villages are full of empty houses."

Viktor accompanies us to see the wooden church of Karavasari, directly under the castle.

"Take a good look at it. It doesn't have even a single nail. Iron was not to be used, as on the old boats. Iron had pierced the flesh of Our Lord. It was built with joints. There's no cement, either, but look how solid it is. Today, they've buried us in tons of cement, and look at how everything is falling apart."

Under the castle walls, there is a small fountain of pure water. The underground vein is the same one that allowed defenders of the city to hold out without having to draw water from the river. The Turks were the ones who opened it laterally so the inhabitants of Karavasari could draw from it freely.

Viktor recounts that, during the retreat of 1944, one of the German soldiers hid inside the niche of the fountain. The Russians killed him, and some bullets are still stuck inside the rocks. He shows them to us.

"What a winter that was. The river thawed without warning and dragged away dozens of people who tried to hang on to chunks of ice. It was March 16. A German tank tried to get through and hit a mine that killed a lot of people."

Today there is only silence, a cool breeze, and the burbling of the water in the twilight.

The first stars come out. Viktor has gone to close his dovecote. Lyuba invites us to come back tomorrow morning to drink some fresh goat's milk. We climb slowly back up to the castle on a labyrinth of stairs. From the top, we look back down on the lights of Karavasari with all the characters of the story—the Turks, the Jews, the Poles, the merchants, the boatmen, and the horses drinking at the river. There's also Lyuba, going back inside the house with her goats, and nearby a group of young people pitching their tent for the night on an emerald-green meadow next to the river. Still farther, a horse grazing. They're all moving inside the same story, written long ago.

"Ah, come on, you don't see the Cold War coming back?" an amazed Maxim asks me at the station in Khmelnytsky, where we're waiting for the train to Odessa in a placid golden-wheat evening. Maxim Apostol is a Ukrainian medical student, cheery and well nourished, with long black hair like Gogol's, and he looks at us with his mouth agape and eyes wide open to mime the fear that's on the horizon. He's an accomplished ham. He hunches his back, contracts his neck, embraces his elbows, and pretends his teeth are chattering, as though a sudden gust of cold wind from the north had turned the season inside-out, sweeping the countryside free of ripe wheat, reapers, and farmers.

"Where do you live, you Westerners? Everybody knows that the Caucasus is about to explode. Putin wants to keep it under control, and the Americans want to build military bases there. Plus there's the oil under the Caspian Sea. . . . See what you think. . . . To me it seems like enough and then some." Then he adds, "We can feel the tension really well. The frontier between East and West passes right through here." He asks me if I know what Ukraine means, and I reply that I know, and how: it means "frontier." In Croatia, too, there was a krajina—a strip of frontier with a Serb majority—that in 1991, instigated by Belgrade, inflamed all of Yugoslavia. "Exactly," he responds, "I see that you've understood perfectly. If Ukraine stops being what it has been for centuries, that is, a buffer, to enter into an alliance with the West, all hell will break loose. The country, which is pro-Russian in the east, will split into two, and then Moscow will intervene. Let's not even talk about the Caucasus. Stalin filled it with enclaves, ethnic mines to foment conflict and facilitate control by Moscow, and Putin can set them on fire whenever he wants."

I know. Since Murmansk, I've been zigzagging down a long *krajina* inhabited by frustrated ethnic minorities ready to let themselves be set on fire. And ever since the Barents Sea, I can feel the growing tension of the East-West confrontation, as though a new Iron Curtain were forming a few hundred miles to the east from the old one: Poles and the Baltic peoples against Moscow, Russian military deployments on the border with Finland, endless complications in getting our visas, the enlargement to eighteen miles of the frontier strip under control of Moscow's police and army, barbed-wire fences between Poland and Ukraine.

What if this visionary is right? For too long, since the fall of the Berlin Wall, we've been living in the atmosphere of a feeble-minded thaw, as if Russia had not become the master of Europe's energy supply, as if it were a flabby giant incapable of reacting. I've been traveling for more than a month along a seismic fault that's only apparently dormant. I've passed through customs, barbed wire, barriers guarded by towers and spotlights. I've experienced seizures of goods, interminable delays, arrests, relentless scrutiny of visas. Crossing the border of the European Union over and over, I've felt chills down my spine more than once, but I've never thought of the Cold War. Now, in the middle of the train platforms inflamed by the sunset, I feel like a cat that has crept by under the bear's nose without waking him up. Maybe Maxim is right; the frontier is moving back into the cold.

I recall Viktor Ivanovich, the pilgrim on the banks of the White Sea who prophesied a war starting at the Beijing Olympics. I can see him now: a meek, robust man with big hands and a Mormon's beard without a mustache, wearing a thick overcoat and carrying a haversack. I had totally forgotten about him. I open my backpack and look through my notebooks. In the second one, on page thirty-one, my summary of that strange encounter. Written in a hurried scribble is: "1 July. Viktor Ivanovich, 1940, born in Sumy, Ukraine." Then, "Prophecy, monasteries, war with Olympic games." And then, "2008 a bad year, 2012 too. Still a month left." Then I noted the names of the monasteries: Svensky Monastery near Bryansk, Torodalmatov, in the Urals. Solovetsky. Everyone in the monasteries knew that a war was about to break out. I asked him where, and Viktor answered, "In the mountains." He said he had given up his Ukrainian passport for a Russian one, and he spoke with irritation about the Chechen mafia, which in his words had taken possession of the port of Sumsky Posad where the Suma River empties into the White Sea. He was one strange pilgrim who knew too many things. I didn't pay him much attention then, but now, here with Maxim, that warning starts to get to me.

It gets to me even more a week later when, on August 7, 2008, the war in Georgia begins.

In front of the station, under the statue of the hetman Bogdan Khmelnytsky, the student goes on. He says that everything is changing, that Russia is becoming a threat again and the West has no idea how to deal with it. "You can't claim independence for Kosovo and then not agree to autonomy from Georgia for Ossetia." Then he tells us about Crimea, which until yesterday was full of vacationing Russians at the seaside but now has no more tourism because Ukrainians don't want to go to a place that has hosted so many Muscovite occupiers. "If you like extreme journeys," he laughs, "go to Crimea. The mountains have again become a wild pastoral land, like they used to be."

It is July 31. The train pulls out of the station, rattling its way across the plain, and I lie down on my bunk to ruminate. Forgotten details from the journey come back to mind: faces and words that initially seemed to be pure, insignificant choreography but now become meaningful. Vadim, for example, the turbo-Orthodox encountered in Estonia. He prophesied unprecedented conflicts between civilizations. Not between Christians and Muslims, but between Catholics and Orthodox. I think back to the drums of war that inflamed Belgrade in 1989, the gatherings of warmongers on the Kosovo Polje, the Blackbird's Field, blessed by Orthodox popes and archimandrites. I recall the tension constructed around the monasteries of southern Serbia. Now again in Ukraine I can smell the odor of incense. Why is it that the Russians who frequent the monasteries know so much in advance?

13. BLACK SEA

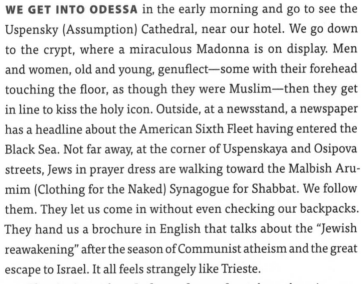

WE GET INTO ODESSA in the early morning and go to see the Uspensky (Assumption) Cathedral, near our hotel. We go down to the crypt, where a miraculous Madonna is on display. Men and women, old and young, genuflect—some with their forehead touching the floor, as though they were Muslim—then they get in line to kiss the holy icon. Outside, at a newsstand, a newspaper has a headline about the American Sixth Fleet having entered the Black Sea. Not far away, at the corner of Uspenskaya and Osipova streets, Jews in prayer dress are walking toward the Malbish Arumim (Clothing for the Naked) Synagogue for Shabbat. We follow them. They let us come in without even checking our backpacks. They hand us a brochure in English that talks about the "Jewish reawakening" after the season of Communist atheism and the great escape to Israel. It all feels strangely like Trieste.

The city is spotless. In front of every front door, there is someone sweeping and washing the sidewalk. At every intersection, there is a sign that says THIS IS OUR CITY. A healthy dose of local patriotism. In Sobor (Cathedral) Square, outdoor tables and chess games. Hundreds of simultaneous challenges. Monika tells me that chess is an Orthodox art form. The Poles don't play. On the iron grating of the Iskusstv Bridge (Bridge of the Arts), above the commercial port (overlooking tugboats, ferries, and mountains of coal), dozens of shining closed padlocks with the names of lovers written on them: Masa and Vadiki; Dunya and Lepa; Valzer and Nasta. Igor and Oksana have hung a whole chain of them and thrown the keys in the water. It's hard to resist the temptation to let this be the end of the journey rather than Istanbul.

On the propylaea of the Vorontsov Palace, not far from the stairway made famous by the film *Battleship Potemkin*, two women friends are looking out at the sea and talking. One looks to be seventy-five, the other twenty years younger.

Monika strikes up a conversation about the beauty of the city.

The older woman responds: "Beautiful but full of thieves. They steal the old houses to build new ones."

Did they steal your house, too?

"They won't be able to until they've finished down below . . . in the catacombs. . . . From my house I can see the water. I've got a terrace with a grapevine. I'll never give it up. I used to watch my husband going out to sea from up there. He was a sailor."

On the Black Sea?

"Yes, on the Black Sea. I didn't used to believe it, but it really is black. I realized it when I went on a voyage with him. But if the wind comes down from Siberia, the black turns green, with whitecaps."

The colonnade is inflamed by the sunset, a rugby-ball-shaped moon is rising, and, carried on the air from some unseen location, we hear the notes of "Blue Moon." The younger of the two women talks about her friends who have emigrated to the West.

"Those who have left here are full of regrets. Even our friend Valentina. We all lived together, helped each other, cooked blini together. Ah, how we love blini; when I cook them, I don't need to buy anything else."

The older woman: "For tonight I've cooked potatoes under the embers. I'll put a little oil on them. Then I'll go out for a walk. Sometimes I walk until two or three o'clock in the morning. Odessa lives by night. You meet people who have come from Russia, Moldova, Belarus. They're not rich. Ordinary people, factory workers even."

Just a few hours left before our departure for Istanbul. A lump in my throat. Leaving behind the Slavic world hurts.

I see it and say, "That can't be it."

The ferry that's going to take us to Istanbul can't even remotely resemble the rust bucket that appears at the bottom of the Potemkin Stairs, on the left side of the Odessa Marine Station. It's so short that it looks like a Venetian water bus, so low that only the smokestack is higher than the upper terrace of the terminal, so anti-aerodynamic that it seems to belong to another era. The inside can hold no more than five or six trucks and thirty or so automobiles. I say to myself, *The farthest this thing can go is to Crimea, around the corner from here*.

But no, this is our ship all right. The letters UKR FERRY on the side erase all doubts. The line for passenger tickets and the one on the ramp for the vehicle deck are both following the sign for Istanbul. Only the name—*Caledonia*—seems to belong to other seas and other latitudes. Who in the world travels from Odessa to the Bosporus? I asked myself that question many times when I was trying to reserve two places for that out-of-the-way crossing. Now I see them, the passengers with whom I'll be bringing to a close my vertical European trip. They come from another world.

Agatha Christie characters: an Ethiopian on foot with an American passport and full of rings and trinkets. A sort of New-Age shaman with a contemptuous look and turbid eyes, a backpack, and a colorful floor-length gown. Two jolly jelly bellies from Kiev aboard a metallic gray Jeep with a space-age trailer of the same color. An Armenian truck driver in clogs and a muscle shirt, dark and sharp-featured the way only an Armenian can be. Three young Muscovite centaurs on their way to Greece with expensive leather biker outfits and American motorcycles. Two Moldovian models who pose for photographs as they whimper and moan, sitting on their suitcases.

A little girl in an orange dress, whose long skirt billows in the wind like a hot air balloon.

The Black Sea grabs us in its tentacles like a jellyfish, and at the first sign of rain, it turns really black, black as coal. Up to a minute ago, it had been windy and greenish blue. Now it is still, oily, and dark, and I finally understand where it got its name. In an instant Odessa disappears behind the mist, and only the colonnade of Vorontsov Palace, above the port, keeps shining for a few minutes, the Nordic propylaea illuminated by a solitary ray of sunlight. The sharpness of the image is absolute. It even seems to me that I can make out the two women whom we met the night before. After that, it's all a soporific pitch and roll. Nothing worth staying on deck for.

Vroom-vroom toward the Bosporus. Four hundred miles non-stop, without a view of the Danube Delta nor even of the coastal hills of Dobruja. Almost a flight, like that of Jason from Colchis. Now it's pouring rain, my travel companion has taken to her cabin to correct the proofs of her book *Boży ludzie*, God's People, depicting the religious of the Other Europe. The dining rooms are empty; everyone is already asleep in the cabins, even the three Russian bikers and the Ethiopian shaman with the U.S. passport. I stay on at the aft disco bar to play cards with a Bulgarian, and he immediately places on the table a small icon of Saint Nicholas, which opens like a book, so that the bearded protector of sailors stands up and I can keep an eye on him, a good-luck charm against storms.

The first boat on this journey—the fishing boat specialized in giant crabs from Kamchatka encountered on the Russian-Norwegian frontier—had an icon on deck of good ol' Saint Nick. I have the impression that he's been with me the whole time on this Slavic journey accompanied by bodies of water, even on dry land, between one lake and another, one river and the next, like the Viking ships that made it to Kiev from the Baltic or like the boat of Väinämöinen, the shipwright bard of Finnic legend, carried on his back amid the birch trees of Karelia.

The next day, in the few hours that we're on board, a lot of things happen. Everyone knows that a ship is an extraterritorial space, where the rules that apply on land are no longer valid. The Bulgarian challenges a Russian to a chess match, and after a well-mannered confrontation that goes on for hours, the two almost get into a fistfight. In the disco bar, on the other hand, a stormy love story is born between a pallid Caucasian (Circassian) woman and a blue-eyed Turk, and the whole ship seems to have been sucked into that clandestine tryst, which the protagonists do nothing to hide. A Ukrainian from Podolia recounts the Gulag epic of his parents. I feel I'm a hundred thousand versts from Odessa. Lost in space.

I take inventory of my personal belongings and discover that the contents of my backpack have changed. There is a new equilibrium between things given and things received. I no longer have my knife, some drawing books, the mosquito net, colored pens, or a book on the White Sea purchased in Murmansk. Instead I have the book on Nordic sagas I received as a present from the wolf-man on the shores of Lake Onega. A necklace from Shungut. The crest of the Russian Boy Scouts, attached to my buttonhole by a soldier in the house of a pope. A box of old coins received from a Lithuanian hitchhiker who works as a joiner.

But a lot of things I have received as presents are not here. They have been consumed along the way. I'm missing the smoked fish of Captain Nikolai with which I crossed over into Russia. I'm missing the reindeer meat I got from the Laplanders, the pancakes cooked by Alya, the sweet queen of the blini in Petrozavodsk. And then the goat's milk from Osipa in the Carpathians, and the awesome distillate of barley (served with fish, butter, and brown bread) offered by Rita and Volodya, the two Russian Lithuanians in their house that was once a synagogue. Not to mention the countless piping-hot cups of chai (tea) poured as a sign of friendship by the world's most hospitable people. The time has come for drawing up the balance sheets.

I received much more than I gave. I encountered a few brigands, but the great majority of those I met along the way were good
people. Many of them, especially the poorest, were ready to offer
the foreigner a roof to sleep under or to accompany him for a part
of the journey. But of all these things, of perhaps the most precious
things I received, nothing remains. Except for shreds of notes dis-
persed throughout seven notebooks. I wonder if I'll really be able
to render the human density of this journey.

It's raining, night returns, the *Caledonia* sails into a curtain
of clouds hovering at the water's surface. Alone on the bulwarks,
I squeeze all the negritude I can from the Black Sea. Coal, oil, cast
iron, ink, squid juice. Thousands of years ago, the Black Sea was a
lake, and the Bosporus, a mountain gorge between Anatolia and the
Balkans. Then, more than seven thousand years ago, a tumultuous
spillover occurred. At the end of the Ice Age, the levels of the seas
grew higher, and the Mediterranean overflowed the thin barrier
of the Bosporus. The gorge became a huge cascade of fifty million
cubic meters of water every day, and the new sea swelled by a meter
every week, forcing the shoreline populations to escape toward the
Danube, the Caucasus, and the Middle East. First it was thought
that the Biblical Flood was an exceptional spate of the Tigris and
Euphrates, but today the overflow of the Mediterranean seems to
be the winning hypothesis. Surveys of the bottom of the Black Sea
confirm it. Underneath, regular strata of lacustrine fossils; above—
with a clear gap datable to about 5000 BCE—disordered strata of
seashells, stirred by an enormous ladle.

As the *Caledonia* sails along on the biblical waters of the flood,
one of the two Moldovian models is cuddled up on the stern,
wrapped in a colorful shawl. The captain walks out onto the bulwarks to smoke. A young Muscovite biker tells me the story of General Alexander Samsonov, defeated by General Erich Ludendorff
at the Battle of Tannenberg, in Poland, during the First World War.
Before surrendering, he tore the epaulets off his uniform in anger,

and now those very same epaulets have been found by chance in a bush, ninety years later, by a farmer.

The Bosporus is getting closer. I've never arrived in Istanbul from this side, and it is the right side, because Hagia Sophia is the perfect head of the line of a Byzantine world that from Constantinople—the Second Rome—has reached Kiev, Moscow, and Saint Petersburg, going up as far as Murmansk, to the edge of the Arctic Ocean. The port where this Slavic and Orthodox journey through Europe began.

A milk-white dawn opens up, and I don't notice right away that the *Caledonia* is sailing between mountains. Gray mountains, suspended over the water. Not until phantasms of immense ships glide by and slip away into the distance do I discover, as my heart skips a beat, that we're in the channel between Asia and Europe. Lighthouses, villages shining with rainwater. In an armchair, a rotund blond woman with her eyes closed is nursing her baby. Maybe she's asleep, exhausted. The little guy follows me with his eyes, never losing his concentration on that act that guarantees his survival.

My journey along the new Iron Curtain is over. I went looking for a real frontier, and I found it. At times it coincided with national borders; at other times, not. In Ukraine I had the impression that it was dangerously threatening to split the country in two, and now in Istanbul I have the impression that this white line runs right through me and is cutting through my soul like barbed wire. I wonder what will become of the old Europe, of its martyred peasant and Jewish heart swept away by too many wars. The train for Belgrade is waiting for me at the Sirkeci Station. I've got very little time to close the circle.

Only the Turk and the Circassian seem not to pay any heed to the clock, not even to the calendar. They kiss, oblivious to the city, the people, the rain.

Translator's Notes

1. Karadeniz is the Turkish name for the Black Sea; Chorne More, the Ukrainian name; *chernozyom* means "black earth" in Russian; *ochi chorniye* means "black eyes" in Ukrainian, but is often translated "dark eyes" or "brown eyes" so it doesn't sound like the result of a fistfight.

2. A verst is an ancient Russian measure of length, equivalent to 0.66 miles.

3. A *dazibao* is a large-character, handwritten Chinese wall poster, frequently associated with the Cultural Revolution of the 1960s.

4. The Schengen Agreement, first signed by five countries in 1985 and later adopted by the European Union, allows for residents of its now twenty-eight member countries to cross borders freely, away from fixed checkpoints.

5. The original expression is *"non guadagnerà un becco di un quattrino."* A quattrino was a coin minted in the Grand Duchy of Tuscany in the 1300s. As the name indicates, its value was four denari or four cents. *Becco*, "beak," is the term used in numismatics to describe a pointed imperfection that sticks out on the circumference of the coin. The expression *un becco di un quattrino*—"the beak of a quattrine"—is roughly the equivalent of a "red cent," referring to a copper penny.

6. The exile and deportation of ethnic Germans then living in eastern Poland and Czechoslovakia began in 1944 as Germans fled to the west to escape the advancing Red Army. This flight of refugees became official deportation after the Potsdam Conference in 1945, when the

Allies agreed to deport Germans from the East to the Allied occupied areas of Austria and Germany. By 1950 a total of twelve million Germans had fled or been expelled from Eastern and Central Europe.

7. Pannonia is the name of a province of the Roman Empire bounded on the north and east by the Danube and occupying the territory of present-day western Hungary, eastern Austria, northern Croatia, northwestern Serbia, Slovenia, western Slovakia, and northern Bosnia and Herzegovina.